Women
Reading
Women's
Writing

Women
Reading
Women's
Writing

Edited by Sue Roe

St. Martin's Press
New York

All rights reserved. For information write:
Scholarly & Reference Division,
St. Martin's Press, Inc., 175 Fifth Avenue, New York, NY 10010

First published in the United States of America in 1987

Printed in Great Britain

ISBN 0–312–00952–6

Library of Congress Cataloging-in-Publication Data

Women reading women's writing.

   Bibliography: p.
   Includes index.
   1. English literature—Women authors—History and
criticism.   2. American poetry—Women authors—History
and criticism.   3. Women and literature—Great Britain.
4. Women and literature—United States.   5. Feminism and
literature.   6. English literature—19th century—
History and criticism.   7. English literature—20th
century—History and criticism.   I. Roe, Sue.
PR111.W65   1987   820′.9′9287   87–9494
ISBN 0–312–00952–6

Contents

Notes on Contributors

Penny Boumelha is Lecturer in English at the University of Western Australia, and lives in Perth with her daughter Katy. Her publications include *Thomas Hardy and Women* (Harvester Press, 1982), and her present research is on nineteenth-century Irish fiction. She is currently completing a book on the subject with Tadhg Foley, *In The Shadow of His Language: Gender and Nationality in Nineteenth Century Irish Fiction* (Harvester Press, forthcoming), and her book, *Charlotte Brontë*, will also be published by Harvester Press, in the 'Key Women Writers' series.

Kate Fullbrook studied English literature at the Universities of Wisconsin, London and Cambridge. She is now a Senior Lecturer in English at Bristol Polytechnic. She is author of *Katherine Mansfield*, published in the 'Key Women Writers' series edited by Sue Roe (Harvester Press, 1986), and of *Free Women: Feminism and the Novel in the Twentieth Century* (Harvester Press, forthcoming).

Margaret Kirkham grew up in what is now called Waltham Forest, and went to Oxford in the immediate aftermath of the Second World War. She has spent most of her adult life in Bristol, teaching in a College of Education and the Polytechnic, and bringing up a family. She is author of a number of articles and of *Jane Austen, Feminism and Fiction* (Harvester Press, 1983). She is now a part-time tutor at the Open University, with a research interest in literature and sexual politics between 1700 and 1850.

Gillian Beer is a University Lecturer in the Faculty of English, University of Cambridge, and a Fellow of Girton College. She is author of *The Romance* (Methuen, 1970), *Darwin's Plots: Evolutionary Narrative in Darwin, George Eliot and Nineteenth-Century Fiction* (Routledge and Kegan Paul, 1983) and *George Eliot*, in the 'Key Women Writers' series (Harvester Press, 1986).

Isobel Armstrong was educated in a provincial university and teaches at one as Professor of English at the University of Southampton. She is the author of a number of books and articles on the literature of the Romantic and Victorian period, including *Victorian Scrutinies: Reviews of Poetry 1830–70* (Athlone Press 1972) and *Language as Living Form in Nineteenth Century Poetry* (Harvester Press, 1982). She is working on a study of Victorian discourses in the fields of economics, science and psychiatry and the study of sexuality. She has published poetry and is becoming increasingly interested in the problem of publishing and circulating poetry written by women.

Diana Collecott teaches British and American literature at Durham University, and was a co-founder of the Feminist Network. She has published a number of essays on modern poetry and is working on an intertextual study of H.D. entitled *Images at the Crossroads*, part of which will appear in *H.D.: Woman and Poet*, ed. Michael King (National Poetry Foundation, 1986).

Paulina Palmer is Lecturer in English at the University of Warwick, where she teaches an undergraduate course, 'Literature and Sexual Politics'. She writes fiction and has contributed to *Girls Next Door*, ed. Jan Bradshaw and Mary Hemming (The Women's Press, 1985). She is currently completing a study of contemporary fiction written by women, *Feminist Theory and Narrative Practice*, together with *An Annotated Critical Bibliography of Contemporary Feminism* (both Harvester Press, forthcoming).

Notes on Contributors

Barbara Hardy is Professor of English Literature at Birkbeck College, University of London. Her publications include *The Novels of George Eliot* (Athlone Press, 1959), *The Appropriate Form* (Athlone Press, 1964), *The Moral Art of Dickens* (Athlone Press, 1970), *The Exposure of Luxury: Radical Themes in Thackeray* (Owen, 1972), *Tellers and Listeners: The Narrative Imagination* (1975), *A Reading of Jane Austen* (Athlone Press, 1975) and *The Advantage of Lyric* (Athlone Press, 1977). Two volumes of her *Collected Papers* are forthcoming, from Harvester Press.

Sue Roe is author of a novel, *Estella, Her Expectations* (Harvester Press, 1982; paperback, 1983). Her critical study *Writing and Gender: Virginia Woolf's Writing Practice*, is forthcoming from Harvester Press. Five of her poems appeared in Spring 1986 in *PEN New Poetry 1*, ed. Robert Nye (Quartet Books). She is currently completing a second novel.

Bonnie Kime Scott is Professor of English at the University of Delaware, where she specialises in teaching British and Irish literature, modernist literature, women writers and feminist theory. She is author of *Joyce and Feminism* (Harvester Press, 1984) and numerous scholarly articles on Irish literature, modernist and women writers. She is currently editing a collection of papers from the Philadelphia Joyce Symposium, *Joyce Studies 1985*, and is preparing a new book, *Gender in Modernism* (forthcoming).

Introduction

Women Reading Women's Writing is not a book 'about' feminism, nor does it offer feminist theories of reading. It is not a theoretical book, in any sense, though all of us whose work is here represented have been influenced by recent developments in the comprehensive area of work designated by the term 'feminist theory'.

We all, by now, have at least some indication of the kinds of writing and research implied by this term. Moving on from the attempt, by feminist critics in the 1960s, to identify in literature instances and issues of patriarchal power, more recent feminist writers and critics have extended their field of research to incorporate theories of linguistics, history and, in particular, psychoanalysis, in order to investigate more fully the implications of language acquisition, linguistic structure and literary form. Such research has extended our vision, and deepened our powers of perception, so that one positive outcome of this incorporation of 'theory' within critical practice is that a new style of engagement with our writing subjects has been made possible. We are writing about other women, as well as about texts. Paradoxically, recent styles of research can enable us to look further and more deeply into the tendencies and capacities of a writer as an individual subject and as the product of individual as well as collective sexual history.

But this research can only assist us in very partial, very piecemeal ways. Any one psychoanalyst's practice engages with a network of theories which it is the struggle of a lifetime to develop; any one 'psychoanalytic theory' is perhaps representative of a single stage or aspect of one

1

psychoanalyst's study, and the application of one aspect of a borrowed theory to a work of literature becomes, seen from this point of view, at best useless; at worst, dangerous. We know, now, quite a bit more than we did even ten years ago about 'theories of gender' but, as literary critics, we shall never know nearly as much as we think we do, and meanwhile we owe it to the authors whose work is important to us not to misrepresent their writing by applying piecemeal knowledge as though it were definitive.

In this collection of new criticism by women, what emerges is discreet dissatisfaction with the whole notion of 'feminist theory' — a distinguishing factor of this volume which is, I think, all the more telling because we have *not* produced the work here represented with this perspective initially in mind. *Women Reading Women's Writing* evolved from a desire to investigate the question of *how* women write about women, by inviting a group of established women critics to write as spontaneously as possible about writers whose work has always been important to them personally, in the course of which we would attempt to say how and why we felt the writer's identity as a woman to be significant. The resulting work reveals that, though the influences of recent theory are consistently discernible, we all, implicitly or explicitly, express here a dissatisfaction with 'theory' as it relates to the creative processes which our writing about our reading reflects.

It seems impossible to make a case for experience exclusive to women, or which privileges a gendered point of view, without talking, at least historically, about oppression. Arguably, it is still the case that we are ourselves the products of a highly complicated network of systems which privilege the activities of men, and, more specifically, the sexuality of men: its status, and its place in the scheme of things. Some of the contributors to this volume are anxious to see this state of affairs not only exposed but dismantled, and the writing of a number of the writers whose work is read — and written about — in the course of this volume, develops this view. Other contributors express no desire to disengage from the political structures reflected in the work of the women whose writing they are here engaged with, but there is nevertheless a consistent endeavour to re-think the question of how women writers have engaged with, subverted, been unhappy or anxious within, these structures, and a consistent attempt, too, to relate the question of political structure to that of linguistic and literary form. The question of how to re-shape experience, and of how to re-think our insights to reinterpret the ways in which women have, historically, expressed pleasure and distress in writing, consistently and creatively engages all of us.

Feminism is not, in or of itself, a system, or methodology. Unified in our conviction that our insights and perceptions have status and need to be taken into account, we represent widely diverse positions — socially, politically and in terms of aesthetic judgement — and it is one of the purposes of *Women Reading Women's Writing* to represent this diversity, both in the broad range of women writers under survey, and in our different approaches. The diversity is most usefully represented here, I think, because it emerges not through theoretical preoccupations, but rather through practice, in the process of each contributor's expressing her most deeply felt responses to the work in question, the particular range of issues which emerge, and which continue to engage her.

For we are not, here, talking specifically about political process. There is an important distinction to be made, always, between a literary text as expressive of social, historical or political issues, and any other kind of document-ation, and I think we are just about arriving at a stage in the development of feminist criticism when this again needs to be remembered. We are not talking directly about the political structures which have, historically, oppressed women. We are taking as the objects of our study just the artefacts and artistic forms and structures through which women have been able, over the years, to subvert political issues, through which they have found ways of tunnelling beneath or through them to usurp, expose, and reinterpret them: women have been engaged in this process of reinterpretation, in their art, since women began making works of art. The objects of our study are *already* reinterpretations, reconstructions, revisionary structures, and, as women critics, we are seeking to under-stand both how to communicate with the women with whose creations we are engaged with here, and also how to interpret these new structures, or artefacts, in such a way as to suggest how these reflect our own points of view, our own predilections, our own processes of creativity. Feminist literary critical practice is a creative process which must be distinguished from other feminist practice, and from the exposition of feminist theory within other disciplines, though it has much to learn from them. At its best, feminist criticism can offer a kind of meeting ground, a possibility for confrontation, for reappraisal, for quiet re-thinking and reassessment which it may be important for us to distinguish, at this stage, from feminism's reputation for reductive stridency.

History is not linear. A 'chronology' is a convenient, shorthand form which enables us to see at a glance that events have followed one another systematically, sequentially, independently. As such, a chronology is a highly insufficient rendering of history as it actually evolved, individually or collectively, and the history of women writers — if it were possible to identify such a thing — would probably take on a more kaleidoscopic form than most histories: certainly, it would be a multi-layered, many-voiced structure. I have arranged contributions to this volume not to reflect the chronological order of the writers, but rather to reflect my sense of a growing movement towards *stylistic* change, in the practice of the literary criticism by women. The question of *how* women read — their predecessors, their contemporaries; how they read works not of polemicism but of art — engages me, as it engages each contributor to this volume, because this attention to style can offer us a double opportunity: it can enable us to read in more focused, more fundamental ways, women artists who have created new opportunities for us, and it can enable us, also, to *dis*engage from the structures constraining us. Style — that is, mode of practice — is as suggestive of opportunity as any methodolgy, but it needs to be read in more creative, less dependent ways than theory may allow. This collection of pieces demonstrates, then, the emergence of a network of *styles* of reading and writing about women's writing, reflecting modes of thinking which roam backwards as well as forwards, employing a whole range of methods of critical recall. As a result we are collectively enabled to *shape*, rather than simply to trace methodically forwards, new opportunities for reading women's writing.

*

If we are to intercept the forms of literary criticism, and to learn at all from recent theoretical developments, we need to understand the importance of the process of recollection and recuperation: to tread carefully and quietly, to pick our way backwards, to avoid stridency, and to try to absorb some of the forms and processes of the creative writing of our predecessors, in order to be able to articulate in writing our feminist readings of them, and of our contemporaries. The first piece in this volume is about George Eliot, and Penny Boumelha's chapter on her work expresses most lucidly and comprehensively the conviction that in reading women's writing, we are reading not simply the documentation of women's experience, but a network of complex processes which constitute an attempt to absorb and *re*-shape experience so that it is redolent not simply of a political point of view, but of a process of psychological recollection, an enjoyment of the imagination, expressive of perception and insight which we sometimes dare not share, and sometimes even cannot fully articulate. It will be suggested in this volume that perhaps as women critics we need to devise or develop a gendered theory of pleasure, but as yet we have no access to such a structure, nor do we always have full access to some of the sources of pain and despair which are evoked here by the majority of the contributors to this volume.

Creative writing is not the same as writing *about* polemical issues; it would be literally impossible to evolve a theory of creativity, since the imaginary place from which this process issues belongs within the structure of individual rather than collective history. That the process of creativity is gender linked is clear; the *specificity* of this process is, by definition, the individuating factor of the work of art. Where does writing issue from? We cannot definitively know, though with the hindsight of an increased knowledge of the processes of the human mind we can gain a greater insight into the complexity of the creative process, and look to disciplines such as that of psychoanalysis for new sources or starting points of investigation. Such investigations are not, however, reducible to methodology, and the essentially 'mimetic' forms of traditional criticism are insufficient as ways of interpreting insights and perceptions which cannot be contained in patriarchy's traditional forms. It may be, though, that the

5

structures of recent 'theory' can also be seen to be essentially mimetic in their structure, and this is an area which we as women critics attempting to break traditional form should investigate more deeply.

George Eliot's text — *The Mill on the Floss*, *Middlemarch*, *Daniel Deronda* — is not exactly expressive of the form, style, structure, of the mind of George Eliot. Maggie Tulliver, Dorothea Casaubon, Gwendolen Harleth, 'are' not George Eliot. The autobiographical experience of the woman writer constitutes deeply structured source material. But just as we cannot 'know' George Eliot by reading one or all of her novels, it is not sufficient to look to her women characters as examples of her feminist achievement. In recent years feminist criticism has tended to see the work of women novelists as, at least on some level, doctrinaire, or prescriptive: as such we cannot help but find it wanting. Even in the early work of a nineteenth-century writer such as George Eliot, it is possible to identify within the writing a point at which its vision of feminist possibility must yield to something else, thereby looking both forward to new possibilities for art forms created by women, and reinvoking stages of psychic history suggestive of completely individual imaginary correspondences. If it can be shown that George Eliot was consistently brought up against the limits of her carefully crafted form, then the reasons *why* this was so can contribute a great deal to our current debates about what constitutes, and what constraints are operating on, the possibility of our developing as feminist critics.

Jane Austen, writing earlier, had found a different way of expressing dissatisfaction. Brought up against the limits of her society, she had crafted a form designed both to expose and to undermine these limits. She wrote subversively for her time, and the force of her disdain is revealed through her talent for making fun. She mirrored the social and moral structures of her day, then turned them inside out to reveal the real motivations at the basis of them, exposing the Bad Faith which constituted the foundations of women's only security within the social and domestic structures. Kate Fullbrook shows also the extent to which Austen exposed to ridicule the economics of social life: its cost, to women.

If Jane Austen subverted existing forms in her fiction, the

Brontës invented new forms of expression and analysis. The confusion between what appears to be, and what is — a confusion exposed by the conventions of naming — is one which the work of the Brontës deeply investigates, and Margaret Kirkham's own childhood confusion between two Shirleys — Charlotte Brontë's Shirley and Shirley Temple — highlights this, exposing the powerful implications of social construction for which for her the Brontës' work acts as a trigger.

Virginia Woolf's work demonstrates, in a new context, the main themes explored in the Brontës' writing: gender identity, romanticism, the difficulties of communication, separateness, and the boundaries between them. Gillian Beer's reading of Woolf's work investigates new *patterns* of connection, new artistic forms, new ways of reading the significance and shapes of history. In the relationship between the subject and the self, the self proves always insufficient, and this is an issue which consistently engaged Virginia Woolf. The question of losing perspectival distance is an issue for Woolf's reader, for whom Woolf's own problems of separation regarding the self in relationship with the community are reflected in the difficulties of radical reinterpretation.

Isobel Armstrong's reading of Christina Rossetti takes us from the problems of reading women's writing to those associated with the issue of what might (now) constitute a feminist reading. The question of permission issues, for the first time, in this reading. How might it be possible to look back at the writing of a ninteenth-century woman writer, to review the issues which were ignored by her early critics, and to reclaim some of these issues, both on her behalf, and for ourselves? At this point it might be relevant to think back, not only through the history of women's writing, but also through the very much more recent history of feminist criticism. The individualist feminist criticism of the 1960s (pointing up the ideological repression of women, expressed in female texts) now no longer seems sufficient as a way of investigating women's relationships with created *forms*, and the relationships between ideological structures and the structures of language.

Though we seem subject to the structures of ideology, we can create our own structures of language. Or can we?

Looking back, it seems that this is what Christina Rossetti was doing, what Emily Brontë was doing, and that even Jane Austen, with her inversions of structure, achieved this. Modernist women writers did it; and so do most contemporary women writers. Can we effect such revolutions in language, *as critics?*

Implicated in patriarchal criticism, in all its forms, is a network of censorships, one of which can be interpreted as a silent injunction against exploring a theory of the emotions in reading and writing. Isobel Armstrong's suggestion that perhaps we need to propose a gendered account of pleasure is apposite, but it is not at all obvious how we might go about this. It would pull us up out of the constraining structures which have 'traditionally' bound us, but the twentieth-century women writers, in particular, who are especially aware of those structures and of their implications, remind us just how much work of retrieval and recuperation we should have to do, alongside, if this were to be possible.

Twentieth-century women's writing, together with feminist re-reading of nineteenth-century texts, permits a new kind of critical reading, a new style of engagement, a new relationship between a woman critic and her female writer/subject. The modernist period permitted breakthroughs in style; H.D. was influenced, in particular, by Freud, and his theories of the separation of the psyche; and of the psyche as *process*, which had important repercussions for poetic form. The 'untidy' structure of the female consciousness, and its process through individual history, is reflected in the forms of H.D.'s work, and its deep structures constitute demanding reading. Writing about H.D. may be an experience enabling the recognition and re-expression of deeply felt gender-linked distress and disorientation. The traditional institutions (academe, marriage, the 'institution' of poetry) cannot contain such disorientating experiences, and the experience of creating new forms — new social structures, new ways of living outside the conventional institutions, the attempt to create new critical forms — is a painful and taxing experience, demanding patience, restraint and a scrupulous and courageous honesty. The *courage* to tell what we know about ourselves: this is a quality demanded, seemingly exclusively, of women writers; perhaps we now need to begin to draw on it, as women critics. Again, the only way to proceed is backwards: by tracing the history of poetic voice, and looking at its sources in the history of the developing psyche; by tracing the initiating impulses of symbolic form back towards the articulation of a pre-linguistic voice; a *chora* which seems formless, and demands to be re-shaped in order for the 'institution' of literary criticism to accommodate it; by giving this voice, which H.D. freed in her poetry, critical utterance. Since the reciprocity of communication and separateness seems particularly difficult for women, the challenge presents itself as that of finding a specifically female form: of enabling critical as well as poetic language to reflect the rhythms and shapes of this highly complex reciprocity. It is a challenge which is as daunting, complex and demanding of courage for today's woman critic as it was for the early twentieth-century woman writer. As Diana Collecott demonstrates, it is still a question of inscribing ourselves, articulating our own voice, and reflecting our own psychological processes, and it demands that we cross and break the forms by which our thinking as well as our behaviour in society have long been circumscribed.

To what extent does this re-thinking demand a recognition of those forms, a new representation of them? One way of writing a new feminist literary criticism might be to ignore such structures, concentrating exclusively on the creation of new forms. The other way is still to analyse and subvert the old ones. It might be that, even today, we are still called upon to perform both tasks. Paulina Palmer shows how the writing of a contemporary novelist such as Angela Carter, for example, reflects both utopian and celebratory elements, and in addition, a constraint to 'de-mythologize'. She is primarily concerned to expose the socio-cultural construction of gender, the cultural production of femininity, the development of male power structures so that, as women, even our fantasy is circumscribed. In a sense, then, though a writer such as Carter represents some of the same issues as a writer such as H.D., she also looks back, for her methods, as far as the writing of Jane Austen, in exposing social and psychological structures to ridicule, allowing the possibility of laughter as a form of subversion, and — particularly in her fairy stories — turning the old forms on their heads, in order to expose the extent of their ridiculousness.

Carter as a novelist also looks back to the work of much more recent women writers, and though she does not use poetic form, her writing is reminiscent of the poetry of Sylvia Plath, in that she 'domesticates' violence and — in the opposite spirit — applies her Gothic imagination to the forms and styles of maternity, sexuality and romance. Barbara Hardy stresses that Plath's contribution to feminism may be seen to be not the specificity of her subject matter, nor her use of the 'traditional' imagery of feminist argument, but rather her ability to bequeath a single image with the power to subvert and disturb, so that the individual or localised psychological disturbance of one woman becomes suggestive of psychological or political disturbance on a massive scale: what is happening in the kitchen and what happened in the Holocaust may be compared, because of the ability of Plath's poetry to depict, on a personal and on a public scale, the insidious and far-reaching implications of patriarchal power structures.

Jean Rhys is a writer whose subject matter was the female imagination, and who wrote from an entirely personal and subjective vision. Her work is evocative, at every turn, of the complex and troubling connections between sexuality, creativity, and the power of sustained loss or grief, and as such her writing reflects her own processes of self-discovery. Her work can be seen to reflect the development of an experimental, diarist form, into realism, but her final work is realist only in the sense that it is inspired by her mature understanding of the forms of the imagination, and her recognition of the importance of the imaginary as the source of passion and desire, as well as of anger and protest. It is writing which easily accommodates the primacy of the unconscious mind as the source of reasoning, of gender identity and of the forms which we draw on and adapt for story-telling. Her style and her moral perspective are modishly twentieth-century, though the source of her inspiration for her most mature and most powerful work was in the writing of her nineteenth-century predecessor, Charlotte Brontë.

I think it is true to say that all the women whose work we

are reading here emerge as presences and personalities, as well as the authors of texts. Without writing to any fixed blueprint we have all demonstrated a number of preoccupations in common, in particular our attention to our subjects as struggling with social and historical constraints, and to their difficulties *as* subjects, or presences, whose writing constitutes an outlet for, and expression of, such difficulties.

In line with this approach, Bonnie Kime Scott attends, in the final contribution to this collection, to the issue of Rebecca West's consistent struggle with the paradox inherent in the attempt to represent women's work in a man's world to which she is in some senses stridently opposed, but in which it is nevertheless of tremendous importance to her to be actively involved. The history of Rebecca West tells a salient story: she was politically, personally and artistically ambitious, but passionate at the expense of the very female solidarity to which she sought to give credibility. She entered the publishing world forcefully, creating platforms and vehicles for women's work which enabled women to speak their minds, but she was able to do so only at the cost of singling women out; of always arguing for the work of women as a special case.

This paradox takes us full circle. I began by stressing our need, as feminist critics, to be aware of some of the tensions operating between collectivity and individuality, and Penny Boumelha, in the first contribution to this volume, highlights George Eliot's importance in bringing into fiction the collision of the unsatisfied, and perhaps illimitable, desires of her heroines with the restricted possibilities of the world as it could be imagined by realism. As women readers we are all, as contributors to this volume, positioned at the locus of this collision, roaming back and forth over the highly complicated and highly evocative 'history' of women's writing, still seeking definitions, still seeking new methods of articulating the deep structures of gender identity and its integral interaction with the creative process, still breaking forms. It is in consistently recognising that this is a fluid, essentially unconstraining place to be, evocative of all sorts of perceptual and revisionary possibility, that we hope in this volume to suggest possibilities for the creative, complicated and potentially exhilarating development of feminist criticism, and that we identify ourselves here collectively and individually as women reading women's writing.

Sue Roe

1

George Eliot and the End of Realism

Penny Boumelha

For new, but very dear, friends in Perth

I hope, in what follows, to intervene in two areas of debate, or at least in two critical positions, that have been influential in recent work on Eliot: they are, firstly, the question of 'classic realism', and secondly, the way in which a text can be read not only *by* feminism but also *for* feminism. Before going on to those matters, however, I should like briefly to consider, as I think a feminist critic must feel obliged to do, the whole collection of problems raised by the name 'George Eliot'. It is one thing to talk about, say, 'Virginia Woolf', where the historical individual and the name affixed to the texts are one and the same, though the apparent obviousness of the connection obscures as much as it illuminates the relation between writer and text. Nevertheless, it is different to speak of 'George Eliot' with the image and the history of a woman clearly in mind. Pseudonyms, as Michael Peled Ginsburg has remarked of Eliot,[1] in a way subvert the paradigm of authorship with which, or at least in full awareness of which, we still mostly work: that the author (a coherent historical, biographical, psychological entity) precedes, originates — if you like, authorises — the fiction of the text. Yet in the case of a pseudonym, this apparently commonsensical perception of the relationship is troubled, as it should be: 'George Eliot' is as much the work of the writing as the texts are works of hers (or his — another of the questions that soon presents itself). Before the *Scenes of Clerical Life* were published, of course, there was no George Eliot, there was only Marian Evans. Or Mary Ann Evans. Or Marian Lewes. As, later, there would be Marian Cross. One of the reasons why it may seem appropriate to continue to speak

15

of 'George Eliot' may well be this self-consciousness about naming that the woman and the writer clearly felt. What is interesting about this for a feminist, incidentally, is the element of *choice* that enters into the succession of identities, as she first alters the name given by the father, then opts to become Lewes in the absence of the legal marriage that would normally entail such a switch, and then invents a different name under which to publish.

Even here, though, Eliot's ambivalent and anxious relation to patriarchal authority is evidenced — the act of choosing her name (a kind of self-origination) is counterbalanced by the names she chose. The pseudonym itself may have been derived from the pseudo-husband, though 'George' perhaps owes as much to Sand as to Lewes, and we are not obliged to accept the acrostic version of Eliot ('To L[ewes] I owe it') proposed by Redinger.[2] This possible displacement of the authority of the father on to the husband recalls Dorothea Brooke's belief, in *Middlemarch*, that 'the really delightful marriage must be that where your husband was a sort of father'.[3] Since it is as well to observe what happens in novels as well as what is said, however, it must be remembered that Dorothea is shown to be wrong in this assumption; the truly 'delightful marriage', for her, proves to be that where the husband is a sort of son (certainly so, if you think of both Dorothea and Ladislaw in their relation to the sterile father/author Casaubon). It is surely not for nothing that Dorothea achieves such a punningly-named husband: she is finally allowed to delight in her own Will, and it emerges that not the father but the lad is law. The authority of fathers, and of 'sorts of fathers', is repeatedly questioned in Eliot's novels, and where it is reaffirmed it is only as an act of voluntary commitment: *Silas Marner*, *Felix Holt*, *Daniel Deronda*, are all centrally concerned with the revelation of origins, with the establishment of paternity and with the degree of determination such originations and inheritances may exercise upon the child. In this, Eliot is not uncharacteristic of Victorian novelists: the orphaned protagonist and the problematising of blood-relationships are everywhere from *Great Expectations* to *Jane Eyre*, from *The Mayor of Casterbridge* to *Wuthering Heights*. But in Eliot, the child repeatedly rejects the father of blood in favour of the father of choice: it is as if her characters may or must choose between an origin and a history. The case in *Daniel Deronda* is interestingly different: Deronda's search for an origin (his Jewishness) leads him to the attempt to become himself the originator or father of his people (his Zionism). It also, uniquely, leads him not to the father but to the rejecting artist-mother. It has been remarked elsewhere that Daniel's quest for his racial origins, at least, can remain an enigma only by the suppression of the evidence of his own circumcised penis,[4] and this serves to establish a curious structural equation between the unspeakable circumcised phallus and the (phallic, castrating) artist mother.

So, then, the very name 'George Eliot' brings to light a whole series of issues relating to male or patriarchal authority, from the pen-name to the penis; and this is one reason why it seems to me appropriate to continue to repeat the author's act of choice in using it. With this in mind, I was particularly struck by a sentence in a review-article of George Levine's, whose appearance in the journal *Women and Literature* might lead the reader to expect a degree of self-awareness, even sophistication, in considering questions of gender: 'Even now', he writes 'it is easy to read George Eliot as a "male" novelist'.[5] Not, you will note, as a *male* novelist simply (if indeed that is simple), but as a 'male' novelist. I can imagine no way in which it is easy to read any works as those of a 'male' novelist; it seems to me that the inverted commas betoken no complex awareness of the constructed nature of our categories of gender (is Henry James a male or a 'male' novelist, I wonder? or D. H. Lawrence?), but merely function as a mark of embarrassment, a pair of linguistic tweezers with which to avoid soiling the hands of the critic with the distasteful concept of the gendered author. Still, at least some such degree of unease is probably preferable to complete obliviousness to the question. It remains the case that the critical self-consciousness of the feminist critic with regard to gender is by no means always apparent in work on Eliot. For example, a fairly recent book — which is, incidentally, by a female critic, Rosemary Ashton — considers Eliot's life, work and writing as part of the series entitled *Past Masters*, with no discernible awareness of the irony[6] (not to mention the further irony that Eliot's place in a companion series on *Past Mistresses* might occasion).

We will get nowhere, I think, by considering Eliot as a male (or even a 'male') author. What we can examine, however, is the relation between the male name and the kinds of writing to be found in the novels. There is, for instance, ample evidence of the attempt to create a male narrator, at least in the earlier works. It is striven for rather over-strenuously, I think, in *Adam Bede*, where Eliot clearly thinks it appropriate for her male narrator to adopt towards the novel's only sexual woman, Hetty Sorrel, a tone of gratingly patronising diminishment, a language all fluffy animals and half-opened buds. It may also be relevant to the creation of a male narrator that Hetty's fate in the novel, in addition to such patronage, is to be betrayed, turned into an infanticide, punished, and finally ignominiously bundled out of the text to make way for the more sober charms of Dinah. Again, *The Mill on the Floss* is a novel whose degree of commitment to its female protagonist has often led to its being read as a combination of thinly-disguised autobiography and inadequately transposed wish-fulfilment, but even in that novel the narrator seems to be, however sporadically, male: at least, he remembers his mother's denial to him of a tail-coat, and his comments on the tactics for winning the confidence of boy-children — 'it is only when you have mastered a restive horse, or thrashed a drayman, or have got a gun in your hand, that these shy juniors feel you to be a truly admirable and enviable character'[7] — suggest, in this period at any rate, a male rather than a female narrator. Further, Gillian Beer has pointed out that Eliot's inclusiveness of men (characters or readers) in sympathy and generalisation — the spirit behind the question 'But why always Dorothea?' that informs and troubles the structure of *Middlemarch* — constitutes in itself a kind of claim at the level of commentary: 'Writing of men with the same sympathetic completeness as of women is an effortless representation of women's scope and authority in George Eliot's writing'.[8] These examples suggest another reason why feminists can continue with a reasonable conscience to speak of 'George Eliot'; the very fact of discussing a 'George' who nevertheless takes the pronoun 'she' brings out the double perspective we are so often aware of in reading her work, of a male narrative voice (an implied male author, even) that will, in an apparent paradox resolved by the hierarchies of gender, guarantee the authority of the text's representation of its strong or aspiring female characters.

What I shall go on, later, to say about Eliot's sense of an ending will depend to some extent on this double perspective and on the ambivalence of the transgressive writing woman that it suggests. The tension between the centrality of women in her fiction and her desire to stake a claim within the recognisable and respectable literary traditions and practices of her time will show the form of the novels under a pressure most clearly translated in their endings. This brings me, though, up against the question of 'classic realism', a term that has gained some currency in recent years and one with which Eliot's fiction has become closely identified. The concept is most conveniently and explicitly set out in Catherine Belsey's useful book *Critical Practice*,[9] where it appears to be based on Colin MacCabe's work on film for the journal *Screen*, amalgamated with some aspects of the criteria by which Roland Barthes distinguished between the 'lisible', or readerly, and the 'scriptible', or writerly. For Belsey, and for a number of others, the idea of 'classic realism' is a critical tool with which to expose the bourgeois and humanistic epistemological bases of the 'great tradition' on which the most widely practised understandings of narrative are still predicated. Whereas most previous critical discussions of realism had addressed primarily its formal characteristics, the 'classic realism' argument has aimed to show the political content built into the narrative tactics, and in this it is entirely admirable. Nevertheless, 'classic realism' has too often served as something of a straw figure in such analyses. In this argument, chief among the tactics of the classic realist text is a form of closure — not simply formal, but ideological — by which the reader is continually produced and addressed as a unified individual human subject through such means as the convergence at a single and uniform ideological position of a set of hierarchised discourses of which one is always a controlling 'truth-voice'. The dissembling of fictionality and of textuality, and a theory of language in which words correspond unproblematically to pre-existing referents in the world, are also held to be characteristic of classic realism, and serve, by obscuring the written nature of the work, to consolidate such beliefs as the 'nature of things' or 'human nature'.[10] The problem with this is that it does not explain how such texts can continue ahistorically to enforce and guarantee this particular mode of reading; nor, for that matter, does it correspond to any actual text of the period that I can think of, though it certainly describes some aspects of nineteenth-century realism, and in particular its project, its idea of itself. In that sense, the concept seems to me to be useful at best to identify an aspiration of texts, a self-image which the inevitably less coherent, less unified, more contradictory texts themselves only fitfully achieve as a practice. Now, Belsey's prime example is George Eliot, and of course in this she may seem to have, if not the authority, then at least the concurrence of Eliot herself, at such moments as the famous Chapter XVII of *Adam Bede* or the rather similar Chapter I of Book IV of *The Mill on the Floss*, in which the story pauses a little to allow a consideration of the kind of writing in which the novel is engaged. But it is surely the case that the very fact of interspersing a narrative with a discussion of the principles on which it is constructed and organised can only serve to undermine any pretensions the work may have to that 'illusionism' held to be typical of realism.

The ways in which Eliot's work is realist — if not 'classically' — are evident enough, and in any case have been fairly extensively canvassed in critical discussions, though even here it should be remembered that she also wrote such things as the profoundly non-realist typological 'half' of *Daniel Deronda*, the Gothic short story *The Lifted Veil*, and other works that do not fill the realistic bill,[11] including many of the epigrams and moral axioms, snatches of verse and apparent extracts from dramas that serve as epigraphs to the chapters of some of her novels. The ways in which she clearly transgresses the boundaries of the 'classic realist' mould also deserve some attention, however. There is, for example, the obviousness of *voice* and of a narrator's presence in much of her writing. *The Mill on the Floss*, after all, begins by establishing its narrator as immersed in dream and memory,[12] rather than starting with what Belsey calls 'a privileged, historic narration which is the source of coherence of the story as a whole'.[13] The fact that he is 'in love with moistness' and 'envies' the ducks with their heads in the water (*Mill*, p.54) establishes a closeness to Maggie and her fate that recognises the partiality (in both senses) of the narration. It could even be argued that the very end of *The Mill* — the evocation of 'the days when they had clasped their little hands in love, and roamed the daisied fields together' (*Mill*, p.655) that is presented as if it were a shared recall but in fact corresponds to nothing of the tense and anguished sibling relationship that the novel has displayed — is so clearly inappropriate as a final commentary as to cast an ironic light backwards over the authority and impersonality of the narration as a whole. We are dealing, then, less with some objective chronicle of truth than with an incomplete, positioned and contradictory account that in any case draws on saints' lives, fairy-tale and legend as well as on the conventions of mimetic realism.

Then again, those epigraphs that I have already mentioned quite flagrantly advertise the textuality of the work and its unsettling relation to the putative authority of other texts, as well as suggesting the range of other possible genres and modes in which the work could have been conceived. Something of the same effect is achieved by the frequency with which characters in the novels themselves draw upon the vocabulary of literary forms and genres, of 'tragedy', 'comedy' and 'romance', to describe and assess their own experience.[14] The importance of reading and of literary models in, for example, *The Mill* is important too; Maggie's fluctuating and contradictory impulses towards self-assertion and self-abnegation are situated in a context distinctively of writing by her similarly contradictory reading, mirrored in the rebellious feminism of Mme de Staël's *Corinne* and in the asceticism of Thomas à Kempis. The same novel demonstrates a self-conscious knowingness about its deployment of stereotypical representations of women — the revenge of the dark upon the blonde heroine, the witch in the book who is drowned if she is innocent and damned if she survives, the gypsy, the Medusa — that shows it knows itself not to be a neutral transcription of a pre-existing reality. Finally (at least for the purposes of this brief survey), there is the degree of

21

metaphoric and symbolic organisation in the novels: the image of the web in *Middlemarch*, for instance, has been quite widely discussed as a mark of the novel's commitment to organicism, but it seems to me that the emphasis could fall as heavily (and just as accurately) upon the metaphoric nature of that commitment. The point here is not to insist upon a non-realist or protomodernist Eliot to stand in the place of the Aunt Sally of classic realism, but to show how, while staying largely within the conventions of nineteenth-century realism, Eliot was able to challenge its limits, question its premises and unsettle its practices.

I want now to go on to use this question of realism as the basis for examining the assumptions implicit in some of the feminist critiques of Eliot's fiction. It is true to say that Eliot has long occupied a privileged, if problematic, place in feminist criticism. The reasons for her pre-eminence are not far to seek. To begin with, she is one woman writer whose place in that great collection of set-texts we have come to call the canon has never been in doubt. She is, too, a formidable figure personally, with her unconventional yet somehow respectable life, the prodigious nature of her self-education and the undeniably monumental scale of her achievement (the disparaging talk of 'triviality', 'domesticity' or 'miniaturisation' so apt to dog criticism of works by women could never have seemed appropriate, though those desperate at all costs to patronise have usually been able to fall back upon her lack of beauty and some fancied causal connection between it and her 'masculine intellect'). There are also good reasons in her writing itself, of course, why feminists have long enjoyed the novels and found them fruitful for discussion: the space she makes for women's ambitions and anger, and the rare combination of passion and wit with which she is able to expose the restrictions and expectations bounding that ambition and suppressing that anger. The scenes of momentary recognition of mutual worth and respect that occur between her apparently polarised pairs of women (Dinah the preacher and Hetty the 'fallen' woman, dark Maggie and delicate Lucy, the ardent Dorothea and the worldly Rosamond) are also of considerable interest for the feminist critic. One aspect of her writing of particular relevance for feminism, too, is its frequent refusal of the consolations of romance; Will Ladislaw and Stephen Guest, thin and under-characterised as they are often seen to be, seem to me effective partly by virtue of their very perfunctoriness. There is something profoundly anti-romantic in the suggestion that the romantic hero has no more to offer than this. The inferiority of such men to the women they nevertheless deeply attract serves to point up the narrowness of the options available to the heroines. Again, the way in which the novels repeatedly set up a couple as apparently obviously destined for romance, only to veer away from that fulfilment, is an effective critique of the romance paradigm. In the cases of Dorothea and Lydgate, or Gwendolen and Daniel, the shared prominence that refuses to reduce itself to romance serves to stress at once an equality of ambition and potential, and a gender-determined disparity of opportunity and achievement.

In all these ways, then, Eliot's novels have commanded the attention and respect of feminist critics. And yet, she has also proved frustrating — even enraging — to some feminists; there is, indeed, an article on the subject which forcefully points out this fact in its very title, 'Why Feminist Critics Are Angry With George Eliot'.[15] The reasons for this anger can fairly readily be demonstrated, and some of them conceded without dissent. She makes women the centre of her novels and yet names almost all of them after the male protagonists (*Adam Bede*, *Felix Holt*, *Daniel Deronda*) or after their locations (*The Mill on the Floss*, *Middlemarch*). She displays the abuses and injustices that press upon the lives of her women and then seems to refuse the logic of the insights offered by her own texts, apparently resolving the conflict between romantic, individualist rebellion and the power of community morality all too easily in favour of the latter. Patricia Meyer Spacks puts this case, when she argues that 'George Eliot's feminism recognises the social injustice of women's position only to declare its irrelevance to the more important matter of personal fulfilment'.[16] Again, Eliot may deplore the restricted lives of her heroines, but she appears to celebrate the morality of martyrdom to which they give rise; Elaine Showalter has commented with as much aptness as asperity that she 'elevates suffering into a female career'.[17] Eliot, furthermore, shows her women to be capable

23

of intellectual and social achievement and aspiration, but offers them no field in which to exercise their abilities, consigning them finally only to death or marriage; Lee R. Edwards, in a consideration of *Middlemarch*, feels affronted by the conclusion of that novel. 'The objection', she says, 'is not that Dorothea should have married Will but that she should have married anybody at all.'[18] Most offensive of all, for some, is Eliot's refusal to bestow upon her heroines the opportunities that she so fully and joyously seized for herself; for Kate Millett, Eliot 'lived the revolution . . . but did not write of it',[19] and Zelda Austen enlarges (albeit on behalf of others) on the same theme: 'Feminist critics are angry with George Eliot because she did not permit Dorothea Brooke in *Middlemarch* to do what George Eliot did in real life: translate, publish articles, edit a periodical, refuse to marry until she was middle-aged, live an independent existence as a spinster, and finally live openly with a man whom she could not marry'.[20] The whole tenor of such criticisms is summed up in a comment by Jenni Calder: 'Sadly, and it is a radical criticism of George Eliot, she does not commit herself fully to the energies and aspirations she lets loose in these women. Does she not cheat them, and cheat us, ultimately, in allowing them so little?'[21]

It is a serious question, and a sad catalogue of complaints, but I must doubt whether they add up to a 'radical' (at least in the sense I mean) criticism of George Eliot. All of these comments share a number of assumptions about fiction, and in particular about its relation to reality, that I suspect cannot be justified. Feminist criticism, after all, is not in itself either a theory or a methodology, but rather a set of varied and often fiercely divergent critical practices identifiable under this general heading by virtue of their shared commitment to the broader political principles and struggles of feminism. The interpretation of those principles and struggles is often the sharpest point of contention between the various tendencies. All the comments on Eliot that I have quoted originate from and exemplify broadly the same kind of criticism, long dominant within English and American feminism, and marked by the attempt to evaluate representations of women in texts by their degree of correspondence to the experience of actual, individual women. In this, it leans heavily upon the presupposed ability of the reader — always, I think, a female reader — to recognise on the basis of her own unproblematised experience the 'authenticity' (or lack of it) in the work under discussion. There are a number of quite evident problems with such an approach: it privileges, without arguing for it, the most reflectionist model of realism and thereby drastically reduces the number and variety of texts it can usefully address, for example. That is one reason why Eliot, already very closely identified with realism, has figured so largely in this kind of image-based criticism, and it is also the reason why those aspects of her writing that refuse or question the mimetic have often met with a blank rejection or a puzzled inadequacy of response. Even when dealing with realist elements, however, this kind of criticism evidences its theoretical problems. It tends on the one hand to approach novels for their sociological content — for their depiction of the injustices and abuses suffered by women — but on the other hand it contains a strongly prescriptive strain, looking above all for positive role-models with whom contemporary feminists can be expected to identify. The resulting requirement of, in effect, fantasy heroines within realist textual environments places unanswerable and anachronistic demands upon the possibilities of writing within mid-nineteenth-century realism. The problem is often raised most acutely by fictional endings: realism, bounded more or less by its project of depicting the real conditions of social existence, has tended to reduce the options for its female protagonists effectively to either marriage or death. Of course, the virtual interchangeability of the two is itself telling. Now, 'images of women' critics have been apt to see a final marriage as a cop-out and a final death as a victimisation of the heroine, and yet they work throughout with an implicit privileging of realism that sees fantasy or romance as inauthentic and evasive. A critical double-bind is thus established by which virtually all novelists, male or female, writing before the expanding opportunities for women of the twentieth century must be judged and found wanting.

It is noticeable, too, that the feminist criticisms of George Eliot that I have quoted above are often damagingly author-based, in more than one way. First, they posit an inexplicit homology between author's life ('living the revolution') and work ('writing about it') that can only help to shore up and revalidate those biographical and confessional models of writing produced by women that have so often served to limit and trivialise it. The patriarchal critical practice by which women's texts are constantly returned to their sex, in a kind of autobiographical treadmill that denies textual production, is not significantly different in its procedures and effects. Perhaps more importantly, the author-centred nature of such critiques is also likely to set us off up what appears to me to be a blind alley: the assumption that we should seek and can find in or through a work of fiction the consciously or unconsciously held views of its writer, for which she or he can then be held responsible to contemporary feminism, is surely only a recycled intentionalism disguised as political criticism.

I want to propose that a feminist reading of any text, whether it is by a woman or a man, needs to know and accept that it is an *appropriation* of the work for feminism rather than a revelation of any pre-existing belief or intention of the author. A feminist reading is a reading made for ourselves by the needs and interests of contemporary feminism, but it must be grounded in an awareness of the historical and formal possibilities of writing and reading if it is genuinely to explore the relation between the work and the society that produced it — and that seems to me a task that no materialist criticism can afford to abandon, even in the name of *jouissance* and polysemy. So it is, for example, that the criticisms of Eliot for not granting her heroines the relative freedom and success of her own life rest partly upon a misunderstanding of the concern of realism with typicality. Eliot's life, after all, makes a singular enough narrative, and it is precisely because her protagonists are not Thomas à Kempises, not St Theresas — not, even, George Eliots — that their histories are exemplary.[22] Maggie Tulliver causes the form of the novel so many problems precisely because Eliot allows her to step so far outside typicality, and because the novel allows her far more of romantic aspiration and egotism than any of Eliot's other women. That is why, ultimately, she forces the novel to the point where its realism must yield to something else, and in that *The Mill on the Floss* prefigures some of the more generically experimental and politically polemical feminist fiction of the end of the century.

It is, then, in the light of this double concern, to read the work for feminism and to situate it within its historical and generic constraints, that I should like to discuss *The Mill on the Floss* in a little more detail. I am not concerned to establish that Eliot was or was not a feminist (though I do not mean to say that that is a question without interest),[23] but rather to examine the ways in which the novel's focus upon a strong female protagonist troubles its form and brings it up against the limits of its own realist project. The novel sets out as a *Bildungsroman*, a form that more characteristically concerns itself with the growth of a male protagonist. That this form becomes problematic when it centres upon a girl rapidly becomes easy to see; after all, *Bildung* — culture, education — is the very thing most bitterly denied the novel's heroine. The form of the *Bildungsroman* has built into it a requirement and an affirmation of the values of autonomy and self-definition — values by no means always considered appropriate for women. It is an almost inherently individualistic fable of identity whose considerable appeal to Victorian readers depended partly upon its confirmation of the integrity and coherence over time of the individual, and in this it posits character rather than social determination as the motive force of its narrative development. Eliot's concern, by contrast, is to show, through the device of compared and contrasted brother and sister, how powerfully determination by forces and expectations not generated within the individual character affects the growth of Tom and Maggie. This central contrast is obviously an effective vehicle for feminist commentary, and again it is one that will be picked up by several of the more polemical women writers of the 1880s and 1890s.[24] Its usefulness is made more explicit in some cases by making the divergent siblings a pair of twins; Sarah Grand's hugely successful novel *The Heavenly Twins* (1893) will be a case in point. But in *The Mill*, Eliot's use of the contrast between brother and sister is particularly poignant in that *both* are shown to be shaped by stereotypical gender expectations. Tom is as clearly damaged and abused by the imposition of a classical education for which he is unsuited as Maggie is by the denial to her of anything more than a shallow quickness of intellect. I do not want to suggest that there is a complete equality here, of course; that would be to strip the novel of its feminist protest. It is obvious that Maggie's life is more cruelly restricted, her ambitions more thoroughly frustrated, than her brother's. Still, Tom's struggle to conform and to make his way reinforces the point, that the differing expectations working upon girl and boy do not simply distort character, they bring it into being.

It is Maggie alone, though, who increasingly becomes the protagonist of the novel as the children are progressively separated by education and puberty (*Bildung* and sexuality, the poles of the novel). The violence of the collision between the ideological underpinnings of the form and the range of possibilities for the fictional heroine becomes evident in the ardour of Maggie's espousal of Thomas à Kempis and the renunciation of the self. Of course, this novel of the growth of the individual self is caught in its own trap, and Maggie's self-abnegation must inevitably reveal itself to be an inverted form of the self-affirmation that the *Bildungsroman* demands. Feminine self-suppression and heroic self-affirmation enter into contradiction with one another, and the result has been diagnosed by some character-oriented critics as masochism. But as Maggie grows into adulthood, another problem becomes pressing: within the conventions of realism, the novel can offer Maggie — or the middle-class woman in general — no vocation, no meaningful work to match that of the *gebildete* male protagonist. We are back at the crossroads: marriage or death. It is here that Eliot's refusal of romance comes into play. The paltriness of the temptation provided by Stephen Guest, the unsatisfactory nature of the romantic escapade (Maggie's is a sexual fall only by the rules of community interpretation), enact all over again the restriction of the opportunities available to her. It is sufficient to rule out the possibility of marriage, however, and only death presents itself as a conclusion. It is important, though, that Maggie does not, for example, gently expire of one of those quasi-symbolic brain fevers so apt in this period to strike down heroines with brain enough to become enfevered. Instead, she is at once vindicated and annihilated by the flood which, however well-laid the clues of imagery and rhetoric may be, strikes the reader each time anew as sudden, arbi-

trary. This ending to the novel has occasioned a great deal
of commentary, interpretation, and often disappointment. It
has been seen, by feminists among others, as evasive, abrupt,
improbable. The reunion with Tom that the flood effects has
likewise been deplored as sentimental, undeserved by him,
too transparently a wish-fulfilment of Eliot's longing to overcome the disapproval of her own brother. For some feminist
critics, the ending has combined a cop-out (reconciliation
with the oppressive brother) and a victimisation (sacrifice of
the woman). But the plot-ending is not necessarily the
destiny of the text — it may be only its destination. There
is more to be said about Maggie's death (as there will be
about Dorothea's marriage) than simply that it happens.

And, indeed, quite a lot more has been said. A large and
varied range of interpretations of the events of the flood has
been offered: in my own and other people's readings, it
has figured as (among others) a revenge murder of Tom; a
narrator's murder of Maggie; the destruction of the restrictive
community; the fulfilment of an incest fantasy; regression to
a pre-pubertal age without sexual difference; the re-emerg-
ence of catastrophist theories of evolution as a series of
creations; the reconciliation of male and female elements;
anal rage (in this classically Freudian reading, the 'dark
masses' floating in the river are, of course, faeces); the projec-
tion of Maggie's impulses towards martyrdom and heroism
on to the forces of nature; and a moment of sexual release,
the 'little death' of orgasm mimicked by the larger death.[25]
Any or all of these interpretations might be correct. But
more important, I think, is the sheer excess of the text over
such interpretation, the flagrantly fantasied and contrived
nature of the ending. It acknowledges and makes unusually
visible the formal-cum-ideological impasse that the novel has
reached by virtue of its concentration on the development of
a woman for whom no meaningful future — no 'end' in its
other sense — can be imagined. It breaks out of this impasse
only by sweeping the novel out of the realist mode altogether.
The irreconcilable contradictions of ideology and form bring
the novel hard up against the very limits of its own realism,
and the flood that crashes through those barriers submerges
the world of history (and of mimetic realism) along with St
Ogg's, bringing with it the victory of symbol, legend,

fantasy. This, it seems to me, is the most exciting feminist point to be made about *The Mill on the Floss:* the dammed-up energy created by the frustrated ambitions and desires, intellectual and sexual, of the woman is so powerful that it cannot be contained within the forms of mimesis — it is the repressed and thwarted potential of Maggie that conjures into being that destructive, vengeful, triumphant flood. It confers upon Maggie those possibilities of heroism that will be withheld from Dorothea and Gwendolen, but there is an ideological price to be paid, as Gillian Beer has argued: 'The subversive vehemence of Maggie's fate both releases from the bonds of social realism, and yet neutralises its own commentary by allowing her, and so us, the plenitude which is nowhere available in her society.'[26] It is the only occasion in these major novels on which Eliot will console us with such fantasied plenitude for the narrow, unjust, oppressive world that social realism has to depict.

Middlemarch, after all, explicitly eschews such transcendence by the individual. The novel repeatedly cautions against the consolatory illusions of egotism, and enacts through its metaphors of web, stream, and connective tissue as much as through its plot the imbrication of the individual character in its social medium. It is a novel in which simplifying and synthetic hypotheses of interconnectedness — Casaubon's *Key to All Mythologies*, Lydgate's search for the 'primitive tissue', Bulstrode's version of Providence — are satirised by the baldly material and frankly melodramatic connections established at the level of plot, by money, parentage, shared acts committed in the past — by inheritance, that is, in all its forms.[27] *Middlemarch* uses a relentlessly materialist vocabulary of health and disease, microscope and lens, inheritance and debt in its analyses of feeling and moral quality. The effect of this is partly to unsettle character, in its more traditional conception, as the engine driving the plot, and partly to frustrate romantic individualist notions of heroism. True, Dorothea is a belated St Theresa, with no order to found; but it is also true that by the end of the novel she is only one of 'many Dorotheas'. Typicality is pre-eminent over singularity in this text.

It has by now become almost unnecessary to point out the elements of explicit or implicit feminist protest in the novel:

its depiction of what Elaine Showalter has called 'The woman's text in *Middlemarch* . . . the fall of Dorothea',[28] in the gradual domestication of her energies, the vicarious fulfilment of her ambitions, the restricted scope of her opportunities. Nevertheless, it is worth looking once more at the ending that the novel offers its heroine. In a sense, it is conventional enough, and certainly more conventional than Maggie's flood. The 'Finale' chapter, with its more or less direct address to the reader and its closing tour of the marriages, seems reminiscent of the tidying-up operations at the end of a Jane Austen novel — a closed ending if ever there was one. And yet, the conventionality and the tidiness are somewhat undercut by the acknowledgement of the reader's probable discontent, through the opinions of Sir James Chettam and of local gossip. But the reader is pre-emptively rebuked as well as being the object of sympathy: 'Many who knew her, thought it a pity that so substantive and rare a creature should have been absorbed into the life of another, and be only known in a certain circle as a wife and mother. But no one stated exactly what else that was in her power she ought rather to have done — not even Sir James Chettam, who went no further than the negative prescription that she ought not to have married Will Ladislaw.' (*Middlemarch*, p. 894) In this 'negative prescription', of course, Sir James prefigures many subsequent critics. The comment stresses the absence of alternatives 'in her power', but if Dorothea cannot have power, she can at least have Will. The pun is embedded in the novel itself, and surely to some effect in a work where wills are otherwise associated with patriarchal authority, with the 'dead hand' of law, prohibition and patrimony. Dorothea must give up her inheritance in order to marry Ladislaw: that is, she must defy the will of the father-husband in order to choose a new Will for herself. In this there is some parallel with Ladislaw himself; descended from rebellious women, negating the primacy of origin by 'prefer[ring] not to know the sources of the Nile' (p.106), Will too has renounced what is for him a birthright rather than a right of marriage, a conditional inheritance from Casaubon. In this double refusal of the weight of the 'dead hand' of patriarchal precedence, there may be faint hints of what a later feminist George, the short-story writer George Egerton, will call 'The Regeneration of Two',[29] of a new imagining of relationship between women and men.

Daniel Deronda, an extraordinary novel in so many ways, manages to bring together a number of different kinds of ending. It combines in its last chapter two formal closures (Daniel's wedding and the death of his spiritual father Ezra) as well as two more open endings centred upon its female and male protagonists. Daniel's decision to commit himself to the struggle to establish a Jewish state in the East is still, of course, an open ending; the fact that it has been 'closed' for us by history should not obscure the visionary uncertainty that it embodied in its own time. Equally, it suggests that the gestures realism makes towards history can be prescient as well as mimetic. Daniel, then, as male protagonist and bearer of the novel's title for his name, is allowed an open ending of at least potential commitment and achievement in the public world of politics.[30] The novel's female protagonist, Gwendolen, on the other hand, must confront an ending more radically and exposedly open — an ending that feminists must continue to hope will also be closed for us one day by history. The novel imagines nothing, and therefore leaves open everything, for her. Gwendolen, in a final letter to Daniel writes: 'I have remembered your words — that I may live to be one of the best of women, who makes others glad that they were born. I do not yet see how that can be . . .'[31] We do not have to subscribe to the ethics of Daniel's faith, nor indeed to his authority as mentor and judge of 'the best of women', to find in these words an affirmation of hope, of visionary possibility ('I do not *yet* see . . .') as well as an acknowledgment of limitation. In these words, with their avowal of the unimaginable nature of such transformations, we can read for feminism the importance of Eliot's testing of the potentialities and limits of the realist mode for the representation of the desires and aspirations of women. In the ambivalent fantasy of Maggie's extinction and transcendence, in the equally ambivalent acquiescence of Dorothea's commonplace fate, and in the frank uncertainty of Gwendolen's future, Eliot's endings bring into fiction the collision of the unsatisfied, perhaps even illimitable, desire of her heroines with the restricted possibilities of the world as it could be imagined by realism. It is in this sense (not, I know, her own) that I should like to end with Virginia Woolf's comment on Eliot's heroines: they are, for her, the transcription of a consciousness of women that 'seems in them to have brimmed and overflowed and uttered a demand for something — they know not what . . .'[32] Eliot's endings bear witness to the struggles of her realism to imagine, to bring within the grasp of representation, that 'something', even as it concedes that it 'knows not what'.

Notes

1. Michael Peled Ginsburg, 'Pseudonym, Epigraphs, and Narrative Voice: *Middlemarch* and the Problem of Authorship', *Journal of English Literary History* 47 (1980), 542–8.
2. Ruby V. Redinger, *George Eliot: The Emergent Self* (New York, 1975; Bodley Head, London, 1976), p. 331.
3. *Middlemarch*, ed. W.J. Harvey (Penguin Books, Harmondsworth, Middx., 1965), p. 32. In view of the relative inaccessibility of the Cabinet edition and the uncompleted state of the Clarendon edition, references to Eliot's novels throughout are to the Penguin editions.
4. For example, in Cynthia Chase, 'The Decomposition of the Elephants: Double-Reading *Daniel Deronda*', *PMLA* 93 (1978), 215–27.
5. George Levine, 'Repression and Vocation in George Eliot: A Reveiw Essay', *Women and Literature* 7, 2 (Spring 1973), 3.
6. Rosemary Ashton, *George Eliot*, Past Masters (Oxford University Press, Oxford, 1983).
7. *The Mill on the Floss*, ed. A. S. Byatt (Penguin Books, Harmondsworth, Middx., 1979), pp. 152–3.
8. Gillian Beer, *George Eliot*, Key Women Writers (Harvester Press, Brighton, 1986), p. 18.
9. Catherine Belsey, *Critical Practice*, New Accents (Methuen, London, 1980), pp. 67–84 and 112–17.
10. I ought perhaps to add a brief note of self-criticism here, since I have myself used the term in just this sense in my work on *Thomas Hardy and Women: Sexual Ideology and Narrative Form* (Harvester Press, Brighton, 1982).
11. This has, of course, been remarked elsewhere. *The Lifted Veil*, in particular, has received recent critical attention; see, for instance, Sandra M. Gilbert and Susan Gubar, *The Madwoman in the Attic: The Woman Writer and the Nineteenth-Century Literary Imagination* (Yale University Press, New Haven, 1979), pp. 443–77.
12. Cf. Sally Shuttleworth, *George Eliot and Nineteenth-Century Science: The Make-Believe of a Beginning* (Cambridge University Press, Cambridge, 1984), pp. 51–3.

13. *Critical Practice*, pp. 71–2.
14. Cf. Kenny Marotta, 'Introduction: George Eliot and Genre,' *Genre* 15 (1982), 353.
15. Zelda Austen, 'Why Feminist Critics Are Angry With George Eliot', *College English* 37 (1976), 549–61.
16. Patricia Meyer Spacks, *The Female Imagination: A Literary and Psychological Investigation of Women's Writing* (Allen and Unwin, London, 1976), p. 46.
17. Elaine Showalter, *A Literature of Their Own: British Women Novelists from Brontë to Lessing* (Princeton University Press, London, 1977), p. 125.
18. Lee R. Edwards, 'Women, Energy and *Middlemarch*', *Massachusetts Review* 13 (1972), 235.
19. Kate Millett, *Sexual Politics* (Rupert Hart-Davis, London, 1971), p. 139.
20. Austen, *loc. cit.*, 549.
21. Jenni Calder, *Women and Marriage in Victorian Fiction*, The World of Literature (Thames and Hudson, London, 1976), p. 158.
22 Cf. Susan M. Greenstein, 'The Question of Vocation: From *Romola* to *Middlemarch*', *Nineteenth Century Fiction* 35 (1981), 487–505.
23. For a good discussion of this question, see Gillian Beer, *George Eliot*.
24. These writers and works are discussed in my *Thomas Hardy and Women*, pp. 63–97.
25. In this brief conspectus, I am drawing on discussions of the ending in critical works mentioned elsewhere in these notes, and on: Gillian Beer, 'Beyond Determinism: George Eliot and Virginia Woolf,' in *Women Writing and Writing About Women*, ed. Mary Jacobus (Croom Helm, London, 1979), pp. 80–99; Laura Comer Emery, *George Eliot's Creative Conflict: The Other Side of Silence* (University of California Press, London and California, 1976), pp. 5–54; John Goode, ' "The Affections Clad with Knowledge": Woman's Duty and the Public Life,' *Literature and History* 9 (1983), 38–51; Mary Jacobus, 'The Question of Language: Men of Maxims and *The Mill on the Floss*', in *Writing and Sexual Difference*, ed. Elizabeth Abel (Harvester Press, Brighton, 1982); pp. 37–52; Jane McDonnell, ' "Perfect Goodness" or "The Wider Life": *The Mill on the Floss* as Bildungsroman', *Genre* 15 (1982), 379–402; John P. McGowan, 'The Turn of George Eliot's Realism', *NCF*, 35 (1980), 171–92; Judith Lowder Newton, *Women, Power, and Subversion: Social Strategies in British Fiction, 1778–1860* (University of Georgia Press, Athens, Ga., 1981), pp. 125–57; Dianne F. Sadoff, *Monsters of Affection: Dickens, Eliot and Brontë on Fatherhood* (Johns Hopkins University Press, Baltimore and London, 1982), pp. 65–118.
26. *George Eliot*, p. 104.
27. Cf. Leo Bersani, *A Future for Astyanax: Character and Desire in Literature* (Boston, 1976; Boyars, London, 1978), pp. 63–6.
28. Elaine Showalter, 'The Greening of Sister George', *NCF*, 35 (1980), 306.

29. George Egerton, 'The Regeneration of Two', in her *Discords* (London, 1894); repr. with *Keynotes* (1893) (Virago, London, 1983) pp. 163–253.
30. Cf. Lyn Pykett, 'Typology and the End(s) of History in *Daniel Deronda*', *Literature and History* 9 (1983), 65–6.
31   *Daniel Deronda*, ed. Barbara Hardy (Penguin Books, Harmondsworth, Middx., 1967), p. 882.
32. Virginia Woolf, 'George Eliot', in *Virginia Woolf: Women and Writing*, Intro. Michèle Barrett (The Women's Press, London, 1979), p. 159.

2

Jane Austen and the Comic Negative

Kate Fullbrook

For Susan West

The aspect of Jane Austen's art that I have always relished most (and it is difficult to choose what to *most* relish in such a ravishingly great author) is her humour — her absolutely fierce and subversive wit. Now that we've done with the gentle Jane — the ignorant spinster incarcerated in a cottage in the depths of Hampshire, loved *because* (so very womanish) she knew nothing of the world — we seem in danger of inventing another, no less skewed Jane Austen who is more to the taste of the present generation. The 'revised' Jane Austen seems to be a curious cross between Burke and Mary Wollstonecraft: a politically sophisticated and highly committed Tory idealist, who crusades equally against the abuses of sentimentality and the libertarian and morally-relativist positions that threaten the stable, Christian squirearchy she loves, *and*, simultaneously, a passionate supporter of contemporary radical ideas relating to the nature and rights of women.[1] Jane Austen has changed from being an author conceived of as having no politics to one who works consistently through the major political debates of her age.

In regard to Jane Austen it seems odd that it has taken so long to register the critical truism stated by Henry James in 'The Art of Fiction' in 1884, that while art must be based on experience, the kind of experience an author draws on is a matter of mind and consciousness, and this, for the artist, is the only kind of experience that matters. In response to Walter Besant's advice that authors should 'write from experience', and that young ladies, in particular, should stay away from subjects that entail treatment of purely male preserves, James could only revise the terms of the question. 'It is equally excellent and inconclusive to say that one must write from experience', he replies.

> What kind of experience is intended, and where does it begin and end? Experience is never limited, and it is never complete; it is an immense sensibility, a kind of huge spiderweb of the finest silken threads suspended in the chamber of consciousness, and catching every air-borne particle in its tissue. It is the very atmosphere of the mind; and when the mind is imaginative — much more when it happens to be that of a man of genius — it takes to itself the faintest hints of life, it converts the very pulses of the air into revelations. The young lady living in a village has only to be a damsel upon whom nothing is lost to make it quite unfair (as it seems to me) to declare that she shall have nothing to say about the military. Greater miracles have been seen that, imagination assisting, she should speak the truth about some of these gentlemen.[2]

Jane Austen, who certainly qualifies as a *woman* of genius, would have had to be buried somewhere more remote than Hampshire to miss the debates attendant on the French Revolution. One scarcely needs to be reminded of a few bare facts about her personal life — that she had two brothers in the Navy (both rose to the rank of admiral), that another brother married a cousin whose first husband had been guillotined, that she was compulsively interested in the economics of private life, that education was one of the key subjects in her fiction, that she was a voracious reader — to realise that an ignorance of the major social questions of her time would have been far more startling than her knowledge of them and engagement with them. The kind of intellectual isolation fondly created for the author by a previous generation of readers was never a possibility.

But while we're undoubtedly better off imagining a Jane Austen who could think her way past the vicarage shrubbery than one who couldn't (and for a critical generation obsessed with theory, intelligent consideration of Jane Austen probably depends on establishing some credentials for her along these lines) this order of analysis strikes me as about as interesting, and about as important, to an understanding of Jane Austen's art as the question of placing Shakespeare's views on the monarchical rights of the Tudors does to his ('from politics', remarks the narrator in *Northanger Abbey*, 'it was an easy step to silence'). The truth is that Jane Austen is a much bigger figure than such political discussions suggest. It is not her theoretical consistency, nor her progressive politics, that forms the basis of her excellence, nor, though it may seem wild to say so, is it her reaction to the late eighteenth and early nineteenth centuries that secures her reputation; rather, Jane Austen survives, and survives to delight, because she speaks with the pure voice of comic negation — the voice that undermines everything that feels itself secure, that collapses the complacency of authority with laughter, that tears what *is* to shreds while it insists that life will and can go on in spite of repeated deflation of established rights to power. The very essence of classical comedy (the traditional scaffolding on which Jane Austen builds all her fiction) is that life will proceed: the lovers will marry, children will be born, the struggle for decency will not end. This timeless comic vision refuses the sometimes simpler comfort of tragedy — that death will bring an end to suffering, that pain will ensure eternal peace. Comedy is rather marked by its tenacity. It doesn't leave out pain; comedy is as impossible as tragedy without suffering. But comedy refuses death, it subverts from within life itself, it is the literary mode of endless struggle. And Jane Austen, with her illusion-piercing attention to her era's and class's enactments of the most universal human experiences — courtship, marriage, parenthood, friendship — and her mockery of both the form and substance of the most cherished charades of polite behaviour, is the greatest comedienne in the language. She speaks precisely in the voice of the culture she mocks — hers is one of the most civilised voices in English fiction, and one of the most subversive.

It is exactly in the role of comic subversion that Jane Austen is most interesting as a woman writer, and interesting in a way that seems as appropriate to the late twentieth century as to the early nineteenth. Freud was right to stress the ferocity and hostility of humour, as well as seeing its fundamentally liberating and civilising aspects. In *Jokes and Their Relation to the Unconscious*, Freud emphasises laughter's function as a replacement (and at times a more effective replacement) for physical aggression. 'By making our enemy small, inferior, despicable or comic, we achieve in a round-about way the enjoyment of overcoming him — to which the third person, who has made no efforts, bears witness by his laughter.' A joke, he argues, 'will evade restrictions and open sources of pleasure that have become inaccessible.'[3] Comedy, which imaginatively takes to pieces the order which it ostensibly allows to persist, has been and is one of the most significant weapons in the imaginative armoury of those excluded from privilege, or alienated from power. Through the mechanism of 'witnessing' which Freud so crucially notes, comedy changes from a source of appeasement for the otherwise powerless and frustrated unconscious self and enters the public domain. It demands participation — the participation of emotion and intellect combined. What Jane Austen asks us to laugh at most often are the power structures of her world — wealth, social status, patriarchy. The devils of her age are also the principal demons of our own; and these elements rank high, if not always supreme, in the catalogue of institutionalised sources of human abuse in every age we know anything about. Jane Austen turns her hostility on the complacencies of power in both its cruel and hypocritical manifestations with a cynical irony that evidences a rare understanding of the roots and ends of power. And in our assent — for laughter always implies assent, and reason follows quickly on the comic response — we witness and affirm that hostility and join her search for the alternative pleasures which are always presented by Jane Austen as the discovery of equality and complementarity.

The experience that Jane Austen wrote from was of course a woman's experience, and it is scarcely a surprise that she speaks as directly to the woman reader of today as she spoke to her own time. The truth seems to be that as women we are part of the *same* time, that despite amelioration in the legal and social position of women in the past two hundred years, the typical woman's experience remains one of financial dependency, status definition in terms of social alliances with men, closure in the realm of language, and deficiency in education — a general lack, in short, in the resources of power that even women who participate in power in some way cannot help but realise is their intended heritage. These are the 'givens' from which Jane Austen's comedy proceeds and there is no difficulty in taking our places as witnesses at the starting points for her demolitions.

All the major novels are structured around courtship — itself a traditionally 'comic' phase of life in which sexual display is allowed to become overt and in which absolute female powerlessness is temporarily suspended in the light of the conventional supposition that a 'lady' can always say no to a proposal of marriage. This phase of sexual and gender 'irrationality' and misrule in which the usually hidden and always dangerous manifestations of desire are permitted public performance and in which female subservience is temporarily qualifed by the right of refusal is always treated by Jane Austen as the occasion for her analysis of social values and pressures. Courtship represents a borderline state, one outside the normal strictures of culture, in which otherwise unthinkable changes can take place. Traditionally, in both literature and life, female 'freedom' of sexual refusal is joined with an ideal of essential female passivity: the conventional female character does not change but merely affirms or denies sexual access, and the male suitor wins or loses a 'prize' that is no more likely to turn into something else than any other sort of jackpot. Most of Jane Austen's heroines do exercise the right of refusal, they say no to an offer of marriage in one way or another, and their refusals mark rejections not only of particular suitors but of the values and power structures those suitors represent. That their refusals are commonly accompanied by the outraged howls of the society that supposedly allows them a free right to the disposition of their persons is Jane Austen's comment on just how real this freedom is meant to be. But Jane Austen offers an alternative view of successful courtship based not on a combination of feminine stasis and masculine activity that is directed only to prize-winning. Her men and women are equally presented as changing, in a process of learning to understand and to accommodate the other. The males and females are seen and judged on the basis of a fundamental equality. The same components go into the composition of their personalities, their manners, and their morals. As moral beings they must educate each other for suitability to love, and they must do so equally hampered by the crudities and false advice that surround them.

The rules for marriage in Jane Austen's world (which are the targets for her most consistent comic attacks) are simple and utterly crass: money must marry money (preferably more money and preferably *old* money), and the same holds true for rank. The principle of equal exchange is still active, though weakened, when it comes to beauty, that is, to sheer sexual attraction, which is more likely to be seen as an unfair and irrelevant snare when unaccompanied by status or wealth. Love, affection, or commonality of mind are scarcely mentioned in the rulebook. Men and women play by the same clear rules though the male characters are allowed more freedom to move about the board, and, of course, they don't have to win or even take part in this particular game if they don't like (though they all *do* like), whereas this is the only game worth playing for the females. Both men and women like to suppose they are making their own moves while they are in fact often pushed about through the manoeuvres of petty dynasties which enclose and threaten to engulf them.

Jane Austen had no thought of throwing away the marriage game but she did want to rewrite the rules. While she never fell for the cant that dismisses power as unimportant, whether that power be derived from wealth or status (in one of her most revealing letters she complains of people's willingness to read her books but not to buy them: 'tho' I like praise as well as anybody, I like what Edward calls *Pewter* too'), she nevertheless *inverts* the sequence of importance of the courtship rules as she ironically exposes the moral squalor of the dominant patterns of human valuation that cripple the intellects and emotions of her characters. 'Anything is to be preferred or endured rather than marrying without Affection' she states categorically in a letter to her favourite niece. It is the process of learning what affection is in a world in which it is so little valued, and in what it sanely might be grounded, that is the major difficulty for her characters who are surrounded, taught, and guided by the dragons of convention.

This is not to say that Jane Austen is a romantic individualist. Her characters must live as a part of a society that will neither go away nor be magically transformed into something entirely other overnight. They are not inoculated against hostile social judgment and Jane Austen never undervalues the weight of even fools' opinions when fools are in control. It is not so much that she insists that society with all its idiocies *should* stand, as she assumes it *will* stand, and her moral realism always reflects this belief. More importantly, though, she creates a voice and an attitude in her narration that makes living under such conditions possible. The conventional idyll of courtship is transposed to a complex ironic mode, the mode of the survivor who must speak the truth indirectly, and pay service to the very proprieties that evoke a hostile response. Actually, Jane Austen immensely respects proprieties, and for much the same reason that Freud valued repression. Her humour repeatedly focuses on the infringement of politeness and hypocritical or hysterical acts of deference rather than on politeness or deference themselves. This is because she sees the world as so savage that without such rules survival itself would be doubtful. Her funniest characters are the most potentially barbaric. One feels that Mrs Bennet would kill to marry her daughters; that Sir Walter Elliot, if he wasn't so indolent, would gladly erase from the scene anyone who wasn't listed in the Baronetage; that the Rev. Mr Collins would commit atrocities for Lady Catherine de Bourgh with a whimper of gratitude for the privilege; and that Mrs Norris is a cannibal by nature and by inclination. Cruelty and egoism govern great tracts of Jane Austen's world, and her central characters must contrive to live, with humour and grace, within this territory. Her women, in particular, are most at risk with their single game to play and their chances of failure high. This tends, not unnaturally, to make them lose their sense of humour — one instance of gravity that Jane Austen rarely mocks. Many more of the women lose than win, and their men lose with them. And it is the very ordinariness, indeed the likelihood of spectacular failure in any given individual's life, that provides the underlying note to Jane Austen's comedies of success. Her irony is founded on stoicism, and it is as a stoic who concerned herself with reform of moral consciousness and saw such reform as being of equal significance for both sexes that she speaks directly to us.

Experience, for Jane Austen, is the experience of day-to-day, commonplace, garden-variety living, which she quite rightly saw and presented as being so dangerous that she successfully effected a revolution in the history of the novel by throwing out the idea that heroism and virtue could only be demonstrated in extravagant situations. The mockery of Gothic extremity in *Love and Freindship*, *Lady Susan*, and *Northanger Abbey* stems from the conviction that life is always extreme, that everyone lives on the razor's edge whether they want to or not, and that the greatest dangers are less likely to appear in the shape of horrid contents of old oaken chests or as incidents in run-away chases as in the extravagances of minds that refuse to look at the world, and in morals guided by convenience rather than by any notion of the good. In *Northanger Abbey*, her most open attack on the Gothic, a ground-clearing exercise so successful that she afterwards left the subject behind, Jane Austen calls her heroine to order through the intervention of her good suitor, Henry Tilney. Catherine Morland has acted on the fanciful ideas derived from her beloved 'horrid' Gothic thrillers. She first decides that Henry's father has murdered his wife and only rejects this idea to imagine that he's locked her up instead. Henry catches Catherine as she sleuthes about the Abbey in pursuit of verification for her hypothesis, and appeals to her reason for grounds to control her imagination.

> Dear Miss Morland, consider the dreadful nature of the suspicions you have entertained. What have you been judging from? Remember the country and the age in which we live. Remember that we are English, that we are Christians. Consult your own understanding, your own sense of the probable, your own observation of what is passing around you — Does our education prepare us for such atrocities? Do our laws connive at them? Could they be perpetrated without being known, in a country like this, where social and literary intercourse is on such a footing; where every man is surrounded by a neighbourhood of voluntary spies, and where roads and newspapers lay everything open?
>
> (Volume II, Chapter 9)

This is the comedy of fancy run wild, and not a slur on fancy itself. Catherine's notions, which provide her at first with delightful *frissons* and then with terror, hold an honourable place in Jane Austen's catalogue of pleasures — earlier in the novel Henry Tilney himself glories in his taste for Gothic fiction, while his sister is shown to be deficient in playfulness by her aversion to such literary fripperies. Playfulness of all kinds is valued in *Northanger Abbey*, and Catherine begins as a tomboy heroine who 'was fond of all boys' plays', and who prefers 'cricket, base ball, riding on horseback, and running around the country' to books, 'or at least to books of information — for, provided that nothing like useful knowledge could be gained from them, provided they were all story and no reflection, she had never any objection to books at all.' When, 'from fifteen to seventeen she was in training for a heroine', Catherine goes for books in a big way, but only for books that satisfy her earlier propensities in favour of action over contemplation. And as Catherine is a heroine who, astoundingly, 'could never learn or understand anything before she was taught' and who is little practised 'in the habit of judging for herself,' she must learn how to read not only novels but the world accurately. The narrator corrects any view of the lack of seriousness of fiction in the earlier part of the book. Novels are described as 'work in which the greatest powers of the mind are displayed, in which the most thorough knowledge of human nature, the happiest delineation of its varieties, the liveliest effusions of wit and humour are conveyed to the world in the best chosen language.'

What Catherine needs to learn is that the world *is* full of 'atrocities' — General Tilney is *in fact* a cruel and conniving man who neglected his wife and who throws Catherine out of his house when he discovers she is not the heiress he thought she was. 'Spies' *are* in the neighbourhood — it is gossip that separates Catherine from Henry, whom she belatedly discovers she loves for his wit, his kindness, his intelligence, and his common sense. This is horror enough, and Jane Austen makes it clear that the Gothic romances were not *wrong* in their portraits of the mechanics of the human heart, but simply that they supplant probable horror with the improbable. Catherine correctly looks for evil motives in the world and is misguided only about the forms they are likely to take. The final joke in *Northanger Abbey* is not on Catherine — a spirited victim of inadequate education for women — but on those who are so unimaginative as to think Catherine completely misguided in the horrors she fancies lurking within the Abbey walls. For Jane Austen we are *all* inside the walls and only our intelligence will secure our privileges within them. The point of Catherine's education is not to *tame* her into the ways of passivity or to deaden her sense of the world's evil possibilities, but to enlarge her conception of danger and to sharpen both her judgment and her capacity for self-protection. In many ways, Catherine, even in her delusions, is *more* correct in her view of the world than Henry. He must move closer to her sense of extremity in life while she must meet him on the ground of common sense.

Northanger Abbey closes with a characteristic warning from Jane Austen that simultaneously utilises and undercuts the literary convention of the happy (didactic) ending, and points the way to *Sense and Sensibility* and *Pride and Prejudice*. Catherine and Henry marry, and as comic lovers they enter the highly improbable land of unending marital bliss:

> To begin perfect happiness at the respective ages of twenty-six and eighteen, is to do pretty well; and professing myself more-over convinced, that the General's unjust interference, so far from being really injurious to their felicity, was perhaps rather conducive to it, by improving their knowledge of each other, and adding strength to their attachment. I leave it to be settled by whomsoever it may concern, whether the tendency of this work be altogether to recommend parental tyranny, or reward filial disobedience.
>
> (Volume II, Chapter 16)

The irony here is sharp and spiked. It not only prickles with recognition that shared antagonism is a strengthener of attachment and that a common hatred may do more to hold people together than milder aspects of unification, but it takes a pot shot at the rights of parents, that is, of intimate authority, especially patriarchal authority in a hierarchical society held together by the basic unit of the family.

In both *Sense and Sensibility* and *Pride and Prejudice* the varieties of inanity located in the conventional family structure are laid out for comic dissection. False parents, authorities that rule by custom rather than by virtue of either emotional or intellectual precedence, are splashed all over the pages. Again the fiction focuses on the toughening and sharpening of women's consciousnesses as they move out from under the wings of protectors who neither protect nor advise with any degree of intelligence or success. The stakes the characters play for are high indeed — death itself threatens Marianne Dashwood, who with her mother's connivance allows full play to ungoverned sentiment; total ostracism is a possibility for witless Lydia Bennet as she actively pursues satisfaction of sexual desire without due caution (the neighbourhood, enacting its usual role as a pack of choric hyenas, would love to hear she had 'come upon the town', but has to make do with her forced marriage); a sort of insanity lurks in the absurd character of Mrs Charlotte Palmer (a most significant if minor character) who has married a man who neither loves nor respects her, and who lapses into a kind of comic nihilism as she laughs crazily and equally at the death of her plants, the massacre of her poultry, and the insults of her husband. Secrecy, silence, the threat of illness, and the ever-present danger of exposure to ridicule dog each heroine in the quest for a mate who will bring her any promise of happiness. The problem is to find a partner who will combine some degree of right feeling with an acceptable degree of intelligence and who will support rather than destroy the growth of the young mature self. Finding such a person is as difficult for the men as for the women, and both sexes come near to strangulation through the machinations of families who demand the right to determine their children's lives.

Mr and Mrs Bennet in *Pride and Prejudice* must be everyone's favourite rotten parents. Between the two of them they combine nearly every fault that parents who are not actively governed by hostility toward their children could show. They are comic monsters of gargantuan proportions, perfectly balanced in their mutual incomprehension, and the perfect partners in that squalid institution — the 'sound' but miserable middle-class marriage. Mrs Bennet, a paragon of 'mean understanding, little information, and uncertain temper', who is a far more vicious caricature of pristine female ignorance than any man could devise, does at least understand that 'the business of her life was to get her daughters married.' As Fay Weldon notes, she is the only one in the novel 'with

the slightest notion of the sheer desperation of the world.'⁴
This, however, is about all she knows, though she is also
possessed of a certain primitive (and really quite lurid)
certainty that if young men and women are thrown together
sexual sparks will surely fly. Mrs Bennet is a thorough
barbarian, utterly without education, terrified of thought,
given to reminiscences about the days when she was an officer
groupie, and her cultivated husband who locks himself in his
library and allows his wife to simply get on with making fools
of herself and their children is the epitome of irresponsible
knowledge that declines to share itself with the rest of the
world (especially *male* knowledge and especially the *female*
world). The history of Mr Bennet's affections is one of the
most interesting things in the book, and the chief lesson in
the dangers of marriage for Elizabeth:

> Had Elizabeth's opinion been all drawn from her own family,
> she could not have formed a very pleasing picture of conjugal
> felicity or domestic comfort. Her father captivated by youth and
> beauty, and that appearance of good humour, which youth and
> beauty generally give, had married a woman whose weak under-
> standing and illiberal mind, had very early in their marriage put
> an end to all real affection for her. Respect, esteem, and
> confidence, had vanished forever . . . To his wife he was very
> little otherwise indebted, than as her ignorance and folly had
> contributed to his amusement. This is not the sort of happiness
> which a man would in general wish to owe to his wife; but where
> other powers of entertainment are wanting, the true philosopher
> will derive benefit from such as are given.
>
> (Volume II, Chapter 19)

Elizabeth, while not 'blind to the impropriety of her father's
behaviour as a husband', and who knows that her father
makes a 'continual breach of conjugal obligation and
decorum' as he exposes 'his wife to the contempt of her
own children', nevertheless finds pleasure in his 'affectionate
treatment of herself'. Her father's extreme irresponsibility
and heartlessness (covered by a seductive wit that the
narration itself comes close to commending) are tempered
with regard to Lizzie, his favourite child and partial ally, and
it is with extreme hostility that Lizzie responds when she
finds herself treated with contempt, that is, as a woman of

the same order as her mother, when she is first insulted by Darcy at the ball. This exacting portrait of what it means for a woman who has always considered herself exempt from the usual categorisation applied to members of her sex to find herself placed down among the women, remains as devastatingly true today as ever. Mr Bennet chose Mrs Bennet as a wife on purely animal grounds, and when the animal ceases to please he leaves her to her ignorance and mocks her for it. He does nothing to secure his daughters from a similar destiny, indeed, for the most part, he actively contrives that they should be subject to the same fate. The library, an emblem of intelligence and discipline, remains Mr Bennet's alone — the women are not even allowed into it except for occasional visits from Lizzie. The girls are left to the noise, confusion, and jumpy irrationality of Mrs Bennet's territory — the preserve of a silly animal who had not even the luck to breed the male child who would secure the entail for her husband's fortune and consequently ensure her own means for life. A few of the most amusing points in the novel owe their humour to Mrs Bennet's refusal to understand the exact sexist logic of entails — 'How any one could have the conscience to entail away an estate from one's own daughters I cannot understand; and all for the sake of Mr Collins too! Why should *he* have it more than anybody else?' — but her illogical rantings not only brand her as a stupid creature but as a woman who does at least know that she and her daughters will be pauperised if money, which they can do nothing at all to secure for themselves except marry, is not forthcoming.

Mrs Bennet knows, but cannot enunciate, what Charlotte Lucas thinks to herself with chilling accuracy when she accepts Mr Collins' greasy offer of marriage:

Without thinking highly either of men or of matrimony, marriage had always been her object; it was the only honourable profession for well-educated young women of small fortune, and however uncertain of giving happiness, must be their best preservative from want. This preservative she had now obtained; and at the age of twenty-seven, without having ever been handsome, she felt all the good luck of it.

(Volume I, Chapter 22)

As cannot be said too often, Jane Austen is a realist. The good Charlotte's calm analysis of her situation as a woman has not lost its power to shock. 'Respect, esteem, and confidence' which are the missing ingredients in Mr Bennet's marital débâcle are no more considered as necessary for a 'successful' union for Elizabeth's closest and most intelligent friend than they were for her mother. Jane Austen again breaks the mould of literary convention — comic characters like Mr Collins are *not*, as a general rule, awarded as partners to non-comic figures like Charlotte Lucas; the marriage of a realistic character to a grotesque turns our fictional stomachs. It is meant to, and it is meant as well to point up the deadliness of the problem that with Mrs Bennet is always accompanied by laughter.

In this light Elizabeth's marriage to Darcy is not so much a kind of fairy-tale miracle, but a dialectic recovery of what all the failed marriages in the novel are missing. In Darcy Elizabeth finds not only a mate she can regard as her equal ('She respected, she esteemed, she was grateful to him, she felt a real interest in his welfare'), but a man to whom she can bring as much as she takes:

> She began now to comprehend that he was exactly the man, who, in disposition and talents, would most suit her. His understanding and temper, though unlike her own, would have answered all her wishes. It was a union that must have been to the advantage of both; by her ease and liveliness, his mind might have been softened, his manners improved, and from his judgment, information, and knowledge of the world, she must have received benefit of greater importance.
>
> (Volume III, Chapter 8)

The humour of *Pride and Prejudice*, with its tense and brilliant subversion of the received view of marriage — which is seen as an enemy to women, to sense, and to happiness — gives way to the alternate pleasure of the marriage of equality in which both mind and heart of each partner is nourished and expanded by the gifts the other brings. The narrative voice draws back, in this way, from an endorsement of Mr Bennet's philosophy — to let the idiots get on with it and catch one's laughs as one may. Jane Austen comes out of the library (in *Pride and Prejudice* that solitary observation post for the disaffected mind) and lays her moral cards on the table. The ironic laughter of stoic attack is transformed with the marriage of Elizabeth and Darcy into the laughter of delight and affirmation.

The comedy in *Mansfield Park* scarcely suffers from being 'too light, and bright, and sparkling' — Jane Austen's comment on the defects in *Pride and Prejudice*. This is the author's bleakest novel, the one that is most difficult to reconcile with the rest of her writing and one in which her comedy, while it never disappears, is the most bitter, the least accessible. Fanny Price is a difficult heroine; she needs to be bracketed with Jane Austen's other grave women — Elinor in *Sense and Sensibility* and Anne Elliot in *Persuasion* — rather than with the light and agile Catherine Morland, Elizabeth Bennet, or Emma Woodhouse. Fanny is not only a grave figure, she is a debilitated one, who suffers a kind of sympathetic illness with the fine but ailing values of permanence, meditation, and taste sanctified by ancient usage, as symbolised by Mansfield Park itself. She is the most totally respectful to authority of any of Jane Austen's heroines, and her (misplaced) trust bring her close to disaster as she lays her happiness on the line in a passive defence of tradition. Fanny is too sad, sick, and vulnerable for even Jane Austen's comedy to touch; we never laugh at her though we may smile wanly at her faith in a patriarchal protection that is so truly good and just and merciful that its persistence is the greatest blessing. But a comic storm rages around Fanny, and when the sophisticated city wit of the Crawfords pales as we realise the danger it poses to the heroine (and it is much harder to snicker along with Mary Crawford than with Mr Bennet) there remains Mrs Norris.

The comedy that surrounds Mrs Norris is the most thoroughly and robustly antagonistic in any of the novels. She represents the sum total of everything Jane Austen loves to hate: deference that is really egoism, stingy greed, multiple varieties of cruelty (petty, sadistic, gratuitous, bullying, vicarious), and lust for power unaccompanied by justice. Laughing at Mrs Norris bears some resemblance to laughing at Hitler. She is a tremendous threat, a completely credible evil woman, a kind of cautionary figure who demonstrates what one reaction to women's powerlessness might be. She covers her uselessness with random movement and sound, and one of her worst moments is when Sir Thomas returns home and she 'felt herself defrauded of an office on which she had always depended, whether his arrival or his death were to be the thing unfolded; and now was trying to be in a bustle without having anything to bustle about.' To Fanny, the only figure more truly vulnerable than herself, she is remorselessly cruel:

'. . . I hope you are aware that there is no real occasion for your going into company in this sort of way, or ever dining out at all; and it is what you must not depend upon ever being repeated. Nor must you be fancying that the invitation is meant as any particular compliment to *you*; the compliment is intended to your uncle and aunt, and me. . . . Remember, wherever you are, you must be the lowest and last. . . . And if it should rain, which I think exceedingly likely, for I never saw it more threatening for a wet evening in my life — you must manage as well as you can, and not be expecting the carriage to be sent for you. I certainly do not go home to-night, and, therefore, the carriage will not be out on my account; so you must make up your mind to what may happen, and take your things accordingly.'

(Volume II, Chapter 5)

The figure that Jane Austen defeats by making ridiculous in the person of Mrs Norris is, it seems to me, an enemy that every woman still carries within (and the author obviously knew this figure intimately). Mrs Norris is the embodiment of the woman who turns her rage at her own condition of powerlessness outward onto others, who reacts to her suppression by trying to suppress the next most vulnerable person who presents herself. Racial, ethnic and class hatred, as well as sexual suppression, spring largely from sources that bear a family resemblance to this familiar compensatory mode of behaviour. Mrs Norris is not wrong to hate and fear her own position of extreme vulnerability. But her reaction to it is abominable. Her comic defeat in *Mansfield Park* is an exorcism of the highest psychological order.

'Emma Woodhouse, handsome, clever and rich, with a comfortable home and happy disposition' might seem a character about as far removed from Mrs Norris as possible.

Emma, rather than being a powerless woman, is one of the largest figures in her local landscape. But *Emma*, too, is a comedy constructed around the deficiencies in women's condition. Emma begins as a snob and a meddler with a crass regard for money and rank that Mrs Norris herself would have found creditable; she has too little to think about, and too small a knowledge of the wider world to make it easy for her to revise her sense of her place within it. She is like a fish in a tank that has never heard of the ocean, and that would prefer not to. Emma, however, escapes becoming a richer Mrs Norris not only because of her liveliness of mind but because of her capacity for adjustment and change through self-criticism. In her enclosed world she has a propensity for openness; the daughter of a whining, hypochondriacal father who snatches away the sweetbreads and asparagus in favour of a little thin gruel, she retains a life-enhancing generosity. And when the prize of Mr Knightley is awarded to her like a rosette at a county show we feel she has cultivated her own garden sufficiently to deserve her win. For all her wealth and position within Highbury we always remember that London is only ten miles away and that in London Emma is nothing. In relation to the greater world just down the road, Emma's garden is almost as small as those of the other women in the novel who, like Miss Bates, can no longer construct a sentence in the face of the starvation that awaits her without the gifts of her neighbours, or, like Jane Fairfax, who is saved in the nick of time from a living burial in the governess trade. Again the brilliant surface of Jane Austen's writing only thinly covers a substratum of danger and threat. In *Emma*, in particular, comedy flashes as a sign of high courage, a refusal to succumb to limitation and abject dependency.

Persuasion is perhaps the saddest of all the novels, a melancholy, autumnal comedy with Anne Elliot as the heroine who has lost her 'bloom' and who is almost overcome by the silence and secrecy that must surround her love for Captain Wentworth, whose proposal of marriage she refused in her youth in obedience to the worldly advice of her cautious mother-substitute, Lady Russell. The world's trumpets nearly blare out the quieter music of the heart in *Persuasion* and the loudest trumpet of all belongs to Anne's father, Sir

Walter Elliot, the vainest, silliest, most stupefyingly awful father in all of Jane Austen's novels. The Elliots' life is one of 'prosperity and nothingness'. Anne's father lives for vanity only:

> Vanity was the beginning and end of Sir Walter Elliot's character; vanity of person and of situation. . . . Few women could think more of their personal appearance than he did; nor could the valet of any new made lord be more delighted with the place he held in society. He considered the blessing of beauty as inferior only to the blessing of a baronetcy; and the Sir Walter Elliot, who united these gifts, was the constant object of his warmest respect and devotion.
>
> (Chapter 1)

More complex than Fanny Price, and in a sense even more unjustly thwarted and disdained, Anne Elliot is Jane Austen's final stoic heroine, and when her constancy to her lover draws out his faithfulness in spite of the vanity in which the world of *Persuasion* nearly drowns, there is a moment of intense relief and triumph as the heroine finally speaks. Once more we stand as witnesses, and what we witness is a quiet, steady, and inexorable attack on the conditions of power that so nearly wipe out love.

Anne Elliot, in putting the case for the integrity of her affections, refuses to admit the evidence of literature as a guide to women's capacities and feelings. 'Men have had every advantage of us in telling their own story. Education has been theirs to so much higher a degree; the pen has been in their hands.' Jane Austen is the first unarguably great woman figure in English literature who begins to redress the balance. It is a matter for continuing pleasure to see the mainstream of fiction by women in English begin with a mind as tough, as intelligent, and as civilised as Jane Austen's. 'With due exceptions' says the narrator in *Sanditon*, 'woman feels for woman very promptly and compassionately.' We are lucky that Jane Austen's compassion took the form of comic subversion of the mechanics of power, and that she invites us to laugh as well as destroy.

Notes

1. The two most important (and opposing) recent studies of Jane Austen's political views are Marilyn Butler, *Jane Austen and the War of Ideas* (Oxford University Press, Oxford, 1975), and Margaret Kirkham, *Jane Austen, Feminism and Fiction* (Harvester Press, Brighton, Sussex, 1983).
2. Henry James, 'The Art of Fiction' in *Partial Portraits* (Macmillan, London, 1888), p. 388.
3. Sigmund Freud, *Jokes and Their Relation to the Unconscious*, trans. James Strachey (Norton, New York; 1960), p. 103.
4. Fay Weldon, *Letters to Alice on First Reading Jane Austen* (Michael Joseph, London; 1984), p. 76.

3

Reading 'The Brontës'

Margaret Kirkham

'But what ARE brontïes? . . .'
'*The* Brontës. It's a family. They lived at Haworth . . .'
'What were they famous at?'
'They all wrote books . . .'[1]

The speakers in this dialogue are children; a younger brother interrogates an older sister. They start where most of us started, before we were women, with the awkward name, the family biography, the legend. Like Helen Taylor, I find that 'almost every female and virtually no male student has read at least one of [Charlotte Brontës] novels in adolescence.'[2] It is usually *Jane Eyre*. Students of both sexes have frequently read *Wuthering Heights* as an examination text and then there are the films and television serials, even the comic-strip versions of *Jane Eyre* and *Wuthering Heights* which some will have read in teenage magazines for girls. What is certain is that we begin reading the Brontës young, and in many cases, as Rachel Browenstein argues, we form ourselves as we form a view of the novels, or more strictly, of their heroines.[3]

Perhaps this is why some of the most enjoyable and stimulating feminist criticism has been strongly personal, like Adrienne Rich's essay on *Jane Eyre*, or Gilbert and Gubar's chapters on the Brontës in *The Madwoman in the Attic*, where the excitement of a personal discovery of the pattern of imagery in a sequence of works by women novelists comes across still glowing. For women whose ability to make any personal response to the Brontë novels had been dulled by academic studies, such works as these have brought back life.

For it is hard to say whether the dismissal of Charlotte Brontë from the ranks of major English novelists of the nineteenth century, or the reading of *Wuthering Heights*, as though it were a modernist text by a genderless author, has been more discouraging, more productive of critical schizophrenia in women readers. It is unfortunate that Marxist criticism in the early 1970s perpetuated attitudes established earlier in orthodox academic criticism. I have found Terry Eagleton's *Myths of Power* enlightening in many ways, but his limited handling of 'the problem of the author' does not take sufficient account of the Brontës as women authors, whose orientation to literature itself, as well as to society, is different from that of male authors.[4]

In pursuing my own interest in the Brontë novels in their historical feminist context, the critics I have found most helpful are those like Inga-Stina Ewbank, Harriet Björk and Lawrence J. Dessner, whose works take account of women's traditions of writing as especially important. I have of course also drawn on such general treatments of nineteenth-century women writers as Ellen Moers' and Elaine Showalter's.[5]

In the introductory part of this chapter I discuss realism and romanticism in relation to women's writing in the early nineteenth century, suggesting that the conflict apparent in writers from Jane Austen and Germaine de Staël to the mid-century novelists, like George Sand and Charlotte Brontë, is politicised in particular ways connected with the ideology of gender and *sotto voce* with the movement for women's rights. I then consider *Shirley* as embodying a transformation of the 'myth of Corinne' and end with a discussion of the problem of Nelly Dean in *Wuthering Heights*. Lacking space to deal with everything, I have not attempted to write on either of Anne Brontë's novels, though what is said at the start is relevant to them. I should have liked to discuss the treatment of the unhappily married woman in *The Tenant of Wildfell Hall* with that of Mrs Pryor in *Shirley*.

In *Myths of Power* Eagleton speaks of *realism* and *romanticism* as politically ambivalent terms. Romanticism may amount to 'a heady celebration of the heroic, a luridly slipshod exaltation of the patriotic, the traditionalist . . .'. And, while realism is associated with 'bourgeois ambition', it may emerge as 'a critical refusal to be mystified by the regalia of rank and despotic power; and as such it incarnates a liberal-egalitarian ethic' (p. 76). This is apposite to Charlotte Brontë especially, but for women novelists there was a further ambivalence about realism and romanticism, rooted in the history of Enlightenment feminism and the contrary kinds of liberation associated with the novel of sense and the novel of sensibility. As Zillah Eisenstein shows, the movement for women's rights originates in liberal theory.[6] By the mid-century, Harriet Martineau was its foremost advocate in England. The essays of Harriet Taylor and J. S. Mill were to appear in the 1850s and '60s; *The Subjection of Women*, after Mill's election to Parliament on a platform including women's suffrage. 'Rights for Women' was thus unambiguously connected with radical reform and the extension of liberal democracy, and thus with the political grouping most under attack in the work of conservative and romantic social critics like Carlyle, Disraeli and the Dickens of *Hard Times*.

To suggest that the realist novel of domestic life, of manners and morals as they concerned ordinary, middle-class women, was closer to the ideology of rational feminism than the romantic novel, may seem strange, but I think it is true. One may see the connection through the writings of Harriet Martineau, who thought the best advocates of emancipation were 'women who are obtaining access to real social business', among them, doctors in America and 'the hospital administrators, the nurses, the educators and substantially successful authors of this country'. With these, however, she brackets women whose role in life is confined to the family:

> every woman who can think and speak wisely, and bring up her children soundly, in regards to rights and duties of society is advancing the time when the interests of women will be represented as well as those of men.
>
> (Harriet Martineau *Autobiography* (1877; Virago, 1983, pp. 401–2)

Martineau's beliefs made her sympathetic to the tradition of domestic realism in fiction as practised by novelists like Maria Edgeworth and Jane Austen, and continued by, among others, Mary Russell Mitford in *Our Village* and Elizabeth Gaskell in *Cranford* and *Wives and Daughters*. To

Martineau, Austen was 'the Queen of novelists' and her own novel, *Deerbrook*, belongs to the genre of feminist realism, capable at its best of exposing prejudice and of transforming such important stereotypes as 'the old maid' and 'the governess'.

Still conscious of the need to oppose the view that women are by nature less rational than men, feminists like Martineau could find support in the realist novel as women wrote it because it represented ordinary women as capable of reflective thought and rational conduct. Heroines of feminist realism are necessarily 'women of sense' in the making, however vulnerable their hearts. Martineau, as her review of *Villette* shows, was torn between admiration of Charlotte Brontë's realism and impatience at her romanticism.[7]

The anti-heroine of feminist realism is Sophie, the 'perfect wife' of Rousseau's *Emile*, whose portrait, according to Mary Wollstonecraft, had shown contempt for women.[8] But, as Ellen Moers shows, the Julie of his *Nouvelle Helöise* was the inspiration for Madame de Staël's *Corinne* and, 'in spite of logic', for many later nineteenth-century women novelists and poets from Elizabeth Barrett Browning and George Eliot to Harriet Beecher Stowe, Emily Dickinson and Kate Chopin. Rousseau 'threw wide the gate . . . to woman's world of love'.[9] As de Staël formed the romantic heroine, her need of love was a distinguishing mark of the *femme de génie*, along with her exceptional talents in literature or the performing arts. The heroine of sensibility, transformed into the nineteenth-century romantic heroine, was now accredited with largeness of soul, imagination and passion. Through her the liberty essential to the romantic artist could be shown as necessary to a minority of exceptionally gifted women. Feminist romanticism could show heroines in whom desire and imagination made restriction to a limited, domestic role unbearable. Thus de Staël, and after her George Sand, enlarged the idea of the feminine and, through their own literary achievements, made more acceptable a public role for women. It did not, however, lead them to support the movement for women's rights. At worst, the romantic heroine's attraction of adulation and her acceptance of it could bring her closer than was comfortable to the stereotype of woman as childish, vain and egotistical, her 'genius' degenerating into 'accomplishment'. The preference for aristocratic greatness (especially in heroes) and unspoilt peasants could distance the literary woman from the political struggle of her sex, centred as it was at this time on 'ordinary' (i.e. middle-class) women.

There has been a tendency in some feminist criticism to associate emergent feminist awareness almost wholly with romanticism but, as Rosemary Jackson says in her study of *Fantasy* as 'the literature of subversion', not all fantasy is subversive. 'To attempt to defend fantasy as inherently transgressive would be a vast, over-simplifying and mistaken gesture.'[10] This is as true of women's writing as men's and, I should also wish to add, it is a mistake to suppose that realism is always conformist in an anti-feminist sense. The justifiable ambition of some middle-class women novelists to see the condition of their sex as a whole improved leads to an emphasis on 'duty', 'usefulness' and thoughtful 'reflection', which is less conformist than it appears, if considered in the light of feminist argument about women's rights in the nineteenth century.

Feminists in pursuit of literary sisterhood and a single tradition of literature which women might call their own, have sometimes neglected differences of importance. The nineteenth-century novel, as written by women, shows a common concern with the ideology of gender, but the novelists were not all on the same side. On the contrary, differences of language and literary culture, religion and national history, as well as political differences abstracted from these things, come into a serious history of women's writing, as they must into our perception of present-day trans-Atlantic differences of emphasis and approach in feminist criticism. What makes the Brontës, and especially Charlotte Brontë, so interesting and central to feminist contextual studies, is that they stand in a critical relationship to both the English (British) and the European (French and German) novel, at a point when, in the hands of women authors, fiction was the most important form of writing for exploring and changing ideas about female human nature, sexual and family relationships, and the ideology of gender.

In seeking to point out opposing views among different groupings of women in the nineteenth century, I do not wish to locate the true feminist impulse in one or another. Divisions, still largely derived from differences of language and nationality, continue to plague us, and it is more important to understand their historical roots than to adopt a partisan approach. It seems right to speak of 'feminist realism' and 'feminist romanticism' because both contributed, though in different ways, to 'the cause of women'. K. K. Ruthven says that 'historians of continuity, who wish to avoid constructing earlier feminisms on our terms . . . must operate with a "weak" (or generalised) definition of feminism'.[11] He then notes the impossibility of bringing everything from *Lysistrata* to *Sexual Politics* under a single definition. It is also true that *feminism*, if it is to be the term used in connection with the pressures for change in the status of women, in the history of Europe and America in the eighteenth and nineteenth centuries, cannot have a single meaning. If attempting to give women a modern history means anything, it means accepting diversity and sometimes confusion, as well as solidarity. Even literal sisters, writing out of largely shared social and literary experience, did not necessarily hold identical views, nor did their imaginations work in the same way.

Wuthering Heights and *Shirley* both came out of Haworth Parsonage in the late 1840s, and in both there is a tension between realism and romanticism, but it is not at all the same. I have chosen to start with *Shirley* because it is addressed more directly than *Wuthering Heights* to 'the cause of women', and to the 'myth of Corinne' as the literary focus of divisions about gender ideology.

Shirley

Shirley was written in 1848, the Year of Revolutions, and it is set in an historicised Yorkshire, where Luddite riots stand for contemporary conflict between masters and workers. Yet it is not primarily an 'industrial novel', for the 'woman question', seen in a nationalist context, is central. Eagleton has little good to say of *Shirley*, which is not surprising since he recognises its treatment of gender ideology only as an awkward sideline, but he does see it as a novel 'which confronts from the outset its own problematic character as a piece of fiction', and as a novel in which friction between realism and romanticism 'manifests itself not only as a theme but also as a problem of how to write.' He convicts Charlotte Brontë of falling back on 'a ready-made lineage of literary devices' at points of ideological impasse, but this does not do justice to the transformation of literary *schemas* through which the feminist themes are structured.[12] The two most important are the role reversal which makes Shirley squire of Briarfield and the revision of paired heroines of sense and sensibility.

The figure of the good squire, as representative of an idealised, traditional ordering of society, goes back to the eighteenth century and, for women, *Sir Charles Grandison* was the crucial novel. Writing partly at the behest of his circle of literary ladies, and with their active co-operation, Richardson employed a partial reversal of roles by making his hero exemplify the strict 'virtue' normally expected only of heroines. But, more important, the 'Good Man' was created to demonstrate how the country gentleman of influence could, and should, secure for women their rightful place in society. What Charlotte Brontë does is to reverse this, giving her heroine the power to secure for her former tutor *his* proper place. Her exceptional status enables her to make a noble sacrifice of her autonomy in the interests of her lover. Together with her Rousseauist visions, this sacrifice is a mark of her superiority.

Charlotte Brontë was familiar with Richardson's novels and *Sir Charles Grandison* is one of the sources of *Shirley*.[13] It is possible that the heroine's unusual Christian name carries an echo from *Sir Charles Grandison*, where emphasis is put on Harriet Byron's maternal lineage and especially her grandmother, Mrs Shirley, of Shirley Manor. Richardson divides his characters into 'Men, Women and Italians' and the novel sets up an English version of paired heroines later to become important to nineteenth-century women writers through its revision by Madame de Staël. Such a pair provides the central *schema* in the construction of *Shirley*.[14]

Paired heroines were used in realist works after *Sir Charles Grandison* and before *Corinne*. Edgeworth's *Letters of Julia and Caroline* and Austen's *Sense and Sensibility* are examples where the *schema* is used to examine the head/heart question, with the heroine of sense acting as mentor to the heroine of sensibility. In these instances both heroines are English, but the romantic ones have names associated with French works of the sentimental or romantic school. The title of *Shirley* gives pre-eminence to the romantic heroine, but it is arguable that 'Shirley and Caroline' would have been more appropriate.

Corinne, like the works mentioned above, was written in war-time and de Staël polarises her Rousseauist and anti-Rousseauist heroines in terms of nationalist as well as gender ideology. Corinne and Lucille are half-sisters, the daughters of Lord Edgermond, but whereas Corinne with her dark beauty and literary genius is the child of his first, Italian wife, the fair and ordinary Lucille is the child of a second, conventional English marriage. Lord Nelvil falls victim to the pressures of his family and English background and marries Lucille, leaving Corinne to die of grief. The satirical chapters on the pettiness and hypocrisy of English society owe something to French national feeling. English nationalism, as well as anti-Rousseauism, come into Jane Austen's most clearly anti-Corinne novel, *Mansfield Park*.

Charlotte Brontë was alienated from Austen, partly I think by G. H. Lewes' tactless praise and partly by the hagiographical account of Austen's life, which she read at the same time as the novels.[15] Yet she did hold some important attitudes in common with Austen: they are clear enough in the 'realist' themes articulated through Caroline, and in her English nationalism. She 'corrects' de Staël through her representation of Yorkshire as the true England, while abandoning the south in general and Sympson Grove in particular, to stuffy hypocrisy. English remains for her the 'language of truth' and England a better terrain for women than French-speaking Belgium. Hortense is caricatured as a grotesque portrait of Continental confinement of women to domesticity, the obverse side of the *'femme de génie'*.

Nationalist, or regionalist, feeling is important in the sympathy shown between Shirley, Caroline and William Farren, which Helen Taylor discusses in connection with class and gender in this novel.[16] It is as good Yorkshire people that these three are shown to enjoy some degree of mutual respect, transcending (up to a point) class and gender. By comparison the working-class agitators in Chapter 8 are reminiscent of Christina Rossetti's goblins. It comes as no surprise that the leaders of the attack on the mill are strangers, 'emissaries from the large towns . . . bankrupts, men always in debt and often in drink.' Two of them are reputed to come from as far south as Birmingham. . . .

Whereas in *Corinne* the paired heroines are made representative of different national cultures and societies, in *Shirley* they are not. At the start of their friendship this dialogue occurs, as the two girls halt on 'the brow of the Common', where the air 'was fresh and sweet, and bracing'.

> 'Our England is a bonnie island', said Shirley, 'and Yorkshire is one of her bonniest nooks.'
> 'You are a Yorkshire girl too?'
> 'I am — Yorkshire in blood and birth. Five generations of my race sleep under the aisles of Briarfield Church: I drew my first breath in the old black hall behind us.'
> Hereupon Caroline presented her hand, which was accordingly taken and shaken. 'We are compatriots', said she.
> 'Yes', agreed Shirley, with a grave nod.
>
> (Chapter 12)

This assures us that whatever use is to be made of contrasts between the two heroines, there will be no simple preference of one to the other. Caroline, as well as Shirley, is given the touch of Italy which signifies enlargement of the female mind. In Chapter 28 we read, 'it seemed that in Shirley's heart lived all the light and azure of Italy, as all its fervour laughed in her grey English eye', while in the next chapter Louis Moore speaks of Caroline as having, 'a little Raffaelle head . . . Rafaelle in feature, quite English in expression'. 'Italian' is for Charlotte Brontë romanticism devoid of the hostile associations which sometimes belong to 'French'.

When the novel first came out, one reviewer, who sounds a bit like Lockwood in *Wuthering Heights*, said, 'The women are all divine, and *Shirley* is indeed an intellectual harem.' Another spoke sarcastically of 'Miss Shirley's metaphysical acumen and argumentative powers . . . as . . . beyond all praise', while Rose Yorke was 'a precocious 12 year old whose dialectics would do honour to John Stuart Mill himself'. Neither of these gave any serious attention to what the extensive dialogues were about, but Eugéne Forçade did, seeing clearly the feminist centre of *Shirley*.

> The cause of women is defended throughout the book with a conviction and skill characteristic of those who are pleading their own cause. As a picture of society the novel could have been called *Shirley, or the condition of women in the English middle class . . .*

He finds in Currer Bell qualities which define a rational and a romantic feminism, 'a morality inspired by a powerful and exuberant individualism', together with 'a spirit of insubordination' and a belief in 'the absolute legitimacy of desire. . . .'[17]

The romantic affirmation of desire and dream in *Shirley* and the 'individualism' of liberal England both strike Forçade. In the set-piece dialogues and '*devoirs*', Shirley voices the romantic feminist dream, while Caroline shows the realist preoccupations of women without fortune, adequate education or appropriate employment. The two are partly defined through their attitudes to Rousseau. In Chapter 12 Shirley asks:

> 'Do you like characters of the Rousseau order, Caroline?'
> 'Not at all, as a whole. I sympathise intensely with certain qualities they possess: certain divine sparks in their nature dazzle my eyes, and make my soul glow. Then again, I scorn them. They are made of clay and gold. The refuse and the ore make a mass of weakness: taken altogether, I feel them unnatural, unhealthy, repulsive.'
> 'I dare say I should be more tolerant of a Rousseau than you would, Cary: submissive and contemplative yourself, you like the stern and the practical.'

Shirley is not merely more tolerant, she is a Yorkshire version of the Rousseauist woman of genius, Transposed into an English milieu, her 'rare' dreams are not sung in public like Corinne's; she sings 'the song that has been sung to her' only to Caroline and her tutor, but she is endowed with the creative joy of a poet and 'This joy gives her experience of a genii-life.' She sings with a degree of passion and dramatic expression that offends the conventional Sympsons and Nunnelys. Her vision of Eve as pagan earth-mother and her *'devoir'* on 'La Première Femme Savante' are her equivalent of Corinne's performance at the Capitol. Refusing to enter the church on a fine summer's evening, she imagines an Eve, whose 'forehead has the expanse of a cloud', an Eve who was 'Jehovah's daughter as Adam was his son.' Her 'improvisation' takes its inspiration from Rousseau and confines to Milton alone the anti-feminist prejudice which Mary Wollstonecraft had found in them both.

However, while Shirley imagines women as 'contending with Omnipotence' and as 'sisters to immortality', it is her destiny to display the nobility of her nature through a love into which no question of 'rights' can enter. She would 'scorn to contend for empire' with a husband thought of as 'the first of created things'. For a woman in love not to welcome the possibility of sacrifice is unthinkable. When Charlotte Brontë read Harriet Taylor on women's rights, she said:

> I think the writer forgets that there is such a thing as self-sacrificing love and disinterested devotion. When I first read the paper, I thought it was the work of a powerful, clear-headed woman, who had a hard, jealous heart, and nerves of bend leather; of a woman who had longed for power, and had never felt affection.[18]

Shirley's extraordinariness is thus defined through her free, unslavish imagination, but also through her willingness to give up the power which her position as landowner gives her.

Caroline, having no power to give up, is in the more usual position of nineteenth-century women, and she questions Shirley's romantic conception of love. 'Are men above us?', she asks in Chapter 12, reminding Shirley that 'Men and women, husbands and wives quarrel horribly,' and adding, 'But we are men's equals, or are we not?' Caroline in love is as dominated by her feeling for Robert Moore as Shirley is by hers for Louis, but there are differences. Caroline's love is connected with care and service. At the end of the novel she promises, to Robert's surprise, to 'take faithful care' of him. At the one point when her feelings lead her to want to make too open a display of them, after the attack on the mill, it is because she sees Moore as hurt and in need of her. Having just accepted Moore's proposal of marriage, she tells him she cannot desert her mother, even for him. Despite his image of her as a dove, her language shows her as preserving her own judgment and moral responsibility.

The similarities between Caroline and her mother are stressed, though the daughter does not ally herself with her mother's high Toryism. Mrs Pryor, for all her dislike of mannish behaviour, has acted in a most unfeminine way in abandoning her child out of moral revulsion at the conduct of the father, and this is not condemned, but presented as a mark of her rectitude. It is Caroline who seeks the friendship of the difficult Miss Mann, as well as the more congenial Miss Ainley, and Caroline who earns the respect of the village girls she teaches.

> Her knowledge commanded their esteem when she taught them; her gentleness attracted their regard; and because she was what they considered wise and good when *on* duty, they kindly over-looked her evident timidity when off: they did not take advantage of it. Peasant girls as they were, they had too much of her own English sensibility to be guilty of the coarse error . . .
>
> (Chapter 17)

Caroline and her pupils are Englishwomen and, though Charlotte Brontë can't bring herself to the creation of a 'heroine of sense' able and willing to claim entitlement to the rights of citizenship, she does show her as able, with difficulty, to 'think and speak wisely' and to instruct the young in 'the duties of society'. 'Duties' and 'rights', however, could not easily be separated in discussion of women's education by the mid-nineteenth century. Where Brontë would not use the two terms together, the writings of those who did are a part of the context of *Shirley*. Caroline belongs in a humble way with Martineau's women 'who are obtaining access to real social business . . . the educators . . .'.

At the end of the novel, Robert Moore envisages a new day school, to be financed out of the profits of the mill and managed by Shirley, Caroline and Miss Ainley. It is difficult

to imagine Caroline, even when a little older, exercising some
authority and responsibility outside the family, but nervousness did not always come amiss, as women began to emerge
in public through their role as educators. There is, for
example, the story of how Miss Buss, giving evidence to
a Royal Commission in 1869, was almost speechless with
nervousness, but impressed the commissioners all the same,
'We were all so struck by her perfect womanliness. . . . Why,
there were tears in Miss Buss's eyes!' Even Miss Beale of
Cheltenham Ladies College, who had once taught at the
school made infamous as 'Lowood' in *Jane Eyre*, was
horribly nervous.[19] Given the actual condition of women in
early Victorian England, Caroline's seriousness about her
studies, her descent from Mrs Pryor and her ability to relate
to the Yorkshire girls in her class, are not insignificant. Her
role as educator is also connected with another important
theme of the novel, the unfitness of the clergy to carry out
pastoral or educational functions, especially in relation to the
female part of their flocks.

Conservative social critics were not averse to the idea of
women as disseminators of a vaguely religious cultivation —
one need only think of Disraeli's Sybil — but in *Shirley*
female participation in education is associated with active
criticism of the clergy. The novel starts with a strongly
satirical 'shower of curates', curates with little concern for
the 'cure' or 'care' of anything much, except their own boyish
social gatherings. The author hounds Malone out of her final
chapter 'The Winding-up' and Shirley, aided by Tartar,
throws Donne out of Fieldhead. But their superiors are not
always much better. In so far as the Church is shown as
ministering to either the poor or women, it is through Cyril
Hall, the affectionate brother of the only cheerful 'old maid'
in the parish, apart from Hortense, who also has good
brothers. Since Charlotte Brontë was a good churchwoman,
shocked by Martineau's atheism, she gives her good parson
an important part as guide and mentor to women, but also
portrays him as their friend. While Helstone sees his flock
as his troops, Hall is capable of a fraternal role. While
Helstone's clerk delights in the 'piercing song' of caged
canaries, Hall stands near an open window, 'breathing the
fresh air and scent of flowers, and talking like a brother to

Miss Ainley'. Mr Hall's parish, Nunnely, is the oldest of the three depicted and there is a suggestion, quite in accord with conservative romanticism about the Church, if not altogether in line with Brontë's anti-Catholicism, that it stands for an ancient form of true religion, in which women were not disparaged. Briarfield Rectory is old, but 'Nunnely's low-roofed Temple and mossy Parsonage, buried in coeval oaks, outstanding sentinels of Nunwood, were older still.' Mr Hall befriends the Farrens without injuring their proper, York-shire pride and insists on Caroline overcoming her shyness in order to teach in the Sunday-school. The implication, surely, is that he has taken in scriptural teaching about the right use of talents, as applicable to both sexes.

Shirley is about very young women in love, and about the use of female talents. It does not solve the contradictions which Charlotte Brontë, as a novelist of the mid-century, felt between the two, but it does represent them in such a way as to encourage women of later generations to ask more and want more. The resonance of this novel is greater than its formal artistic achievement, though it is less of a mess than is sometimes said, if its feminist centre is perceived. Even the 'magic mirror' passage which reveals the futures of Rose and Jessie Yorke, is not the irrelevance it has sometimes been thought. It may reflect the author's personal sorrow and her relationship with Mary Taylor, but it is used to set up further vibrations of the central thematic chords of the novel. Jessie, as a young child, has the makings of a *'femme de génie'* and is to die early, apparently in Italy, her flame spent after 'frequent sorrows' and 'much loving'. Rose, who resembles her radical father and shares his independent spirit, had, at twelve, a mind 'full-set, thick-sown with the genus of ideas her mother never knew'. The 'magic mirror' reflects for her no love except the love which provides comfort for her dying sister, and then a future which cannot yet be envisaged, outside Europe altogether. Jessie's short, intense life, figurative of artistic genius, is that of another Corinne-Shirley. Rose's exile from an England where it is hard not to end up burying God-given talents, is the future of a bolder Caroline, as the association between them established in Chapter 23 suggests, with its discussion of *The Italian* and

Rose's declaration that she will not bury her talents in 'the dust of household drawers', or 'a broken-spouted tea-pot'.

Shirley, I suspect, would be worth some historical research to uncover its influence on women readers between the time of its publication and the early 1930s. I remember a distinguished woman M.P. coming to give away the prizes at my school near the end of the last war. She was a well-known feminist and delivered a rousing address on the theme of girls not wasting their abilities. Later I found out that our prize-giver had a daughter called 'Shirley'. I thought it odd, until I mentioned it to our history mistress, whose mother had known Mrs Fawcett. 'Shirley Temple?', she said, 'don't be ridiculous, haven't you read Charlotte Brontë?'

Wuthering Heights

Writing at the end of the nineteenth century, Mary Ward said:

> *Wuthering Heights*, then, is the product of romantic imagination, working probably under influences from German literature, and marvellously fused with local knowledge and a realist power which, within its own range, has seldom been surpassed. . . .[20]

The realism of *Wuthering Heights* is centred in the figure of Ellen Dean, about whom critical opinion is much divided. Charlotte Brontë called her 'a specimen of true benevolence and homely fidelity'; Q. D. Leavis said she was 'the normal woman' of 'truly feminine nature'. Gilbert and Gubar call her 'patriarchy's paradigmatic housekeeper' and James H. Kavanagh casts her as 'the phallic mother'. Perhaps a reconsideration of her literary ambience will suggest something more about the kind of realism she represents.[21]

That Emily Brontë was not a naive writer, unacquainted with a range of the romantic and realist literature of the period in which her novel is set, can now be taken for granted.[22] *Wuthering Heights* may be said to enact changes of literary style and emphasis over the period it covers. The Gothic love story of the first Catherine and Heathcliff belongs to the years 1771 to 1784 (though it might be seen also as extending to 1802, when Heathcliff dies), but a world stretching back into the distant past, before 1771, is evoked through allusion and the folk-tale element in Heathcliff's introduction to Wuthering Heights. Nelly is part of the older world disrupted with the gift of a whipping-boy, when only a whip had been requested and she is still there, good for another thirty years or so, in the nineteenth century. What she stands for has a good deal to do with her permanence.

The earliest date in *Wuthering Heights* is '1500', carved with the name 'Hareton Earnshaw' over the door of the house. The latest date is New Year's Day 1803, when the young Hareton and new-made (restored?) Catherine Earnshaw are to leave the Heights for the Grange, Nelly Dean going with them. The whole story therefore reaches back before the birth of Shakespeare and ends in the year when *Northanger Abbey* was advertised. One of its narrators, Lockwood, belongs in Jane Austen's world, the other in a time-perspective which stretches both fore and aft. The language of *Wuthering Heights* ranges from Joseph's biblical Yorkshire dialect to Lockwood's fashionable cliché, amd Nelly's language from the ancient to the contemporary. Recognising the young Hareton, after her vision of the child Hindley, she cries, 'God bless thee darling! . . . Hareton, its Nelly — Nelly, thy nurse.' At other times, talking to Lockwood in the present, she uses a style indistinguishable from the narrative prose of turn-of-the-century moral or domestic fiction.

At one level, *Wuthering Heights* is structured like a late Shakespearean romance, where the new life of children redeems the losses of their parents, but here no reconciliation between actual children and parents takes place: instead it is the nurse and the young people 'in a measure' her 'children' who are restored to one another. When the novel starts she sits eating her porridge with Catherine and Hindley, her foster-brother; when it ends she is again to be part of a household in which, though a servant, she has the status of foster-mother. I do not think her meanings are adequately elucidated without reference to her placing in this structure and to allusion within the novel itself to *King Lear* and *Romeo and Juliet*, the first stated, the second implied. And we need to bear in mind that Emily Brontë did not read our

Shakespeare, but the early nineteenth-century Shakespeare, felt as close to the mediaeval romance *and* to 'Truth' and 'Nature'. Emily Brontë responded to both aspects of Shakespeare and they are at the heart of her representation of Heathcliff and Nelly Dean. I don't agree with much of Kavanagh's re-reading of *Wuthering Heights*, but I am sure he is right in asserting that Heathcliff and the Housekeeper are the central, curiously aligned, protagonists.

Between 1771 and 1803 the household of Wuthering Heights undergoes destructive change. The great kitchen, known as 'the house', which has formerly been the communal living space of family and servants, is divided when Hindley becomes its master. It is he who turns out the servants, who include his foster-sister and his 'bastard'/adopted brother, inaugurating a new régime where division between siblings and between family and servants is symbolised by a hearth and a table, no longer shared. At the end of the novel, Wuthering Heights is abandoned as no longer inhabitable by the new generation. Joseph and 'a lad' remain in the old kitchen, the ghosts of a daughter and a disbarred servant/son haunt the rest.

The story Nelly tells to Lockwood is sometimes thought of as the story of Catherine and Heathcliff, with the tepid appendage of the second Catherine and Hareton, but the title of the novel suggests that the history of a house, as a building and a family, is the central subject. Looked at in this way, the importance of Heathcliff and Nelly, as parallel and contrasted figures, becomes clear. Each is a quasi-child of the Earnshaws, each is rejected by the 'true' child of opposite sex, with whom a bond transcending social distinctions once existed. Each is forced to serve a master or mistress with whom there was once a familial relationship. Both stand for hidden but integral aspects of the house of Earnshaw, Nelly for a female principle or presence, not acknowledged in a genealogical table, but necessary to its survival; Heathcliff, for male disbarment under patriarchal law, where younger, or bastard sons become allied with daughters. It is his rage which completes the destruction of Wuthering Heights begun by Hindley.

If we moralise this rage as evil we must expect to find Nelly Dean as the embodiment of goodness, but that does not quite fit the way she is shown. Nelly's dislike of the first Catherine, which she does not attempt to hide, is little less than hatred, so that when Catherine, in her illness, perceives Nelly as 'my hidden enemy', she is right. Nelly no more forgives her for 'trampling us like slaves' than Heathcliff forgives Hindley. If she is not responsible for Catherine's death, she does not act effectively to prevent it and she does not mourn her. Yet it is a mistake to see Nelly as generally malign, for neither she nor Heathcliff are created to fit conventional moral categories. An unconscious wish on Nelly's part to see the first Catherine's death is parallel to Heathcliff's open wish to destroy Hindley, the inevitable consequence of oppression, but this does not prevent a genuinely life-sustaining role towards the next generation — even Heathcliff shows 'a natural impulse' which preserves Hareton's life in face of his father's brutality. Yet 'benevolence' is part of a moral vocabulary which does not apply to Nelly, since her recognition of the necessity of nurturing the young, irrespective of the wrongs of the nurturer, arises less from duty that instinct, or 'Nature' itself.

It is here that the origin of her familial status in the Earnshaw household is important. She is the same age as Hindley and her mother has fed them both at the same breasts. This is what bonds her with him as 'foster-sister' and at the level of folk tale such a relationship may carry ties little less than being carried in the same womb, but it also suggests that something lacking in the Earnshaw household can come only from outside. The first and second Mrs Earnshaws both seem negative, fading figures. Old Mrs Dean, on the other hand, whose milk sustained the heir and her own daughter, lived to be eighty, 'a canty dame' to the last, though a poor man's wife. Nelly shares her robustness and, though she does not marry, and neither bears nor suckles children herself, through association with her mother she carries the role and meaning of 'nurse' in its primitive sense, and the realistic level at which she functions includes that of a Shakespearean character of 'low life', like Juliet's Nurse. Despite the reading on which she prides herself, her 'wisdom' is the wisdom of practical experience, which teaches her that food does not prepare itself, fires do not blaze without fetching in wood and children do not thrive if not cared for. Like one of Shakespeare's shepherds, she is there to remind her 'young ladies' of the material basis of human existence and her shrewdness is rooted in the working life of a farming community and the seasons of the year. She remembers, 'It was the beginning of harvest', or 'we were busy with the hay in a far away field', as well as 'I was all flour with making the Christmas cake'.

Nelly is connected with the old ways of Wuthering Heights and a realism that belongs with an older kind of literature, but, through her narrative function, allusions to more recent literature are made. The English novel begins with *Pamela*, the story of a literate servant who is her own heroine and acquires familial status by marrying her master. Nelly is also a reading servant, a woman of sense, who does not marry and is not the heroine of her story. Her low social status is part of the means by which Emily Brontë changes the terms of the realist/romantic dichotomy. The Mrs Dean whose tale is told to Lockwood is a woman in her mid-forties, accorded the title of 'Mrs' as a mark of respect for her independent status and acceptance as a 'matron' rather than an 'old maid'. She has saved enough to secure a cottage of her own if need be — not having married her master or anyone else, she gets wages for housework.

At the end of Chapter 8, Lockwood attempts to place her as a Wordsworthian figure of 'low and rustic life', observing that 'people in these regions . . . live more in themselves, and less in surface change and frivolous external things' than those in towns. But Nelly rejects this way of defining her:

> I certainly esteem myself a steady, reasonable kind of body, . . . not exactly from living among the hills, and seeing one set of faces, and one set of actions, fron one year's end to year's end: but I have undergone sharp discipline which has taught me wisdom . . .'.

The discipline undergone is revealed in her story and her wisdom is not so much moral wisdom as knowing how to survive and how to cherish new life against the possibility of better times.

Some emphasis has been put upon Nelly's controlling influence upon the stories of the two Catherines, with the suggestion that Emily Brontë means us to see that she distorts them. While I should not wish to deny that she tells the tale from her own point of view, and that this is to be taken into account, more attention needs to be paid to the fact that Lockwood actually inscribes the whole story and the main narrator. The ironies at work here tend to validate Nelly's view rather than his. At the start, Lockwood appears as a silly young man who might almost have walked out of the sea-coast as it exists in Austen's *Sanditon*. Like Sir Edward Denham, he has read too much sentimental literature and fancies himself as:

> . . . a dangerous Man — quite in the line of the Lovelaces . . . entitled (according to his own views of Society) to approach any pretty young woman with high Compliment & Rhapsody on the slightest acquaintance.
>
> (*Sanditon*, Chapter 8)

Emily Brontë cannot have read *Sanditon*, so there is no question of direct allusion, but of allusion to a familiar type, Lockwood makes use of hackneyed and affected language, his seaside flirtation was with 'a most fascinating creature', a 'real goddess' who was also 'a poor innocent'. He speaks of Catherine as Heathcliff's 'amiable lady', then Hareton is 'the favoured possessor of the benificent fairy'. Supposing her to be Hareton's wife, he fantasises himself as seducer,

> . . . she has thrown herself away upon that boor from sheer ignorance that better individuals existed! A sad pity — I must beware how I make her regret her choice.

Lockwood's mistakes here and in comparing himself with Heathcliff are paralleled by mistakes about Mrs Dean. At first she is a human 'fixture, taken with the house'. Later he calls her 'My friend, Mrs Dean', yet this is patronising and when she treats him in a non-servile way, requesting him to take a letter to the Heights, if he is going there, he is absurdly put out. In his world servants carry the letters of their masters, not the other way about. He does not refuse, however, 'for the worthy woman was not conscious of anything odd in her request.' The irony here, of course, is against Lockwood, who does not understand the more egalitarian manners of Yorkshire, compared with the south of England.

If we can see through Lockwood's inability to understand Nelly because she is a servant, I do not think we find her anyone's agent but her own, and more like 'Nature's' astringent housekeeper than 'Patriarchy's'. Finally, it is misleading to take what Shirley Keeldar says about Milton's cook as a clear guide to the meaning of Nelly Dean, as Gilbert and Gubar do. The author of *Wuthering Heights* was not the same as Charlotte's fictional portrait, even if it was partly drawn from her. Emily, it should be remembered, preferred to stay at home and housekeep to the misery of governessing, even if it did mean propping Goethe up against the flour bin. And it was she who would not let Tabitha Ackroyd, the family servant, be thrown out of the Parsonage when she broke her leg, insisting that she remain to be nursed in the household of which she was part. In a novel about brothers, sisters and servants within the patriarchal family, that bit of authorial biography seems relevant.

Notes

Places of publication are all London where not given.
1. Pauline Clarke, *The Twelve and the Genii* (Faber and Faber, 1962).
2. Helen Taylor, 'Class and Gender in Charlotte Brontë's *Shirley*', *Feminist Review* 1 (1979).
3. Rachel M. Browenstein, *Becoming a Heroine* (Penguin, 1984) *passim*.
4. Terry Eagleton, *Myths of Power* (Methuen, 1975) Introduction.
5. Inga Stina Ewbank, *Their Proper Sphere: A Study of the Brontë Sisters as Early Victorian Novelists* (Edward Arnold, 1966). Harriet Björk, *The Language of Truth* (C. W. K. Gleerup, Lund, 1974). Lawrence J. Dessner, *The Homely Web of Truth* (Mouton, 1975). Ellen Moers, *Literary Women* (Doubleday, New York, 1976; Women's Press, London, 1978). Elaine Showalter, *A Literature of Their Own: British Women Novelists fron Brontë to Lessing* (Virago, 1978).
6. Zillah R. Eisenstein, *The Radical Future of Liberal Feminism*, (Longman, 1981) Part II 'The Historical Origins of Liberal Feminism'.
7. Unsigned Review of *Villette* in *Daily News* (3 February 1853); Item 41 in *The Brontës: The Critical Heritage*, ed. Miriam Allott, (Routledge & Kegan Paul, 1974).
8. *Vindication of the Rights of Woman* (1792) Chapter 5 and *passim*.

9. Moers, *op. cit*, p. 153.
10. Rosemary Jackson, *Fantasy, The Literature of Subversion* (Methuen, 1981), p. 175.
11. K.K. Ruthven, *Feminist Literary Studies* (Cambridge, 1984), p. 17.
12. Eagleton, *op. cit.*, pp. 86–7.
13. See Dessner, *op. cit.*, p. 5 and *passim*; Björk, *op. cit.*, p. 123.
14. My use of the term *Schema* is taken from E. H. Gombrich's *Art and Illusion* (Phaidon, 1960) p. 29. The anaolgy between the painter's use of *schemas* from art, 'corrected' by drawing from life, and the novelist's transformation/revision of literary models or *schemas*, underlies a good deal of my discussion of *Shirley* and *Wuthering Heights*.
15. Her letter to W. S. Williams (12 April 1850) with its reference to 'Chinese fidelity' and 'miniature delicacy', makes clear that she had read Austen in an edition which included Henry Austen's Biographical Notice. The Bentley edition of 1833 was the most widely available and included the 'piece of ivory' letter.
16. *Revue des deux mondes* (March 1853). Item 52 in Allott, *Critical Heritage*.
17. *The Brontës: Their Lives, Friendships and Correspondence*, ed. T. J. Wise and J. A. Symington (Oxford, 1932), Vol. III, p. 278.
18. Ray Strachey, *The Cause* (1928; repr. Virago, 1978), p. 137.
19. Item 116, Allott, *Critical Heritage*.
20. Charlotte Brontë, 1850 Preface to *Wuthering Heights*. Q. D. Leavis, 'A Fresh Approach to *Wuthering Heights*', Lectures in America (Chatto and Windus, 1969), p. 93. Sandra M. Gilbert and Susan Gubar, *The Madwoman in the Attic: The Woman Writer and the Nineteenth-century Literary Imagination* (Yale University Press, New Haven, 1979), p. 291. James J. Kavanagh, *Emily Brontë* (Blackwell, 1985), Chapter 2: 'The Phallic Mother and the Sadism of Control'.
21. See F. S. Dry, *The Sources of 'Wuthering Heights'* (1937); E. T. Apter and J. F. Goodridge in *The Art of Emily Brontë*, ed. A. Smith (Vision Critical, 1976) and Patricia Thomson, *George Sand and the Victorians* (Macmillan, 1977).
22. Kavanagh, *op. cit.*, p. 82, interprets this as another example of Nelly's pro-patriarchal machinations. I see her wish to send a note to Catherine as needing no excuse. Its contents are, of course unknown.

4

The Body of the People in Virginia Woolf

Gillian Beer

As Virginia Woolf began imagining the work which was to become *Between the Acts*, she foresaw the enterprise. She implored herself not to 'call in all the cosmic immensities' or 'force my tired and diffident brain to embrace another whole — all parts contributing'. Instead she wanted 'a centre: all lit[erature] discussed in connection with real little incongruous living humour; & anything that comes into my head; but "I" rejected: "We" substituted: to whom at the end there shall be an invocation?'[1] The alternation between 'I' and 'We' is the living quarrel of Virginia Woolf's art, particularly in her later career. Her subject-matter is often isolation, and she excels at recording the repetitive, fickle movements of an individual's thought and feeling at levels beneath self-criticism. But she was fascinated by communities: the family, groups of friends, the nation and history. These groupings control the form of her work in the novels from *Mrs Dalloway* on to *Between the Acts*. The need for a certain autonomy, 'a room of one's own', is set alongside the need to find a creative standpoint which will be less merely personal, less preoccupied with private relationships. To be alive on the same day in London may be a deeper bond, her writing in *Mrs Dalloway* suggests, than any of the individual choices of love and friendship which narrative fiction ordinarily privileges.

She saw the movement away from the particular to the broader inquiry as especially important for women writers. In 1929 in 'Women and Fiction' she predicts that future women writers will 'be less absorbed in facts' . . . 'They will look beyond the personal and political relationships to the

wider questions which the poet tries to solve — of our destiny
and the meaning of life.'[2] In 'The Narrow Bridge of Life'
(1927) she wrote of the need to 'stand further back from
life.'[3] We may temper these rather sibylline critical utterances
with the evidence from her life of close involvement with the
women's movement, with socialism and with the network of
friends and ideas we call 'Bloomsbury'. And the process
of the novels indicates that the 'standing further back' she
recommends is not withdrawal but a means of observing
patterns other than those formerly recorded. She made an
early attempt at describing a new pattern, in an entry in her
Diary on Monday, February 21st, 1927, which plays third
persons against each other, notably excluding the first person
singular and plural, neither 'I' nor 'We' participating:

> Why not invent a new kind of play — as for instance:
>
> Woman thinks: . . .
> He does.
> Organ Plays.
> She writes.
> They say:
> She sings:
> Night speaks:
> They miss
>
> I think it must be something in this line — though I can't now
> see what. Away from facts; free; yet concentrated; prose yet
> poetry; a novel & a play.[4]

Only subjects are recorded (woman, he, organ, she, they,
she, night, they). The sentences have no object — the relation
of subject and object appearing to her at this time, it seems,
as the endorsement of 'facts'.

As she wrote *The Waves* and *The Years* she was steadily
reading Dante, reading him in 'the place of honour' at the
end of her own day's writing, quoting the Purgatorio at the
end of the 1911 section of *The Years*:[5]

> Che per quanti si dice piu li nostro
> tanti possiede piu di ben ciascuno.
>
> (canto xv, ll.55–6)

So by so many more there are who say 'ours'
So much the more of good doth each possess.[6]

The deep value which she accords to communality is not a matter only of her sincerely learnt and practised socialism or her forcefully written (if not always practised) solidarity with other women. It has to do with her practice of writing out of the mass and out of the body.

'We' is an elastic pronoun, stretching in numbers and through time. Its population ranges from the exclusive pair of lovers, now, to the whole past of human history. It can welcome or rebuff the hearer. It can also colonise. Virginia Woolf saw clearly that 'we' may be coercive and treacherous. It invites in the individual, the subset, the excluded, who once inside may find themselves vanished within an alien group claiming on their behalf things of no benefit or relevance to themselves.

Virginia Woolf was chary of the 'we' of patriotism, and of the self-gratifying claims of male writers to speak in universals which cover (in many senses) the experience also of women. Her reaction in writing to social communities was sceptical and wary; she needed to find ways of maintaining difference as well as constellation, lest clusters become ordered as hierarchies. Yet her writing emphasises communality and the body. Language itself drives, as Bernard remarks, 'roman roads across experience'. Living in an old linguistic culture burdens the speaker with shared and unshared experience. The autocracy of the inherited tongue may be at odds with the particular. So Mrs Ramsay resents being betrayed into uttering a belief she does not share ('We are in the hands of the Lord') through the power of language to stretch belief beyond reason. Woolf was attracted by assemblage rather than coherence: the slippage, repetition and reversal of oral elements within sentences and within words (the unstable movement of 'b' 'f' 'r' and 's' sounds in passages of which this is a brief example from the opening page of *The Waves:* 'Then she raised her lamp higher and the air seemed to become fibrous and to tear away from the green surface flickering and flaming in red and yellow fibres like the smoky fire that roars from a bonfire. Gradually the fibres of the burning fibres were fused into one haze. . . '). This onomatopoeic emphasis is one means by which she represents the random communities of language, the waves of sound continuing on beyond sense. *The Waves*, in particular, explores various diads: the I/not I; the I/you and the I/we. For, paradoxically, 'we' always recognises separation even while it emphasises congruity. That recognition is epitomised in the line from Cowper's 'The Castaway' which Mr Ramsay obsessionally mutters at intervals throughout *To the Lighthouse:*

We perish each alone.

We/each/all/one: the systole and diastole of human experience is posed upon 'perish' and summarised in 'alone'. Yet only by means of 'the common life which is the real life', as she writes in *A Room of One's Own*, can change be brought about.

*

In *A Room of One's Own* (1929) she identifies first-person and its written sign 'I' with the phallic oppressiveness of the opinionated male writer, observed by the quizzical and insistent other 'I' of her narrator, who is also 'one'.

Indeed, it was delightful to read a man's writing again. It was so direct, so straightforward after the writing of women. It indicated such freedom of mind, such liberty of person, such confidence in himself. One had a sense of physical well-being in the presence of this well-nourished, well-educated, free mind, which had never been thwarted or opposed, but had had full liberty from birth to stretch itself in whatever way it liked. All this was admirable. But after reading a chapter or two a shadow seemed to lie across the page. It was a straight dark bar, a shadow shaped something like the letter 'I'. One began dodging this way and that to catch a glimpse of the landscape behind it. Whether that was indeed a tree or a woman walking I was not quite sure. Back one was always hailed to the letter 'I'. One began to be tired of 'I'. Not but what this 'I' was a most respectable 'I'; honest and logical; as hard as a nut, and polished for centuries by good teaching and good feeding. I respect and admire that 'I' from the bottom of my heart. But — here I turned a page or two, looking for something or other — the worst of it is that in the shadow of the letter 'I' all is shapeless as mist. Is that a tree? No, it is a woman. But . . . she has not a bone in her body, I thought, watching Phoebe, for that was her name, coming across the beach. Then Alan got up and the shadow of Alan at once obliterated Phoebe.

(pp. 149–50)

The humour of the passage is in the alternation of the identical first-person to signify two different views: one, the obliterativeness of the letter 'I' in whose shadow 'all is shapeless as mist. Is that a tree? No, it is a woman. But . . . she has not a bone in her body.' The upright 'I' fillets the upright figure of Phoebe walking, into a softened receptacle of his own views and passions. The 'I' of the body is lost in the Lawrentian pastiche of passion. Phoebe is a lay-figure caught between the frank and sceptical 'I' of the insistently tart narrator 'But — I am bored!' and the imposing 'I' of the male author. At the end of the paragraph Woolf asserts that she is describing the self-conscious virility of the male writer in the face of the women's movement. So the doubling of the 'I' here and their mutual resistance makes for the enclosure and limiting of each. But we will better understand the awkwardness and allure of 'We' for Virginia Woolf if we group together three works which came out of a single creative movement: *Orlando*, *A Room of One's Own* and *The Waves*. First thoughts of *The Waves* preceded the buoyant writing of *Orlando*, and her preparation of *A Room of One's Own* accompanied that work. *Orlando* and *The Waves* are the works in which she most trenchantly surveyed the relationship between the subject and the self. She imagined *The Waves* ending, perhaps, with a 'gigantic conversation'.[7]

Virginia Woolf is seeking a written 'I' which can also move out into 'We' and include a serenely and laterally shifting population. For that she must do away with the insistent phallic 'I' and its blasting properties. She seeks a writing body which will be permeable and expansive:

A very good summer, this, for all my shying & jibbing, my tremors this morning. Beautifully quiet, airy, powerful. I believe I want this more humane existence for my next — to spread carelessly among one's friends — to feel the width and amusement of *human* life: not to strain to make a pattern just yet: to be made supple, & to let the juice of usual things, talk, character, seep through me, quietly, involuntarily, before I say — Stop & take out my pen. Yes, my thoughts now begin to run smooth: no longer is every nerve upright.[8]

She enjoys 'supple' and 'seep'; rejects 'strain' and 'upright'. 'We' includes the body, and Virginia Woolf insisted on closeness to the body as the primary source of humour and communality. She saw moreover that creative writers do not write an ideolect in solitude: '*For masterpieces are not single and solitary births; they are the outcome of many years of thinking in common, of thinking by the body of the people, so that the experience of the mass is behind the single voice*'.[9] (emphasis added)

Mrs Dalloway (1925) is the first of her works which moves about within a community poised in a historical moment, and explores the mass behind the single voice. Virginia Woolf was fascinated by place, that condensing of past and present which subtly controls and changes experience and establishes a common life. In *Mrs Dalloway* she sets out the topography of London as precisely as does Defoe whom she so much admired. Social territories are marked out (Lady Burton in Brook Street, Sarah Bletchley in Pimlico); communal spaces are lovingly articulated, particularly all the details of Regent's Park. The accounts of walks and of districts register the characters' social space as well as their separations. Elizabeth Dalloway 'looked up Fleet Street' and explores its sociogeography as if it were a strange house in which she was a shy visitor.

She looked up Fleet Street. She walked just a little way towards St. Paul's, shyly, like someone penetrating on tiptoe, exploring a strange house by night with a candle, on edge lest the owner should suddenly fling wide his bedroom door and ask her business, nor did she dare wander off into queer alleys, tempting by-streets, any more than in a strange house open doors which might be bedroom doors, or sitting-room doors, or lead straight to the larder. For no Dalloways came down the Strand daily; she was a pioneer, a stray, venturing, trusting.[10]

Alone of the characters, Septimus haunts an absolute world, bare of locality except for the dead places of the war.

The people in the book are inhabitants of the same city on the same day. They lightly bear the weight of a common past sealed in statues, buildings, roadways, and stored in the memories each privately preserves as they walk those open ways. The immediate trauma that unites them is that of World War I, which for Virginia Woolf is also the deep historical separator, functioning as the line down the middle of the picture, represented also in the 'Time Passes' section of *To the Lighthouse* (which occupies the war years), and as the voiding topic of *Jacob's Room*. Septimus Smith endlessly and nihilistically recalls his lost experience of the war. But as we read, that experience is not confined to Septimus alone; it spreads *through our reading* into the whole community described.

The reader becomes the medium of connection, partly through our assumed familiarity with these same places and history, partly through the lateral entwining of the narrative and its easy recourse to the personal pasts of memory, the communal past of an imagined prehistory. Woolf uses several means of representing those impersonal intimacies of juxtaposition and association which usually go unrecorded. The closed car and the aeroplane are seen by the various figures in the book. More subtle and more mysterious are the two old women, of whom one, singing beside Regent's Park tube station, takes us back past language to a semiological cradleland surviving into the present.[11]

Class and even gender may prove ultimately in her work to be ephemeral distinguishers. Nevertheless, alongside the emphasis on the common conditions of life, in *Mrs Dalloway* the two selves of gender are parted. Our response as practised readers is to recognise Septimus Smith and Clarissa Dalloway as the centres of intensity in the book's life, the 'major characters'. The shadow-plots derived from reading earlier fiction lead us to expect connection between them at the level of event. We are disturbed instead by slightness and separation, the connections being formed solely at the level of reading-process and, at the end, in Clarissa's musing consciousness of discrete lives. The contacts between Septimus and Clarissa are oblique and communal. They (like other inhabitants) share the day with the closed car, the commercial aeroplane. They share no personal history; they never meet, never have met. They belong to different social classes, have scarcely read the same books, but they are deeply embedded in common history — the recent past of the war, the longer past of English social stratification, the continuing presence of changing London.

Moreover Clarissa and Septimus are 'as one' in the book's imagination, standing in for each other in the reader's attention. We look for a contingent meeting, perhaps even for a rescue which never takes place. Clarissa cares about her roses not about the Armenians; Septimus about his revelation. Septimus knows nothing of Clarissa. Clarissa reaches out to make a one-way connection in her mind between his fate and hers, as she does also between herself and the woman in the room opposite. She feels his death in her body:

> He had killed himself — but how? Always her body went through it, when she was told, first, suddenly, of an accident; her dress flamed, her body burnt. He had thrown himself from a window. Up had flashed the ground; through him, blundering, bruising, went the rusty spikes. There he lay with a thud, thud, thud in his brain, and then a suffocation of blackness.

His death momentarily allows her absolute intimacy, which everywhere else eludes her: 'closeness drew apart; rapture faded; one was alone. There was an embrace in death.' The language is that of sexuality: Clarissa in fantasy feels the 'rusty spikes' invade her body as they had done Septimus. But the brief sentences succeed each other without lubricious dwelling on the event. Immediately afterwards she acknowledges her separateness, which now feels to her like a punishment:

> Somehow it was her disaster — her disgrace. It was her punishment to see sink and disappear here a man, there a woman, in this profound darkness, and she forced to stand here in her evening dress. She had schemed; she had pilfered. She was never wholly admirable.

(pp. 202–3)

This sense of desolate privilege is assuaged within the space

92

of a page; at last the old lady in the room opposite, whom she had long observed, seems also to observe her: 'She parted the curtains; she looked. Oh, but how surprising! — in the room opposite the old lady stared straight at her! She was going to bed.' Even then it remains uncertain whether the other woman sees Clarissa.

By a magical transposition of persons that narrative can effect, Clarissa's hope of exchange and intimacy substitutes the old lady for Septimus in our experience as readers. But at the level of event Clarissa receives no recognition from Septimus; she simply claims him as her double, the enactor of her shadow-life and preserver of her and his unnamed treasure: 'A thing there was that mattered; a thing, wreathed about with chatter, defaced, obscured in her own life, let drop every day in corruption, lies, chatter. This he had preserved.'

The reader is likely, first, to feel affronted at her claim: much worse has happened to Septimus than to Clarissa. And who is she, society hostess, to claim the life of a shell-shocked, lower-middle-class person, to perceive his experience as somehow her own? The activity of the novel, however, sustains her claim, calmly receives our outrage and leads us to recognise some of its sources in stereotype. Kinship cannot be measured by event, by class, or even by gender, it seems. Separation may even be the condition for recognising kin. The two old women of the book are separate too, though they link London together; one privately goes on with her silent life in her solitary room, the other, open and derelict, sings a song which burrows beneath language and difference:

ee um fah um so
foo swee too eem oo.

'London has swallowed up many millions of young men called Smith' (p. 94): Septimus happens to be the recorded one among them. He and Mrs Dalloway are no mystic pair, but their poignantly repeated coldness allows Woolf in this novel to take the measure of a whole society in its historical moment.

The unforced likenesses between our reading experience of

both characters reveals what is hidden far down beneath social event, personal relationship and individuality: the failure of feeling, and the fear of failing to feel, which marks the community of her time and writing. That fear is registered in the process of thought which is Peter Walsh and Miss Kilman also. The novel creates the sense of an *atomistic gathering* through its piquant vignettes of people, its record of pathways; it has less recourse to the sustained analysis of established relationships. The work finds unity at a level other than that of discredited action, other even than analytical language. It gathers in upon the party-giving solitary, Clarissa Dalloway; and she has become, for a little while, also Septimus Smith and the unnamed beyond him: 'There she was'.

Orlando and *The Waves*, the books at the centre of Woolf's career, are, on the face of it, those most preoccupied with the self. One thing that sets them apart from the rest of her work is the absence of World War I from their pages: from *Jacob's Room* through to *To the Lighthouse* the war shapes, splits, and penetrates the works.[12] In *Orlando* it vanishes; in *The Waves*, despite its ruminating on imperialism and the city, the characters inhabit a world in which all that is traditionally central to narrative has been peripheralised or obliterated: Percival's adventures in India, Bernard's family, Louis' city career, Jinny's lovers, even the crisis of Rhoda's madness and the love affair between her and Louis are present only as fragmentary allusion. The characters inhabit a world devoid of close historical markers, though in a recognisable present day. The other work which forms a single creative flow with *The Waves* and *Orlando* is *A Room of One's Own*. Their composition weaves in and out of each other; but they are quite different, one from the other, each seeking to capture what has not been fully marked elsewhere.

Virginia Woolf much enjoyed biography and autobiography, even while she distrusted their evidences and their determinism. She distrusted the iconoclasm then in fashion in the biographical work of Lytton Strachey and liked autobiography because 'Almost always this comes from autobiography: a liking, at least some imaginative stir'.[13] In her essay on Christina Rossetti she remarked:

As everybody knows, the fascination of reading biographies is irresistible. . . . Here is the past and all its inhabitants miraculously sealed as in a magic tank; all we have to do is to look and to listen and to listen and to look and soon the little figures — for they are rather under life size — will begin to move and to speak, and as they move we shall arrange them in all sorts of patterns of which they were ignorant, for they thought when they were alive that they could go where they liked; and as they speak we shall read into their sayings all kinds of meanings which never struck them, for they believed when they were alive that they said straight off whatever came into their heads. But once you are in a biography all is different.[14]

The knowing biographer is on a par with the realist novelist in her judgment: both claim an authority which stifles their awareness of life.

How to write lives became for Virginia Woolf a more inclusive question: how to write life. In *To the Lighthouse* she had rewritten her own family history, making of it something other than a 'historical' record. At this period she became increasingly preoccupied with the levels at which it is possible to describe life-process, and with the exclusion of women from records which preoccupy themselves with careers and historical triumphs and defeats.[15] She began the exploration novelistically in the twinned figures of Mr and Mrs Ramsay — he so anxious for the survival of his fame: she so concerned for the immediate — and for the survival of her children. How far are they at odds? How much of human longing is wrapt into the longing for survival?

In *Orlando* she elongated the arc of the individual's survival through time; Orlando is not only continuously alive through many historical periods; he never ages, she never ages, beyond thriving maturity. The reader is jestingly made aware of how much we believe our reading. Reading lets us live, apparently, through swathes of history. It allows us, without danger, to take part in past tumult. We sleep it off, like Orlando, and discover a new place, a new book, next day. In *Orlando*, Woolf doubles our reading pleasure by making us aware of the gaps between reading and living and also of how readily we confuse them. In reading we readily shift gender — until the activity is pointed out to us and then it seems strange. When Orlando with much hyperbolic preamble becomes a woman, men and women readers equally are made conscious of a constraint. The writing assumes that we will need to change our relation to Orlando and yet points to the absurdity of doing so, since we made no bones about participating in his earlier adventures, whether reading with men's or women's eyes.[16]

Orlando rests on the surface of the ages she inhabits, teased by the desire to write allayed by great possessions, experiencing as man and woman without guilt or Tiresian pangs. The hedonistic ease with which Orlando keeps just within the constraints of each society, and, when she cannot do so, moves out or moves on is a tribute to Victoria Sackville-West, the 'biographical' inspiration for the work. Its lightheartedness is artfully to represent most things as possible. Its undertow of feeling is to remind us that, *au contraire*, in life, very many things are not. *Orlando* mitigates but also repeats the sad story of Shakespeare's sister which Woolf imagined, at about this same time, in *A Room of One's Own*. In *Orlando* the single self breasts the waves of society — moving at times almost without effort through the subsequences of event.

The triumph of the work is to offer epitomes not of Orlando him/herself, who soon becomes somewhat boring to the reader — transparent and foreknown — but rather of the societies s/he enters. History as Virginia Woolf tells it, becomes a form of biography: a biography of the land and sky as much as of the individuals who pass across its surface. *Orlando* is a tale of the upper classes, of the inertia of the landed as much as the continuance of the land. It is in the vein of dream-work in which the reader, like the dreamer, identifies with royalty and has the freedom of strange lands. Wish-fulfilment here makes us turn our gaze back upon the wishes fulfilled and understand the impossibility of those wishes. The apparent entry which biography offers into another's life is, Virginia Woolf suggests, more often a self-gratifying spectatorship which diminishes the life observed. In *Orlando* she delights in breaking across the reader's expectations. Her work elsewhere, even in dialogue, does not much insist on the spoken voice, but here the clear tones of the assured narrative discourse mock the biographer's enterprise, the reader's choices, and the assumptions both writer and reader bring to the making of a life. By means of biography she explores the written and the bodily self, the self of biographer, reader, and subject. *Orlando* has at the centre of its discourse the body: Orlando's shifting sexual form, certainly, but also temperature, the heat and cold with which we most familiarly and with our whole body gauge the world. The Elizabethan age is characterised by hyperbolical weather:

> The age was the Elizabethan; their morals were not ours; nor their poets; nor their climate; nor their vegetables even. Everything was different. The weather itself, the heat and cold of summer and winter, was, we may believe, of another temper altogether. The brilliant amorous day was divided as sheerly from the night as land from water. Sunsets were redder and more intense; dawns were whiter and more auroral. Of our crepuscular half-lights and lingering twilights they knew nothing. The rain fell vehemently, or not at all. The sun blazed or there was darkness.[17]

Orlando survives, not in Tiresian disenchantment, but brilliantly engaged with the sensory world, even at the final collapse of her ancestral home merely into language. 'The gallery and all its occupants fell to powder. . . . Her own body quivered and tingled as if suddenly naked in a hard frost.' Touch, most direct of contacts, breaks the sealed space between reader and subject. But the body is central to this book as humour, not earnestness: Virginia Woolf's riposte to the literary doggedness about 'natural desire' which she mocked in *A Room of One's Own* is to flaunt both language and body as joke.

> Hail! natural desire! Hail! happiness! divine happiness! and pleasure of all sorts, flowers and wine, though one fades and the other intoxicates; and half-crown tickets out of London on Sundays, and singing in a dark chapel hymns about death, and anything, anything that interrupts and confounds the tapping of typewriters and filing of letters and forging of links and chains, binding the Empire together. Hail even the crude, red bows on shop girls' lips (as if Cupid, very clumsily, dipped his thumb in red ink and scrawled a token in passing). Hail, happiness! kingfisher flashing from bank to bank, and all fulfilment of natural desire, whether it is what the male novelist says it is; or prayer;

or denial; hail! in whatever form it comes, and may there be more forms, and stranger.[18]

The stereotypes of happiness are here jumbled together with the uncelebrated (but instantly recognisable) joys of 'singing in a dark chapel hymns about death'. The curious forms of happiness are less circumscribed than realism or lyricism would have us believe. This book mixes the pleasures of the impossible, 'It's a very fine boy M'Lady' said Mrs Banting, the mid-wife, 'putting her first-born child into Orlando's arms' with hyperbolic double-entendre:

> It was no longer so thick, so watery, so prismatic now that King Edward — see, there he was, stepping out of his neat brougham to go and visit a certain lady opposite — had succeeded Queen Victoria. The clouds had shrunk to a thin gauze; the sky seemed made of metal, which in hot weather tarnished verdigris, copper colour or orange as metal does in a fog. It was a little alarming — this shrinkage. Everything seemed to have shrunk. Driving past Buckingham Palace last night, there was not a trace of that vast erection which she had thought everlasting; top hats, widows' weeds, trumpets, telescopes, wreaths, all had vanished and left not a stain, not a puddle even, on the pavement.[19]

The inordinate fecundity of the Victorian age with its ponderous and imposing imperialist fertility leaves 'not a stain' from its vast erection.

Virginia Woolf wrote in *The Pargiters* of her difficulty in writing about her body, but in *Orlando* she freely moves across the inhabited and the imagined body in a way that challenges gender. Where do we live in our bodies? Can we give or take a few genitalia and remain ourselves, our desires not altered, our will hampered maybe, but the same? In *Orlando* the central self endures the vicissitudes of translation — through time, through gender, through changing language — not itself much changed. Primary allegiances (to 'The Oak Tree', to Sasha) are unmoved. The form of desire is peremptorily inscribed at the start.

In 1929 in Marshall and Snelgrove, Orlando smells a scent which 'curved like a shell around a figure' — and there she is, momentarily back again in Elizabethan England with Sasha. For, the narrator suggests, not only have we each many selves but many simultaneous times within us. Each human being is a full, fleeting history, incommunicable because made not out of public events but from sense-recall and private images. Yet this singularity is composed out of the shared materials of a community in time. How to discover the communal in this singularity is the poet's and, her work suggests, should be the fiction writer's task. In *Orlando* she offers us a sensory history of England: the size of the clouds, the smells, the differing intensity of colours, the weather and the natural growths. By this means she suggests the presence of the individual living in the body. In *Orlando* the two selves of gender alternate and oscillate: in comedy difference can be expressed as collision and joke.

Death is necessary to the economy of all Virginia Woolf's other novels. That is what makes *Orlando* remarkable: it is a jest in the face of death. The seamlessly en-gendered do not die. Death, it seems, finds its way in, at least in fantasy, by the separation of male and female. Orlando skirts death by changing dress. The force of the comedy here suggests anxiety. The biography of *Orlando* meditates on death by emphasising its absurd absence from the text: in this novel it is not the absence and death of a person (Jacob, Mrs Ramsay, Percival) which charges the narrative but the absence of death itself. 'Bio-graphy' — the writing of a life — is the form which ordinarily takes death for granted. At the beginning of *Orlando*, only, death is present in an appearance of life. The figure of the bumboat woman, sealed in ice as if in amber, locked beneath the fires burning on the frozen Thames, is a cruel and perfect reminder of the oppressions and extremes on which art builds.

Near London Bridge, where the river had frozen to a depth of some twenty fathoms, a wrecked wherry boat was plainly visible, lying on the bed of the river where it had sunk last autumn, overladen with apples. The old bumboat woman, who was carrying her fruit to market on the Surrey side, sat there in her plaids and farthingales with her lap full of apples, for all the world as if she were about to serve a customer, though a certain blueness about the lips hinted the truth. 'Twas a sight King James specially liked to look upon, and he would bring a troupe of courtiers to gaze with him. In short, nothing could exceed the brilliancy and gaiety of the scene by day. But it was at night that the carnival was at its merriest. For the frost continued unbroken; the nights were of perfect stillness; the moon and stars blazed with the hard fixity of diamonds, and to the fine music of flute and trumpet the courtiers danced.[20]

The poor provide a spectacle for the rich, the dead for the living. The book then uses this image of death as a punctuation mark, a sealed image of life-in-death and death-in-life from which to start its fugue. The narrative flight of this early episode is never quite fully matched again: the frozen Thames, the sumptuous fires and dances and furs, stark contraries which both represent the vigour of Elizabethan language and satisfy contrary needs in artist and reader: stability and flux. The episode ends with the stability of the ice (which provokes life and rapture) giving way to the death-dealing flow of the river. Time like an ever-rolling stream bears away the many: only Orlando and her faithful retinue back home survive to the end of fictional time. The imperious self cannot credit its own death and in this book it is comforted. Orlando is still there at the book's conclusion, in a thinner atmosphere.

If Orlando seems to have run out of steam at the end, that can be taken as the problem of making the present real on paper. The past is realised most fully in language. The present exists as body and as a semiological mass so current that our acts of interpretation are barely conscious. The past enlists consciousness: we recognise it as we do not do the present: the signs have been sorted, the cards dealt, the patterns established. The self may be known by others in the present, by ourselves in the past; that is the insight Woolf retrieves again in *Between the Acts*.

That is part of the explanation of why history is important to her. But there is another reason. The self is always insufficient. In *A Room of One's Own* she speaks of the communal self as a more enduring mode:

For my belief is that if we [women] live another century or so — I am talking of the common life which is the real life and not of the little separate lives which we live as individuals —[21]

In her diary at around the same time she queried:

> Now is life very solid or very shifting? I am haunted by the
> two contradictions. This has gone on for ever; will last for ever;
> goes down to the bottom of the world — this moment I stand
> on. Also it is transitory, flying, diaphanous. I shall pass like a
> cloud on the waves. Perhaps it may be that though we change,
> one flying after another, so quick so quick, yet we are somehow
> successive, & continuous we human beings; & show the light
> through. But what is the light?[22]

In *Orlando* the male principle turns out to be less different
from the female than it is portentously claimed to be. The
whimsically unsexed biographer of Orlando discovers him
and her not much changed by shifts in gender, though she
experiences the constraints imposed on her sex. He is defined
more by his class than his sex, it turns out. Incorrigibly an
aristocrat with the confidence, blindness, and class-mobility
flatteringly and traditionally ascribed to his clan, he can be
ambassador, gypsy, blue-stocking and traveller. Orlando's
male freedom is *class* freedom and so is Orlando's female
freedom. Orlando is privileged with wealth, beauty, andro-
gyneity, and immortality. In such conditions differences of
opportunity between men and women diminish, but they do
not vanish. The aristocratic woman becomes for Virginia
Woolf a necessary and comic symbol of the power to claim.
Orlando is exterior: the adamant central person is surveyed
throughout in biographical third-person. The joke is on the
ungendered biographer who seeks to plumb the depths of
personality but finds the pen skimming on the surface. *The
Waves* was to be her submarine adventure, a 'mystical eyeless
book' in which the 'eye' and 'I' is multiplied and dissolved,
written from within instead of from without. She began by
thinking of the work as the multiple autobiography of a
woman,[23] though that conception became less important as
the writing advanced.
She had first imagined that roll beneath the waves through
a true episode which she fictionalises in her diary in a way
which is both menacing and farcical. Flight fascinated her.
As always, in her work, humour has an undertow of the
death of the body, a conjunction of human rigidity and
human dissolution which she found artistically irresistibly
comic and touching. The flying Princess seems like a haunting

other imagination for her own fears of flying too high, as well as being a savage pastiche of aristocratic claims to dominance.

> The Flying Princess, I forget her name, has been drowned in her purple leather breeches. I suppose so at least. Their petrol gave out about midnight on Thursday, when the aeroplane must have come gently down upon the long slow Atlantic waves. I suppose they burnt a light which showed streaky on the water for a time. Where they rested a moment or two. The pilots, I think, looked back at the broad cheeked desperate eyed vulgar princess in her purple breeches & I suppose made some desperate dry statement — how the game was up: sorry; fortune against them; & she just glared; & then a wave broke over the wing; & the machine tipped. And she said something theatrical I daresay; nobody was sincere; all acted a part; nobody shrieked; Luck against us — something of that kind, they said, and then So long, and first one man was washed off & went under, then a great wave came & the Princess threw up her arms & went down; & the third man sat saved for a second looking at the rolling waves, so patient so implacable & the moon gravely regarding; & then with a dry snorting sound he too was tumbled off & rolled over, & the aeroplane rocked & rolled — miles from anywhere, off Newfoundland, while I slept at Rodmell, & Leonard was dining with the Craniums in London.[24]

The plane is lost; the bodies vanished; disappeared over the Atlantic without trace. With eerie glee Woolf pictures the scene: the absurdly small and proper statements; the cross-dressed princess in her purple breeches tumbling beneath the waves. The glassy calm of the pictured scene works as a disturbance in her mind which keeps drawing her awkwardly towards it, until at last writing it makes its hallucinating reality ebb and begin to be forgotten. The grandiose flight becomes absurd because failed. The mocked and admired figure of the Princess gives Woolf a means of trying out assertion, and vanishing, and submerging. The comic tone is disquieting but necessary: it provides a means of simultaneously letting go and holding on. As she writes *Orlando* she muses on her loss of the desire to have children.

> This insatiable desire to write something before I died, this ravaging sense of the shortness and feverishness of life, make me cling, *like a man on a rock, to my one anchor*. I don't like the

physicalness of having children of one's own. This occurred to me at Rodmell; but I never wrote it down. I can dramatise myself as a parent, it is true. And perhaps I have killed the feeling instinctively; as perhaps nature does.[25] (emphasis added)

In *The Waves* she lets herself roll under, no longer clinging 'like a man on a rock' to her 'one anchor', but fanning out into the manifold. She represents in Susan the desire for children, the having of natural happiness, and the ebbing of its fullness; she dramatises in Rhoda the fear of embraces, and it is to Bernard that she gives her own 'Fin, in a waste of waters' (p. 307) — the significant vision of the long summer of 1928 which she believed no biographer could retrieve. In retrospect we have a strong sense of the individual identities of her people in *The Waves*, even to the point of caricature. Their sinuously overlapping thoughts and images, however, emphasise the easy abrasions and floatings apart which occur in community. Waves are all the universe contains. The permeable human transmits and is composed by them. Towards the end of the book the separation between the various characters gives way and instead of a 'conversation', with which she first thought of ending, we have Bernard's inclusive monologue.

In *Orlando* the comedy is the immovability of the self as well as its dexterity. Beneath multiplicity there is a remarkable self-conformity: two thousand and fifty-two selves, the narrative reports, may have 'lodgment at one time or another in the human spirit.' The novel enjoys both the vacillations and the integrity of simple Orlando. Towards the end of the work the biographer blithely mulls over the order of selves and the excluding function of the conscious:

these selves of which we are built up, one on top of another, as plates are piled on a waiter's hand, have attachments elsewhere, sympathies, little constitutions and rights of their own, call them what you will (and for many of these things there is no name) so that one will only come if it is raining, another in a room with green curtains, another when Mrs Jones is not there, another if you can promise it a glass of wine — and so on; for everybody can multiply from his own experience the different terms which his different selves have made with him — and some are too wildly ridiculous to be mentioned in print at all, 'the one she needed most kept aloof' . . . 'as happens when, for some unaccountable reason, the conscious self, which is the uppermost, and has the power to desire, wishes to be nothing but one self.'[26]

In this fictional order, where the overweening self is king and queen, the whole community, even the shared discourse of the period, become figments of an organising singleness. In *The Waves*, on the contrary, we enter the iridescent play of communal selves. The spry zest of *Orlando*'s language gives way to ruminativeness.

The Waves punctuates its multiple first-person form with sparse speech tags which become rarer as the book grows. 'Said Rhoda', 'said Neville': once the figures and their concerns are established even such interjections occur only every few pages. Virginia Woolf said that she wanted in *The Waves* to follow a rhythm not a plot: that rhythm is figured in the pressure of the waves moving beneath the surface of the sea, humping themselves momentarily at the shore to break in foam. The pattern can express both long continuity and ephemerality, the single and the common life. At death the waves of the individual break and are drawn back into the sea of shared memory, memory which then itself is loosed and scattered but never entirely lost, since the body of waters remains. That is the seismic level of the metaphor. The lengthening meditations of the people in the book, pitched beneath the level of speech, follow the same pulse.

Rhythmic organisation is far less referential than that of plot and may be seen as part of the movement towards impersonality in her work.[27] This impersonality does not imply a lack of concern with persons, but a dissipation of the intense analysis of developing individual relationships which had been the material of the English novel, and of her own early work in *A Voyage Out*. In *The Waves* characters speak with a liturgical separation, facing inward to the altar of the self or outward to the reader, but never in dialogue — though occasionally antiphonally ordered.

The absence of dialogue takes the reader deep into the submarine intimacy of the book's address. No one answers the diverse meditations, though they may hear and share. By this means Woolf forthwith moves outside binary oppositions. Instead of the two selves of gender, she creates a spectrum: six persons, three male, three female. They are separable, even highly distinctive, but 'at one', atoning for some irreparable loss which at once scatters and yet keeps life (the novel) going. They all lean towards the presence or memory of the lost hero: the unknowing, the clumsy and unreflective Percival who like his namesake Parsifal never asks questions. He goes, he performs, he plays cricket and rides, he sets out for imperial India and dies there in a fall from his horse.

> 'Now,' said Neville, 'my tree flowers. My heart rises. All oppression is relieved. All impediment is removed. The reign of chaos is over. He has imposed order. Knives cut again.'
> 'Here is Percival,' said Jinny. 'He has not dressed.'
> 'Here is Percival,' said Bernard, 'smoothing his hair, not from vanity (he does not look in the glass), but to propitiate the god of decency. He is conventional; he is a hero. The little boys trooped after him across the playing-fields. They blew their noses as he blew his nose, but unsuccessfully, for he is Percival. Now, when he is about to leave us, to go to India, all these trifles come together. He is a hero. Oh, yes, that is not to be denied, and when he takes his seat by Susan, whom he loves, the occasion is crowned.'[28]

Percival is the principle of death as well as of immediate living. He is the seventh, 'Septimus', who converted the six into a magical prime number and continues to make possible the seven-branched candelabra of friendship after his death. He is the male principle, idolised — and dead. He is given no discourse of his own. We know him only through the musings of others. The characters within the work are questioners, meditating on all they see and feel, suffering their insufficiencies and reaching out (save Rhoda) to other needed life. Percival represents the old narrative order. His story is simple: he is the young hero who goes out to the furthest reaches of his country's empire, though he finds not a grail but a grave. His fall is the stable ground on which the novel and the intermittent community of the six is built, the gravity that draws all together. With the death of classical narrative the book can become both an elegy and a release: a play-poem, in all senses. The death of Percival is the sole narrative event which we are allowed to record at its traditional scale.

His death is the condition of the freedom to explore other kinds of 'I', permeable and transitive.

Although *The Waves* has many passages, particularly in the early part of the book, which are humorous, it has always been discussed in profoundly serious terms — and is referred to so by Virginia Woolf herself: a mystical eyeless book. Having no 'eyes' and multiple 'I's, the reader loses a steady quizzical distance.

Yet there is, though in a different mood, play in *The Waves* as much as in *Orlando*. The play of movement, the endless conjoining and dissipation of sea forms, is the rhythm of the characters' overlapping languages. As has often been observed, they have access to each others' thoughts and symbolic systems.[29] Woolf reconceives the act of writing fiction, not as novel but as play-poem, in which the silent voice upon the page allows consciousness to articulate itself with a clarity and panache rarely achieved in speech. Unchastened by the constraints of society, or of reply, the voices assert their presences with all the cadences of speech, so far as syntax can represent them, but without tone, sound or utterance. So they live alongside, dipping into each others' lore, assembling symbols from a common wealth, but always allowed their own full say.

The book points one speech against another and in the earlier parts of the work uses speech-tags to retard or disturb the sense of what is said. Read aloud, the humour of *The Waves* becomes manifest, as the gradings of voice point the distinctions between people and emphasise their inventiveness. But, enjoyable as such reading is, it does away with an important level of the work: its silencing of voice. We enter these speaking minds without satire, so close-in that judgments are never more than half-formed. Humour is there even in silent reading, of course, since humour is the form which makes room for identification and canniness at once. We experience incongruity as pleasure: Neville, even as a child, holds things apart and mocks the inclination to lyricism which is intrinsic to Woolf's work: 'I hate dangling things. I hate dampish things. I hate wandering and mixing things together.' The unwritten common life is essential to humour; it creates and delineates community. The shift from person to person within this book jogs our allegiance and our attention so that the multiple first-person controls our continued immersion in any single character. The movement of such humour can only be shown in a longer quotation:

'There is about both Neville and Louis a precision, an exactitude that I admire and shall never possess. Now I begin to be aware that action is demanded. We approach a junction; at a junction I have to change. I have to board a train for Edinburgh. I cannot precisely lay fingers on this fact — it lodges loosely among my thoughts like a button, like a small coin. Here is the jolly old boy who collects tickets. I had one — I had one certainly. But it does not matter. Either I shall find it, or I shall not find it. I examine my notecase. I look in all my pockets. These are the things that for ever interrupt the process upon which I am eternally engaged of finding some perfect phrase that fits this very moment exactly.

'Bernard has gone,' said Neville, 'without a ticket. He has escaped us, making a phrase, waving his hand. He talked as easily to the horse-breeder or to the plumber as to us. The plumber accepted him with devotion. "If he had a son like that," he was thinking, "he would manage to send him to Oxford." But what did Bernard feel for the plumber? Did he not only wish to continue the sequence of the story which he never stops telling himself? He began it when he rolled his bread into pellets as a child. One pellet was a man, one was a woman. We are all pellets. We are all phrases in Bernard's story, things he writes down in his notebook under A or under B. He tells our story with extraordinary understanding, except of what we most feel. For he does not need us. He is never at our mercy. There he is, waving his arms on the platform. The train has gone without him. He has missed his connection. He has lost his ticket. But that does not matter. He will talk to the barmaid about the nature of human destiny. We are off; he has forgotten us already; we pass out of his view; we go on, filled with lingering sensations, half bitter, half sweet, for he is somehow to be pitied breasting the world with half-finished phrases, having lost his ticket; he is also to be loved.'[30]

Part of the pleasure of this passage is that Bernard, unnoticing, does achieve the perfect phrase for a mind-sensation that I have never seen described elsewhere: the impending knowledge that one must change trains which 'lodges loosely among my thoughts like a button, like a small coin.' Another pleasure is the speed and lucidity with which feelings and

judgments shift: 'He tells our story with extraordinary understanding, except of what we most feel. For he does not need
us. He is never at our mercy.' . . . 'he is somehow to be
pitied breasting the world with half-finished phrases, having
lost his ticket; he is also to be loved.' The background of
slapstick — the lost ticket, the missed train, the satisfying
talk with the barmaid — is held quietly, though without
austerity, at a level with all the other elements in Neville's
musings.

This declarative discourse allows Woolf to include more
and more, without crisis. She makes us acutely aware from
time to time of the mass of unknown others among whom
her named people move. Neville again: arriving at a main-
line station in London:

> What extraordinary adventure waits with me, among these mail
> vans, these porters, these swarms of people calling taxis? I feel
> insignificant, lost, but exultant. With a soft shock we stop. I will
> let the others get out before me. I will sit still one moment before
> I emerge into that chaos, that tumult. I will not anticipate what
> is to come. The huge uproar is in my ears. It sounds and resounds
> under this glass roof like the surge of a sea.

Jinny's exuberant story-making and speeding up of millions:

> 'Thus, in a few seconds, deftly, adroitly, we decipher the
> hieroglyphs written on other people's faces. Here, in this room,
> are the abraded and battered shells cast on the shore. The door
> goes on opening. The room fills and fills with knowledge,
> anguish, many kinds of ambition, much indifference, some
> despair. In one way or another we make this day, this Friday,
> some by going to the Law Courts; others to the city; others to
> the nursery; others by marching and forming fours. A million
> hands stitch, raise hods with bricks. The activity is endless. And
> tomorrow it begins again; tomorrow we make Saturday. Some
> take train for France; others ship for India. Some will never
> come into this room again. One may die tonight. Another will
> beget a child. From us every sort of building, policy, venture,
> picture, poem, child, factory, will spring. Life comes; life goes;
> we make life. So you say.
> 'But we who live in the body see with the body's imagination
> things in outline. I see rocks in bright sunshine . . . I must jump
> up and go . . . I drop all these facts-diamonds, withered hands,

china pots and the rest of it, as a monkey drops nuts from its naked paws.'[31]

Rhoda's horror at crowds takes over Bernard's 'pellets' and Jinny's 'monkey paws' and degrades them:

> 'Life, how I have dreaded you,' said Rhoda, 'oh, human beings, how I have hated you! How you have nudged, how you have interrupted, how hideous you have looked in Oxford Street, how squalid sitting opposite each other staring in the Tube! Now as I climb this mountain, from the top of which I shall see Africa, my mind is printed with brown-paper parcels and your faces. I have been stained by you and corrupted. You smelt so unpleasant, too, lining up outside doors to buy tickets. All were dressed in indeterminate shades of grey and brown, never even a blue feather pinned to a hat. None had the courage to be one thing rather than another. What dissolution of the soul you demanded in order to get through one day, what lies, bowings, scrapings, fluency and servility! How you chained me to one spot, one hour, one chair, and sat yourselves down opposite! How you snatched from me the white spaces that lie between hour and hour and rolled them into dirty pellets and tossed them into the wastepaper basket with your greasy paws. Yet those were my life.'[32]

To Bernard, 'general life' is the pre-language which he seeks and can never fully find, beset as he is with phrase-making. The image he uses for the satisfied loss of individuality is that of the baby replete: 'Having dropped off satisfied like a child from the breast, I am at liberty now to sink down, deep into what passes, this omni-present general life' (p. 122).

In *The Waves* repetition delineates personality, as in Louis's allusive closeness to T. S. Eliot's language of *The Waste Land*: 'I have read my poet in an eating-house, and, stirring my coffee, listened to the clerks making bets at little tables, watched the women hesitating at the counter. I said that nothing should be irrelevant, like a piece of brown paper dropped casually on the floor.'[33] Repetition also generates the relations of body to world. Certain obsessional cries persist: Rhoda's flowers: 'I made of them a garland and gave them — Oh, to whom?' Neville's 'Come closer, closer.' Words cling to particular people, 'blistered' to Louis, 'pear-shaped eyes' to Susan. The key relation of body to world is different for each person: Louis, later to be her lover, says of Rhoda: 'She has no body as the others have'; Susan, who will seek the 'natural happiness' of the farm and childbearing (and weary of it) observes an adult sexual encounter while the maid hangs out washing. The night-gowns are 'blown tight'; Ernest's mouth is 'sucked like a purse in wrinkles' and 'the pyjamas are blown out tight between them . . . the urn roars as Ernest roared, and I blown out hard like the pyjamas.'[34]

Bernard, a child in the bath, feels the water from the sponge run down on him; knowing his body makes language simultaneously a primary pleasure to him:

> Water pours down the runnel of my spine. Bright arrows of sensation shoot on either side. I am covered with warm flesh. My dry crannies are wetted; my cold body is warmed; it is sluiced and gleaming. Water descends and sheets me like an eel. Now hot towels envelop me, and their roughness, as I rub my back, makes my blood purr . . .[35]

At the end of the book, in the long meditation which replaced the 'conversation' she first expected to end with, Bernard feels the same physical well-being, like a loved gross animal within him:

> There is the brute, too, the savage, the hairy man who dabbles his fingers in ropes of entrails; and gobbles and belches; whose speech is guttural, visceral — well, he is here. He squats in me. Tonight he has been feasted on quails, salad, and sweetbread. He now holds a glass of fine old brandy in his paw. He brindles, purrs, and shoots warm thrills all down my spine as I sip. It is true, he washes his hands before dinner, but they are still hairy. He buttons on trousers and waistcoats, but they contain the same organs. He jibs if I keep him waiting for dinner. He mops and mows perpetually pointing with his half-idiot gestures of greed and covetousness at what he desires. I assure you, I have great difficulty sometimes in controlling him. That man, the hairy, the ape-like, has contributed his part to my life. He has given a greener glow to green things, has held his torch with its red flames, its thick and smarting smoke, behind every leaf. He has lit up the cool garden even. He has brandished his torch in murky by-streets where girls suddenly seem to shine with a red

and intoxicating translucency. Oh, he has tossed his torch high! He has led me wild dances![36]

That 'guttural, visceral' inner voice humorously represents the bodily community which is also the unreachable ideal language which Bernard always seeks. Such language is beyond or prior to words, 'a little language such as lovers use'; 'a bark, a groan'; 'a painful, guttural, visceral, also soaring, lark-like, pealing song to replace these flagging foolish transcripts — how much too deliberate! how much too reasonable'. (p. 273)

Bernard seeks the deep stream: 'a rushing stream of broken dreams, nursery rhymes, street cries, half-finished sentences and sights — elm trees, willow trees, gardeners sweeping, women writing'. (pp. 280–1) Bernard knows 'a howl, a cry'; at the end he has 'done with phrases'.

This communal world of the unrecorded — people, parts, cries — is the new writing world of the body, a world which can be represented only by language which is at once silenced and auditory, placing much emphasis on analogous elements. In *The Waves* Woolf explores a new form of communality and impersonality. Words and thoughts in this work move freely between people; sexual images are not reserved in mind to men or women only. Bernard is the man writing women's writing written by the woman writer; Jinny's 'senses stand erect' (p. 298); both pillar and pool are Rhoda's images; Susan's body is a tool: 'The blade is clean, sharp, worn in the centre.' Though each person lives within a separate configuration, gender and personal history converge only evanescently in individuality. Like the waves, the person and people come together, then sink 'into one of those silences which are now and again broken by a few words, as if a fin rose in the wastes of silence.' (p. 299) The pressures of 'I' and 'We' have here formed a work at standing water, without tides. *The Waves* is dense on the page, intensely verbal and articulate, but it searches endlessly, through its rhythms of recounting, for a way of giving utterance to all that is unpossessed by writing. Virginia Woolf is not here creating simply an exploration of individualism; she seeks what is held in common — and as commonly lost.

Death is the undertow of the work: wave-forms dissipate

as water. Social history as she explored it in *Mrs Dalloway*
is unimportant in *The Waves;* finding a new discourse matters
more. Social history, that invigorating element of the
common life, will return as a sustaining force in *Between the
Acts*, the novel in which 'we' is most fully substituted for 'I'.
'We' in *Between the Acts* does not attempt any sentimental
knitting up into accord. 'We' remain 'orts, scraps and frag-
ments', passing shows, skeins of gossip. The only common
passions shown are those of sex, hunting, recall. But what
profoundly connects all the figures in the book is the coming
of World War II. 'We' becomes the only way to keep a
future. The common future is under immediate threat:
'Unless we can think peace into existence we — not this one
body in this one bed but millions of bodies yet to be born —
will lie in the same darkness and hear the same death rattle
overhead.'[37]

Notes

1. *The Diary of Virginia Woolf*, ed. Anne Olivier Bell (Hogarth Press, London, 1980) Vol. V, p. 135.
2. *Collected Essays by Virginia Woolf* (London, Hogarth Press, 1966) Vol. II, p. 147.
3. *Collected Essays*, Vol. II, p. 224. 'It will give, as poetry does, the outline rather than the detail.' 'The psychological novelist has been too prone to limit psychology to the psychology of personal inter-course' (p. 225).
4. *Diary*, Vol. III, p. 128.
5. *Virginia Woolf's Writing Notebooks*, ed. Brenda Silver (Hogarth Press, London, 1973) p. 244.
6. *Ibid.*
7. *Diary*, Vol. III. p. 285 (Sunday, 26 January 1930); Vol. V, p. 135.
8. *Diary*, Vol. IV, p. 124 (16 September 1932).
9. *A Room of One's Own* (Hogarth Press, London, 1929) p. 98. See also 'Memories of A Working Women's Guild, *Collected Essays*, Vol. IV, pp. 146–7; *Collected Essays*, Vol. II, in 'Life and the Novelist', pp. 131–6, (1926). Virginia Woolf characterises the novelist's para-doxical need for immersion in 'life' and withdrawal from it, in terms of the body becoming writing: 'But at a certain moment he must leave the company and withdraw, alone, to that mysterious room where his body is hardened and fashioned into permanence by processes which, if they elude the critic, hold for him so profound a fascination'. (p. 136) How much significance should we attach to the masculine gender here? Is the hardening of the body into writing

to be set over against the passage quoted, or is it a description of a different imaginative phase: 'Stop, & take out my pen'. Her enjoyment of 'the company' of her own body needs to be set alongside the more solipsistic analysis of 'Virginia's Embodiment' in Roger Poole, *The Unknown Virginia Woolf* (Cambridge University Press, Cambridge, 1978) pp. 199–215.

10. *Mrs Dalloway* (Hogarth Press, London 1925) pp. 151–2.
11. Pp. 90–1. See my 'Virginia Woolf and Pre-History' in *Virginia Woolf: A Centenary Perspective*, ed. Eric Warner (Macmillan, London, 1984) and for a more detailed analysis of the semiotic signification of the song, Makiko Pinkney's *Virginia Woolf and the Problem of the Subject: Feminine Writing in the Major Novels* (Harvester Press, Brighton, 1987).
12. In *To the Lighthouse*, Virginia Woolf's most brooding meditation on the family community, about which I have written elsewhere, everything that happens in narrative representation occurs either before the war of 1914–18, in the rich childhood world of the Victorian family with its submerged tensions, or in the post-impressionism of the 1920s. In 'Time Passes' we have the major events of death and war summarised off-centre, flung into square brackets or past participles. With the mother, Mrs Ramsay, dead, the celibate woman artist, Lily Briscoe, now holds the narrative and pictorial line together. She does it by living askance from the family she observes and whom she celebrates at the end in the abstract forms of triangle and line.
    See my 'Hume, Stephen, and Elegy in *To the Lighthouse*', *Essays in Criticism*, 34 (1984), 33–55.
13. *A Writer's Diary*, ed. Leonard Woolf (Triad/Panther, London, 1978). See, for example, 'The Art of Biography' and 'The New Biography', *Collected Essays*, Vol. IV, pp. 221–35 as well as her many reviews of biographies and autobiographies.
14. 'I am Christina Rossetti', *Collected Essays*, Vol. IV, p. 54.
15. 'The history of England is the history of the male line, not the female' ('Women and Fiction', *Collected Essays*, Vol. II, p. 141.)
16. In *The Short Season Between Two Silences: The Mystical and the Political in the Novels of Virginia Woolf* (Allen & Unwin, London, 1984), Madeline Moore offers a celebratory reading of *Orlando* which places the work 'within the coherence of her radical political hopes' (p. 114). I find a darker undertow of pessimism in the work than her attractive reading acknowledges.
17. *Orlando, A Biography* (Hogarth Press, London, 1928) p. 27.
18. *Ibid.*, pp. 264–5. Crowds characterise the modern age, their pleasures expressed in the dexterity of the body: 'Every inch of the pavement was crowded. Streams of people, threading in and out between their own bodies and the lurching and lumbering traffic with incredible agility, poured incessantly east and west' (p. 247).
19. *Ibid.*, pp. 266–7.
20. *Ibid.*, pp. 35–6.
21. *A Room of One's Own*, p. 171.

22. *Diary*, Vol. III, p. 218 (Friday, 4 January 1929).
23. 'Yet I am now and then haunted by some semi-mystic very profound life of a woman, which shall all be told on one occasion'. *Diary*, Vol. III, p. 118 (Tuesday, 23 November 1926).
24. *Diary*, Vol. III, pp. 154–5, (Sunday, 4 September 1927). See also 'Flying Over London', *Collected Essays*, Vol. IV, pp. 167–72.
25. *Diary*, Vol. III, p. 167.
26. P. 277.
27. See 'A Letter to a Young Poet', *Collected Essays*, Vol. III, p. 191, where she writes of 'the most profound and primitive of instincts, the instinct of rhythm . . . let your rhythmical sense wind itself in and out among men and women, omnibuses, sparrows — whatever comes along the street — until it has strung them together in one harmonious whole. That perhaps is your task — to find the relation between things that seem incompatible yet have a mysterious affinity.' (Written in 1932.)
28. *The Waves* (Hogarth Press, London, 1931) pp. 132–3.
29. A process more striking in *Virginia Woolf, The Waves: The two holograph drafts*, ed. J. W. Graham (Hogarth Press, London, 1976).
30. *The Waves*, pp. 74–5.
31. *Ibid.*, p. 77; pp. 190–1.
32. *Ibid.*, pp. 221–2.
33. *Ibid.*, p. 183.
34. *Ibid.*, pp. 24–5.
35. *Ibid.*, p. 26.
36. *Ibid.*, p. 317.
37. ' "Thoughts on Peace in an Air Raid" written in August 1940, for an American symposium on current matters concerning women', *Collected Essays*, Vol. IV, p. 173. For discussion see Mark Spilka, *Virginia Woolf's Quarrel with Grieving* (University of Nebraska Press, Lincoln, 1980) and 'Virginia Woolf and Pre-History' *op. cit.*

5

Christina Rossetti: Diary of a Feminist Reading

Isobel Armstrong

For Jokhim Meikle

'That's it.' I said, or probably felt, this when I was nine and reading Christina Rossetti's 'Who Has Seen the Wind?' for the first time. I was looking for something I called 'real' poetry, which seemed to be very rare. I would not have used the quotation marks which a knowing maturity makes me place round 'real'. This experience, 'That's it', is fused with the smell of a peculiarly sour disinfectant used in country primary schools after the war, when the caretaker spread a kind of disinfected meal of sawdust over the unpolished wood floor, and swept it up again. It comes together with the worn green cloth boards of a poetry anthology, probably some variant of the Child's Golden Treasury, and the tedium, suddenly changed, of silent reading in a hot room.

There were no illustrated paperbacks like Penguin's *Voices* to search through. I was exasperated by class readings of 'The Owl and the Pussy Cat' which was taught to us (we drew pictures of the pea-green boat), as far as I can see, because it was funny, and wasn't poetry. It wasn't funny as well as not being poetry. It never occurred to us to think of homonyms for 'pea'. It was the kind of thing grown-ups and teachers liked, as I did when I became both. Christina Rossetti's poem was quite different. It is a sparse two stanzas long and hauntingly lucid and mysterious all at once. An intransingently impersonal reserve releases intense lyricism. Its directness of address — 'Who has seen the wind?/ Neither I nor you' — gives access to a rush of questioning which 'you' are invited to initiate. Who has *seen* the wind? Who *has* seen the wind? Nobody? It was written for children in a volume of poems called *Sing Song*. It is playful without being condescending because it has a serious respect for the metaphysical, and certainly epistemological, questions it presents with such economy and through such ordinary words. How do we know the wind when we see it only by its effects on other things, trembling leaves and bowed branches? The concord is reduced to the relations between seen, familiar movement and the source of movement. Or is it concord? She does not mention the obvious, sound, which is present only in the 'passing' syllables of the poem itself — 'The wind is passing by'. Such evanescence must make one wonder on what basis the confident and familiar connections of cognitive life are made. A subtle disturbance is effected.

How far these questions were known to me in the energy of discovery and delight (the same delight people later called jouissance?) is inevitably lost. But I now guess that I must have known at some level that this crystal, limpid simplicity did not infantilise. It never occurred to me to question, of course, where I got the idea of 'real' poetry from, or who 'I' was, and what status the 'I' of the poem had in relation to my 'I'. The poem might be subtly questioning assumptions about the solidity of 'I' and 'you', but the primal certainty of 'That's it' was consolidating. That we, the writer and myself, were both women, certainly did not occur to me, let alone that the term 'woman' was a category needing some investigation. There were 'men' and 'women' in the world just as certainly as 'I' and 'you'. Much later a colleague was collecting a gathering of quotations about the 'wind' of inspiration for a light-hearted lecture — Joyce's gross collic, Wordsworth's 'motions of the wind/Embodied in the mystery of words'. I suggested Christina Rossetti's poem but he had not heard of it. Now I think of that poem in the context of feminism and this produces further readings. It is a curiously proud yet self-effacing lyric about the masterful romantic idea of inspiration. Seen, but not heard, to tremble and bow down the head: what is happening to the woman's voice? How guardedly the wind of inspiration, prerogative of male poets, is considered. The tree, trembling in obedience to the wind, may be a root-bound Daphne subjected and unable to flee from Apollo's powerful lyre, but the poem is deeply sceptical of an authoritative relation between wind and lyre.

The excitement about Christina Rossetti's poems, however, was buried for easily twenty years. My resistance to feminist criticism lasted for about the same time.

I had forgotten Christina Rossetti so thoroughly that I asked a graduate student once why he was interested in editing the work of a minor poet.

During public examinations and throughout my undergraduate career no single poem by Christina Rossetti was put before us for close reading. No essays were set on her work. Or, if poems of hers were discussed, I forgot them, which is equally significant. It was as if she and real poetry had never been. Instead there was the effort of discussing Marvell ('The tough reasonableness beneath the lyric grace' (T. S. Eliot): Discuss) and finding an analytical strategy for looking at poetry. T. S. Eliot, I. A. Richards, William Empson, F. R. Leavis, these were the people I learned from. I am not setting up an antithesis between the male analysis of these critics and 'female' intuition. But what amazes me is the narrow understanding of what analysis was, and its extraordinary exclusiveness. I am even more amazed by our unquestioning acceptance of the institution of criticism, its canon and criteria.

We struggled with the Pelican *Guides*, half realising the contradictions of those curious volumes, with their preliminary chapters on 'Background' and subsequent essays on individual authors which never mentioned 'background' once. The Pelican *Guides* were then effecting their revolution in poetry criticism by insisting on what was conceived of as a lost tradition of intellect and cerebral power to be found in seventeenth-century poetry and an account of 'wit' as the play with paradox, ambiguity and logical complexity. The artificial category, 'the metaphysical poets', invented by Grierson, was consolidated. It was not for some years that I realised that the metaphysical poets did not call themselves this. This tradition was allied with an entirely discrepant neoromantic belief in 'vividness', 'immediacy', 'intensity', 'range' (F. N. Lees on Hopkins, Pelican *Guide*, 6). I did not see this discrepancy at the time, probably because the seventeenth-century poets were assumed to be in possession of a 'unified sensibility' (an invention of T. S. Eliot's) in which feeling and thought were fused. And it was assumed we knew, and could distinguish, feeling from thought in a poem.

Above all, the *Guides* asserted the need for authoritative tradition as an ethical imperative, an élite tradition based on 'rigorous standards' (General Introduction): 'Which authors matter most?' 'Where does the strength of the period lie?' The confident judgmental assumptions behind the questions (you *had* to judge, you *had* to choose) dictate the form of the answers required.

Oddly, nineteenth-century poetry coincided with none of the criteria required, as the title of the sixth volume implies — *From Dickens to Hardy* (1958). The authors who 'mattered' most were the novelists, and another 'tradition' (but note the singular) to support them — a tradition which was entirely separate from the one to which the best poetry was supposed to belong — was invoked. It did not occur to me to ask how genuinely historical the tradition was, or how far it was an invention. Other people have looked at the elementary and de-politicised notions of culture and the tradition behind these choices, and at the covert political choices being made in disguise. A tradition guaranteed stability and authenticated one's choice of writer as if it were a pre-given matter which required no investigation. Leavis himself could be a very fine historical critic, but the Pelican *Guides* simplified his positions, as they simplified the account of poetic language explored by Empson and Richards. Novels in particular could always be re-described in terms of universal values and ethical imperatives which did not move into the sphere of the social or engage with the questions of politics. At the very most, nineteenth-century novelists turned out to endorse Fabian socialism. If they did not, like the Brontës, they were thought of as passionate and *psychologically* wayward. This was, of course, a male-created tradition and consisted mainly of male authors. What is interesting is that Christina Rossetti, with the double disadvantage of being a woman and a Victorian poet, should have featured in this critical context. She did, and her work was actually discussed much more fully than that of Elizabeth Barrett Browning. But her poetry is described with an uneasiness I have only noticed recently.

She is frequently called 'Christina', and compared to her

detriment with the 'wit' of Herbert and the force of Hopkins. But it is the uncertainty of the critical language and its collapse into a paucity of vocabulary which is interesting. It is subtly denigrating *praise* which is most striking. All the 'tough' criteria of 'wit', cerebral complexity and logical analysis are abandoned when she is discussed. I take repeated phrases from the work of the two sophisticated critics quoted below. Her work is found to be depressing but praised because it is 'simple and modest'. The strenuous work on the nature of poetic language undertaken by I. A. Richards and Empson which, for all its aestheticised and excessive preoccupation with the trope of ambiguity, was supremely intelligent and impressive, seems to collapse. Nevertheless, both critics are trying very hard to be fair.

Christina Rossetti (1830–94) is in some ways a more interesting and considerable poet than either [Dante Gabriel or William Morris]. Christina continues to attract the modern reader by the general *simplicity* and *delicacy* of her language . . . by her *simplicity* . . . she bears a resemblance to her American contemporary Emily Dickinson (1830–86) . . . ambiguousness of effect disturbs but also rather oddly deepens her work . . . (and there is a significance too in the narrowly missed failure or success of her poems) . . . her *modest* attempts to write . . . her *Poems for Children* contain too much talk of death and transience to be useful in the nursery.
    (E. D. Klingopulos, *Pelican Guide*, 6, pp. 88–9, emphasis added)

It is significant that one finds oneself appraising her work in these *negative* terms . . . an extensive reading of it is *depressing* . . . *exquisite good taste* and spiritual *good manners* . . . The distinctiveness and *limitation* of Christina Rossetti's talent . . . the *shy reserve, tenderness* and *wistfulness* of the speaker are presented *simply* and *truthfully*, and our acceptance of her truthfulness is bound up with our recognition of her authentic speaking voice . . . its *modest* acceptance of very *limited pretension* which makes it seem if not mawkish, a little *mièvre* . . . If we pay Christina Rossetti the archaic compliment of calling her a *lady*, this will be understood to have *no implication of snobbery* . . . *touchingly sincere* and disinterested . . .
    (W. W. Robson, *Pelican Guide*, 6, pp. 364–7, emphasis added)

The snobbery referred to is social not sexual snobbery, as Robson makes clear when describing the 'embarrassing intimacy' of Mrs Browning. I do not offer these assessments to 'over-turn' them in the interests of 're-valuing' Christina Rossetti (as Maud Ellmann has said, you only value something when you want to sell it). That would be to collude with the competitive techniques of male dressage operating in the work of so many critics, whether in the straight fights of Leavis or the Oedipal struggle of Bloom. Gubar and Gilbert in *Mad Woman in the Attic* make a great mistake in re-instating the female tradition in terms of power.[1] What is important here is that Christina Rossetti can only be praised for qualities in which the 'tradition' is not really interested. Or is it? Simplicity, modesty, delicacy, good taste, good manners, shy reserve, tenderness, truthfulness, limited pretensions, touching sincerity, ladylikeness — all these epithets are in effect coercive. The magisterial 'we' of Robson's piece assumes a consensus from which no reader will dissent. This is what women, and women's poetry, should be like. Better modesty and simplicity than 'embarrassing intimacy'. The term 'simplicity' closes discussion rather than opens it. That something important might be going on in the 'simple' lyrics of Blake and Christina Rossetti was vaguely understood, but this criticism had no categories for dealing with 'simplicity'. Christina Rossetti, who as a violent child slashed her arm with scissors, who as an adult wrote *Goblin Market* (not discussed in the *Guide*), a poem so scandalous that it could only be read by children, does not consort easily with these descriptions. Looking back I consider that if intelligent male critics of the late 1950s could read her work so inattentively and with such expectations, how hard it must have been for women to read her work, and how hard it must have been for women trying to write poetry then. It certainly did not occur to us to ask such questions then. We accepted this, just as we accepted being told not to wear trousers in lectures.

I was taught with meticulous care and seriousness in a Department of English which had one very remarkable woman on its staff. Two thirds of the students were women but it never occurred to us to consider why most of our teachers were men. This was the impercipient, apolitical time described in A. S. Byatt's novel, *Still Life* (1985). The scrupulous and thorough teaching we received was informed with Arnoldian values and an Arnoldian view of culture. We were being given something, the best that had been thought and said in the world, a life-giving tradition of thought and feeling and moral values which could somehow contribute to the sum of human goodness. And we ourselves would pass this on. It was a noble enterprise of high seriousness. Its strength was that the Leavisian assumptions were grafted onto an older syllabus with the tradition of literary history and philology behind it. I would never wish to have been in another context. (I'm glad I did not go to Oxbridge.) I still feel deeply disturbed when I read Terry Eagleton's demolition of English Studies in *Critical Theory*, for instance. That the category of literature and culture itself, which Foucault thinks of as appearing at the end of the eighteenth century, was a social construction, was not a conceivable possibility for us then. Raymond Williams' *Culture and Society* came out in 1958, the year of the sixth volume of the Pelican *Guide* which I have mentioned. That literature is all the more important for study just *because* it is a social construct, and must therefore be of critical importance in our history, is an argument I would not have been in possession of. Part of my enterprise in writing this piece is to see where feminist criticism can enable us to stand, both in relation to traditional criticism and to literary theory.

I am frequently asked why I teach 'theory' to students. I always do so with considerable hesitation. But my answer is partly that there are many theories, and that feminist criticism intensifies the questions we should be asking anyway. The questions of consciousness, ideology, history, language, raised in different theoretical debates, will not go away, just as their instigators, Marx, Freud and Nietszche, will not disappear. We have a commitment to our students to show as lucidly and responsibly as we can where debates in the subject are at. The historical movement from practical criticism to critical practice is one in which we and they are formatively involved and to withdraw from the effort of providing students with a framework for dealing with these problems is to disable us both. Founding texts by the authors I have mentioned should surely be discussed. I am convinced that it is possible to engage a range of students with debate. And that is the very reverse of giving them formulas to 'apply'. Our education system encourages the belief that only a minority of students can deal with concepts. Of course we are responsible if a 'weak' feminist student writes naively of patriarchy, but I wonder if this is not any less preferable (at least the notion of patriarchy has some historical base) to our own confident handling of that phantasm, 'the dissolution of sensibility'? All teaching is full of danger because of the power of the teacher, but it can nevertheless help to unbind one from the power of ideology. It is said that an education into concepts is dangerous because of the narrower range of reading undertaken by students now. Is it that narrow? And if so, is it not more necessary, rather than less, to have a framework to read in? *Lear*, Milton, the metaphysicals, George Eliot, isn't that canon as restricting as any? I read Dickens after taking my degree. We can recognise that questions of power enter into the teaching situation, but this is a way to liberate oneself from being controlled by them. That is why feminism needs to evolve a criticism which will recognise but not collude with a power relationship.

'That's it', came again many years later when I came across Christina Rossetti's 'Winter: my secret'. I was amazed by the coldness, almost frigidity of the poem's reserve and by its flagrant coquetry. 'I tell my secret? No indeed not I.' Once you have said there is a secret you have betrayed it. But what it may be is kept provocatively in abeyance throughout the poem. 'It' may be a secret passion, or no secret at all, the poet's virginity, which is paradoxically a hidden and an 'open' secret. 'I wear my mask for warmth.' The mask is a fragile protection which is both disguise and representation. The poem came to seem about a troubled negotiation with accounts of women's sexuality, the devious path of female identity which Freud thinks of as circuitous and mysterious. When 'That's it' came for the second time I was looking out from the fourteenth floor of a tower block, which housed the English Department, onto an informal path plotted by students across the path to the university. It looked like a hair-parting from the height I observed it. The alternative route seemed like the poem, which manoeuvres in narrow space, and the route one had to make through traditional criticism and feminist criticism as well.

When you have decided on a feminist reading, what then? I will pass over my reluctant response to feminist criticism, but this reluctance obviously shaped my approach. I shall write about successive readings of 'Winter Rain' for the rest of this essay, because it poses the problems I experienced more sharply than 'Winter: my secret'.

Winter Rain

> Every valley drinks,
>   Every dell and hollow:
> Where the kind rain sinks and sinks,
>   Green of Spring will follow.
>
> Yet a lapse of weeks
>   Buds will burst their edges,
> Strip their wool-coats, glue-coats, streaks,
>   In the woods and hedges;
>
> Weave a bower of love
>   For birds to meet each other,
> Weave a canopy above
>   Nest and egg and mother.
>
> But for fattening rain
>   We should have no flowers,
> Never a bud or leaf again
>   But for soaking showers;
>
> Never a mated bird
>   In the rocking tree-tops,
> Never indeed a flock or herd
>   To graze upon the lea-crops.
>
> Lambs so woolly white,
>   Sheep the sun-bright leas on,
> They could have no grass to bite
>   But for rain in season.
>
> We should find no moss
>   In the shadiest places,
> Find no waving meadow grass
>   Pied with broad-eyed daisies:

But miles of barren sand,
    With never a son or daughter,
Not a lily on the land,
    Or lily on the water.

To begin with, the poem does not have an overtly 'female' content. I was dissatisfied with restricting myself to poems which could be literalised as accounts of women's experience because this circumscribes and isolates women as special cases, culturally and psychologically. What was I permitted to say? It is significant that an oppressive sense of what was 'allowed' hung over me. The sort of individualist feminist criticism I knew then (Kate Millett) pointed to the ideological repression of women expressed in female texts. Barbara Hardy had shaken me by the scruff of the neck with Millett a few years before but I did not want to resolve the poem into a sexual politics of this kind. It seemed to lead me to rage and anger (though I reflect that a little of this would have been useful in confronting my earlier education). It seemed to be a 'vulgar' feminism, like vulgar Marxism. People were beginning to describe women's writing in terms of its claims to an independent tradition. Though I liked the work of Cora Kaplan and Dolores Rosenblatt I was tentative — too much so — about making these claims. Like the cruder feminist individualism it seemed to make women special cases of oppression. But if you do not take this route, how do you prevent yourself from falling into a stodgy impartiality which is not impartiality at all?

I read biography avidly, trying to find out what Christina Rossetti read. If she belonged to a network of texts one could find one's way back to a set of cultural relationships, relationships with some 'central' discourse, which did not trap her into isolation. But in trying to do this I discovered the extraordinary passionate and traumatic story of her love for William Bell Scott and his casually brutal treatment of her, which is proposed in Lorna Morse Packham's biography. I noticed that Geoffrey Grigson's review of the first volume of R. W. Crump's edition (1979) of Rossetti's work in the *Times Literary Supplement* simply ignores Packham's hypotheses. Did he know of them? He prefers a more credible account of her life which is actually more tortuously ingenious. Was I 'allowed' to deal with this agony, and if so, how? My feeling that the biography was important did not seem to match with any form I could write in.

It is interesting that the sense that I was able or 'permitted' to say some things and not others remained as some undefined coercion even in a feminist reading. I believed, and still believe, that one must talk about a politics and simultaneously about language, but how? The politics must be in the form and in the language, I decided, because that frees one to think of structures which must belong to cultural patterns. And since poetry does not simply reproduce, but creates and becomes the materials of cultural forms themselves, this reciprocity seemed promising for the way out of the impasse which makes women the passive object of a special or marginalised experience. It makes the woman poet an agent.

'Winter Rain' is conjured out of rigorous repetition and the iteration of negations. '*Every valley* drinks,/*Every dell* and *hollow:*/ Where the kind rain *sinks* and *sinks* . . .'. It is one of those pastoral lyrics so familiar in English writing that the form is virtually sourceless, speaking out of an idiom so generalised that it comes from everywhere and nowhere. The voice speaks from conventions which are both hidden and obvious. One meets this simultaneous sharing and not sharing in Christina Rossetti's poetry constantly. It is a scrupulous way of marking community with and dissociation from the pastoral tradition which is after all a male preserve. The action of 'fattening' rain appears to follow a conventional course, as it irrigates the concavities of dell and hollow, bursting buds, creating a natural environment for fertility, though the pregnant solidity of 'fattening' works oddly with the diffusing nature of rain. But then comes a systematic deviation into the denial of negatives — 'But for . . . But for . . . no . . . never . . . never . . . no . . . no . . . no . . . never . . . not.' Without rain the natural processes of birth and propagation would cease, the poem says in its 'simplicity'. The frightful matching sterility of land and water, which would not be water but desert, is the final negation. The simple statement of lack goes much further however, questioning expectations about the teleological necessity of recurrence and regularity. What is 'natural' when this is denied?

It seemed that much could be understood when I got to this point. If the teleological order and the 'natural' is being questioned, so implicitly is the cultural. If the 'natural' order which exists in interdependence with the teleological order turns out to be neither natural nor ordered, then a great deal has been said about the coercive force of accepted assumptions. The constant action of doubling, repetition, iteration and duplication seemed to me to create an intransigently restricting order which the poem disrupts by using the processes of order themselves. It was tempting to think in terms of Kristéva's antithesis between the semiotic and the symbolic. The subversive, semiotic freedom of 'fattening' rain, which keels over from the sheer physicality of organic growth to the idea of fattening for slaughter, is in opposition, perhaps, to the repressive abstract patterns of symbolic 'masculine' syntax and repetition. But I was not happy with this. The 'repressive' pattern, if it was that, was overwhelmingly dominant and seemed to be tested in its capacity to sustain itself by showing that it collapsed of itself. There seemed to be a play in and with pattern which made order both restricting *and enabling*. Thus the antithesis between semiotic and symbolic maintained by Kristéva was not sustained, in this poem at least.

The idea that an order could be restricting *and* enabling took me some way for I saw that one could regard the dominant Victorian poetics of expression in a parallel way that seemed both psychoanalytically and politically important. Victorian poetics (Keble is an obvious example) assumes that expression occurs when the barrier of the customary restraints of consciousness is broken. Emotion breaks out of the self into representation. But by the same token, though this is never consciously theorised, the barrier constitutes repression. Each needs, and is predicated on, the other. Though there are significant differences, this does not seem far away from Freud's account of repression as effecting a continual displacement and indeed, creation of energy. I did not wish to use Freud at that time because the two sets of theories don't converge in very important ways, but I am bolder now. We can bring the two theories together. After all, without Freud one would not conceptualise any form of repression. Victorian poetics could be seen as a paradigm for both sexual and political life. I saw that in playing so daringly with the barrier of the symbolic and in recognising the inter-dependence of expression and repression, Christina Rossetti was both confirming and questioning the limits of both.

Goblin Market, where the 'good' Laura smears the goblins' forbidden fruit on the face of the 'bad' Lizzie, who had been denied the fruit she once bought with a piece of herself, her own hair, took on a new meaning. That there is a market price for the glory of Lizzie's experience which is paid for with one's identity is one gross fact. But we are not asked to 'choose' between a bad and a good girl because there is in reality no *moral* opposition here. The play of desire and restriction, Lizzie and Laura, create one another and the play of opposition is enabling. But Christina Rossetti chooses to distort and intensify the opposition between Laura and Lizzie in this poem because she sees that the play of desire and repression is subjected to a fierce economic and ethical code in their world. The dripping fruit crushed against the faces of both girls, one resisting, one rejoicing, becomes both outrage and orgy, a deliberate demonstration that what is literally 'expressed' here can only be so in the context of violation, abuse, scatological fury and aggression. For a structural condition has been turned into a moral order. The morbid aspect of Victorian culture is in this poem, but, it seems to say, can these facts ever be 'neutral'?

This is something I felt I 'could' say. I took a lecture to America on the problems of full-frontal feminism and its preoccupation with content at the expense of language and form. Elaine Showalter rose in majestic disagreement. She argued that I was colluding with a central academic discourse which always assimilated women to men's concerns. I was too ready to show that Christina Rossetti was part of a dominant Victorian aesthetics of expression. I was not making claims for a feminine tradition. After a long argument I said, 'But *I* want to write poetry which men will read.' 'Ah', said Elaine. She was right to feel that I had not used the sanctions of feminist criticism powerfully. But there is a problem. What can be said about Christina Rossetti ought to be relevant to Tennyson, Browning and Hopkins.

Back again, I read more Kristéva, the French feminists, Derrida, the English translators of Lacan, Juliet Mitchell and Jacqueline Rose, *m/f*. I also read Bachelard in the hope that he might provide a new and more free way of writing which women could use to break out of conventional criticism. This is a telescoped account of reading which took place over a period. What I read sifted a series of questions. I did not read this in order to 'use' it, and often did not see the relevance of what I read for some time. This should make us beware of asking students to 'use' theory. In the end it was Christina Rossetti herself who helped, through the Preface to 'Monna Innomenata'. Klingopoulos reminds his readers in 1958 that Christina Rossetti there talks about the happy condition of Mrs Browning as against her own depressive art. However, he did not see that the Victorian euphemism for the spinster is to call her *unhappy* in contradistinction to the 'happy' married woman. In that Preface Christina Rossetti is boldly describing herself as an unmarried woman, i.e. an 'unhappy' spinster who writes of sexual as well as religious feeling under all the constraints of her society. Such poetry, she writes, must be 'less dignified' when it is written by a woman. So much for Robson's ladylike poetess and Elizabeth Barrett Browning's 'embarrassing intimacy'. If it was clear that Christina Rossetti was fully aware of her position as a woman poet, her boldness must make her readers as bold.

What could one do, then? Going back to 'Winter Rain', the dells and hollows where the generative principle of rain 'sinks and sinks' seemed more emphatically female declivities. I could never see what writing the female body was really about, whether literally or figuratively, but the sexuality of this and the bursting buds with their viscous gluey coats, seemed more insistent. Certainly the infinitely sinking rain could seem like the flow of the female body described by Madelaine Gagnon, but this seemed altogether too literal, and anyhow didn't collaborate with the logic of the poem. The poem rests upon dysymmetry, on the principle of subtraction, a world 'without'. Take one element, the flow of water, from the precarious hierarchical harmony of nest and egg and *mother*, mated birds, lambs and sheep, the protecting and the dependent, allow rain to 'sink and sink' *away*, and an empty world will follow as inexorably as spring once followed winter. But the scepticism also hovers round the idea of rain 'in season'. Rain out of season is as devastating as none at all, leading equally to a sterile world all 'water'. The cold strategy of denial begins to investigate itself further in the last stanza.

The poem ends when the logic of denial, with its successive hypotheses of a world of lack, supersedes all else, and the consequential shifts become progressively enormous. The lack is total.

> But miles of barren sand,
>   With never a son or daughter.
> Not a lily on the land,
>   Or lily on the water.

I began to understand that the poem was about, not denial, not the repressive withdrawal of the principle of fertility, but the logical consequences of *seeing* the world in terms of lack and negation. That is why 'Winter Rain' is in the subjunctive — 'But for' — to denote the hypothetical, as so many of the poems are. Ultimately the 'barren sand' of negation will not even produce the hierarchical order of 'sons and daughters' which is founded on the principle of denial and upon which it itself is founded. It will simply produce itself. That the definition of lack might be the product of a masculine order — think of Derrida's account of woman as 'non-identity, appearance, simulacrum' — is nowhere to be found in the poem. That is one of its strengths. It is the principle of negation which is important rather than its origin. But the sudden appearance in the last stanza of 'sons and daughters', human progeny and the taboos of sexual difference, prompts a reading which pays attention to gender if only because of the traditional identity of lily and virginity. Both sons and daughters are caught up in the principle of negation. It differentiates at the same time as it includes them in its anxieties. The world of lack is delicately and searchingly generalised. It is grossly clumsy to literalise a reading in terms of the phallic lack of Freud's subsequent Oedipal theory. But castration theory, defining both sons and daughters as 'without', but giving the daughter no way to surmount this, does help here. Part of the difficulty of writing this piece has been to introduce these ideas in a way which is faithful to the poem's lyric 'simplicity' and austerity. They are not there as literal presences but as buried, subliminal *structures*. I hope that the poem's bare, overwhelming understanding of emptiness overwhelms a facile reading. I cannot sneak Freud and Lacan into a footnote, as I might in a more conventional piece of criticism. Nor can I take it for granted that everyone knows them. 'Lack' for some people indicates the notion of the Oedipal 'without'. For some people it does not. I am reduced to this clumsy expedient by the need not to seem arcane. At the same time I run the risk of making these ideas literal presences in the poem.

The final deprivation, the last stanza, refuses a facile reading. The mirror image of the lily on the land, the lily on the water, is not an image of anything because the lily is only phantasmally conjured by its absence. There is a consummate shift of the male Narcissus myth here. Lilies grow on land and in water: they are also reflected in water. But here the absent lily faces the absent, illusory lily. The water is a mirror without a reflection, or a desert without a reflective surface. 'The woman does not exist', Lacan said. It follows that a no-thing cannot be reflected and find an identity. The lily cannot be in love with itself or discover its being through self-reflection. But it also follows, as the poem pursues an inexorable logic, that the virginity of which the lily is a symbol may also be an illusory thing. It may cease to exist and cease to be necessary in another alternative order. After all, the strict reflective concordance and perfect equalisation arranged in the final stanza is fallacious. It is a representation in language of a condition which is not 'true'. And here the poem's virtuosity achieves another turn out of the negation it describes by following its own logic. If the lily of virginity is illusory, the double lily *has* been represented in language, even if paradoxically through the language of negation. The virginity of the double lily is a verbal artefact, just as the proposition that rain could be systematically absent from the economy of nature is a hypothetical fiction, the represen-tation of an alternative world. It depends on a contract between poem and reader to sustain a logic which seems on the face of it contrary to experience. The deconstructive

movement, however, opens up two further possibilities both
of which 'follow', but which are antithetical to one another.
One possibility is that if this world of intransigent negation,
the 'non' or 'nom' of the father as the Lacanian pun has it,
is an order constructed in language it must be possible to
redefine, re-construe and shift these rigid negations. It must
be possible to construct another order of language through
language even at the cost, or gain, of seeing all orders as
constructs.

The beauty of the poem's logic is that it defines the world
of 'non', not as a norm but as an aberrant artifice, deviating
from what we know of experience. The entire absence of rain
is not a norm, though it is thinkable. But, on the other hand,
the second consequence of regarding the world of 'non' as
an alternative world is in opposition to the first possibility I
have described, and not so consoling. What is it alternative
to? Is there an unalterable world beyond language from
which the self-referring processes of words deviate at their
cost? After all, we 'know' rain does not disappear. Is that
unalterable world 'the bower of love' described at the start
of the poem? The bower of love, where birds 'meet each
other', as the non-reflected lilies do not, is a seductive and
enticing world of pastoral concord and security. But it is
nonetheless fixed in repetitive cycles in which all things occur
'in season'. The pattern can never be changed. Or, as the
pastoral convention of conscious artifice may denote, is this
a fiction, too? The pastoral may simply be the reverse side
of the order of 'non', an enclosed world on which the
economy of negation is predicated. The *soaking, fattening
rain*, the bitten grass, are curiously threatening. The poem's
pursuit of the possibilities which 'follow' from its premises
is so complex that I have had to resort to the clumsy forms
of 'But', 'And yet', 'On the other hand', 'both . . . and . . .',
in order to describe the shifting dialectic it both sustains and
stands aloof from. There is both boundlessness and limit in
this last stanza as it moves through self-created cycles of
endless hope and despair, neither of which can be decisive.
To have experimented so resiliently with these endless questions in such a fragile form by taking the idea of limit to the
limit is remarkable. The poem seems to perform structurally
what Derrida calls the 'operation' of the woman, or the idea

of woman. The idea of woman is a function, not a content and disrupts because it suspends 'decidable oppositions', as this poem does. But we should not forget that there *is* a content to the decidable oppositions themselves, something that an abstract Derridean reading too often forgets.

A good many things worry me about this discussion. I did not want to simply dump the Lacanian idea of lack in the poem in an unhistorical way: the Lacanian idea is far more specific than anything in the poem. It can only be invoked as a marker. His and Derrida's are descriptive formulas which can make every poem the same. I do not like the idea of 'applying' theory to texts in some technological way, for the form in which theory and texts relate is subtle and indirect. But Lacan and Derrida seemed to illuminate the poem's questions. I do not think my early training in ambiguity could have got me here. My reading, I hope, is informed by, but does not 'apply' their work. But what I found fascinating was the poem's resistance to their very essentialist strategy and the integrity with which it considers the possibility of the coercive 'non'. The world of 'non' is intransigent and yet, conceivably, alterable. Christina Rossetti seems to go round behind Lacanian determinism. I would like to think further about Victorian patriarchy to embody this reading in history. All this must have repercussions for Christina Rossetti's religious poetry, but that is a discussion for somewhere else. Certainly it helps one to see the force of the coda to *Goblin Market*. Laura and Lizzie bury their experiences, which are transmitted in terms of an admonitory fable to their children. They are absorbed into a cultural order of marriage and the family which allows them to interpret their experiences by limiting them to the moral; they fall to one side of a decidable opposition.

Other worries concern language. Though it seems to me that the poem understands oppression in language very well, I do not want to settle for the politically dangerous notion of a female language which circumvents phallogocentrism by separatism. The strength of the poem is that it negotiates directly with the power of repressive language, using pastoral in a way which recognises that pastoral conventions can be both liberating and coercive. Again, for the first time in my criticism I have talked of deconstruction. It seems to me that wrongful Derridean readings revolve on their own axis round the perpetual abstract sameness of the nature of the sign, of absence and presence, just as the Lacanian postulates of lack can be abstracted. Christina Rossetti's opening up of endless and very particular interrogations is not like this at all. The poem has a deconstructive movement because it reveals contradictions by putting pressure on its own logic. It seems to me that 'real' Derridean readings are deeply inward. Because they must deal with particular complexities of contradiction in a particular way, the unique form in which questions are asked in any text must be controlled by 'the process of its own becoming', to think for a moment in the Hegelian terms to which deconstruction is heir. Perhaps my formative days in 'traditional' criticism, which I have often talked about with Gillian Beer, have persuaded me towards this reading. If so, so much the better. There is no need for a feminist deconstruction to collapse into sterile negations and abstractions. Derrida's thinking on the suspension of 'decidable opposition' is interesting for feminist criticism in repudiating power, but Derrida is so provocative and ingeniously evasive as a writer that I am not certain about this. His game with power reintroduces it.

I am still struggling with Kristéva's work on abjection and with new layers of reading, or changed readings, of 'Winter Rain'. Kristéva's exploration of abjection as 'the recognition of the fundamental *lack* of all being, meaning, language and desire',[2] as a constant dissolution and creation of limits which must therefore provoke a 'narcissistic crisis' because it disrupts the self-sufficient order of self-reflection, must bear upon this poem and those doubled but non-existent lilies. Her association of the incommensurable of abjection with religious constructions may well be a way into Christina Rossetti's religious poetry and back from that to the other poems. It is not proper to sever her religious poems from the rest of the work. Kristéva's association of abjection with 'the rite of impurity' deepens the cultural and psychological implications of defilement in *Goblin Market*, the pulped fruit smeared on the women's faces. And yet I am worried by Kristéva because the notion of abjection does without history. One would have to wonder about Victorian abjection, perhaps Carlyle's 'everlasting No' in *Sartor Resartus*, before exploring what relation her work might have to Christina Rossetti's work. The same worry pursues Derrida's cunning conceptualisation of woman in terms of disruption through suspension of decidable oppositions. And I still wonder if you can say this only if you are a man.

Where does the alternative hair-line path lead now? It still seems to me that women's criticism has to think more deeply about language and politics. If we are in dialogue with a male discourse, this will be different in different historical periods, or patriarchy would be of the same order as the universals of traditional criticism. Voloshinov's account of language in terms of an ideological struggle for the sign in *Marxism and the Philosophy of Language* is surely suggestive for feminist criticism.[3] Its dialogic project can be extended into inter-textual dialogue. The politics of Christina Rossetti's language would become far clearer if we read her against the work of other women poets — Landon, Hemans, Greenwell, Ingelow. The discourses of male-produced theology, the language of the social theories which clustered round Christina Rossetti's work with fallen women, the evolutionary discourse of Darwin and above all, the men she must have been perpetually in dialogue with, her brother and the Pre-Raphaelite brotherhood, all these would enable us to read her relation to Victorian ideology and culture. And this is also a way of rereading the relations of biography and culture.

Does this inter-textual project look too much like 'ordinary' criticism? In that case, feminist criticism subsumes ordinary criticism, not the other way round, because ordinary criticism is too often blind to questions of gender. Does that mean that men will write feminist criticism? Yes. We can never become post-feminists. I began by saying that the idea of literature as a 'new' cultural construct was unknown to my early education, but that does not make it disappear. Literature, Laura Marcus said in conversation, seems to be the marked off area where the writer is both deeply and unconsciously coerced by the hardened forms and discourses he or she finds in experience and is strangely enabled to experiment with them and with language. The idea of experiment gets us out of the discourse of power because it suggests that experiment can be free from oppression. Feminist criticism can move freely among these experiments with hardened form on the understanding that its interest in gender must make it part of the experiment. It can put pressure on inflexible and petrifying assumptions and, whether they are unconsciously held or not, test out the conventions of criticism itself.

I have used the word coerce too much, but I do so unapologetically. My reading of Christina Rossetti makes me aware of the degree to which I have colluded with coercion. This diary form with its holiday from footnotes and references to friends is a way of expressing my tentativeness by escaping from conceptions of the legitimate form for literary essays. It also tries to escape from accepting the notion of criticism both as mastery and as disinterested discussion. One hidden censorship is a silent injunction against exploring a theory of emotions in reading and writing. Barthes' 'jouissance' was an attempt to reinstate and theorise a (masculine?) theory of pleasure. Women's criticism should take this further. Perhaps we need a gendered account of pleasure. One need not return to naive expressive and psychological theories or to a doctrine of sincerity or to a simplified conception of the text and consciousness to do this. The task is infinitely complex. But in order to undertake it, it will be necessary to be bold — and probably un-'dignified'.

Notes

1. Sandra M. Gilbert and Susan Gubar, *The Madwoman in the Attic: The Woman Writer and the Nineteenth-century Literary Imagination* (Yale University Press, New Haven, 1979).
2. *Oxford Literary Review* 5, 1982, 128.
3. V. N. Voloshinov, *Marxism and the Philosophy of Language* (Seminar Press, 1973; reprinted Harvard University Press, 1986).

6

A Double Matrix: Re-Reading H.D.

Diana Collecott

For Nan

Introductory Note

Three years ago, I was preparing to spend nine months in the United States on a research fellowship and looking forward with delight to my first prolonged period of intensive study since working for a doctorate some ten years before. In the interim, as part of a larger change of orientation, my main academic interest had shifted from the male poets of Anglo-American modernism to the female ones — especially H.D. (1886–1961). As it turned out, I had to remain in England for three months during the autumn of 1983, under the care of my recently widowed mother, to recover from surgery that removed my womb. For both of us it was a painful period of loss and recovery, a time of silence and gestation: of the new work and the next phase of life. Removed from my contemporaries and professional milieu, I was once again in the family home I had left in late adolescence, confronting her wifehood and motherhood while I lived through my own 'failure' to bear children. In spite (or because) of this, there was a renewed continuity between the child I had been and the adult I had become. My only writing at this time was an introduction to H.D.'s memoir of childhood, *The Gift*, so a resonance was set up between my work on her and her work on herself.

In consequence, the six months of 1984 that I spent among the H.D. papers at Yale were very fruitful. Besides, they were 'time out' from my uncomfortable but more or less continuous commitment, as a student and then as a teacher, to the British academic system. It was an occasion for what

Adrienne Rich has called 're-membering': in this case, a double act of recovery, of a woman writer marginalised by a literary history defined and mediated by men, and of my own womanliness, which was suppressed as part of the internalisation of patriarchy in the universities. 'We think back through our mothers if we are women' wrote Virginia Woolf; but for those whose social and intellectual formation took place in the 1950s and 60s, no less than for her generation and H.D.'s, this is hard to achieve, given the overwhelming influence of male mentors and literary forefathers. So that re-reading H.D. came to involve interrelated recognitions: of the bond with the mother, whether real (biological, emotional) or ideal ('the woman artist', the Goddess), and with other mothers; these include the French intellectuals Simone de Beauvoir and Julia Kristéva, who helped me to understand what it means to be a 'subject in the making', the American feminist critics Rachel Blau DuPlessis and Susan Stanford Friedman, who helped me to begin to see H.D. whole, without privileging the early over the late work, the poetry over the prose, the published over the unpublished writings.

Two poets, both of whom in their different ways acknowledge *their* maternal inheritance, also stand at the threshold of my renewed interest in H.D.: Denise Levertov and Adrienne Rich. Together they inspire the interplay of vision and revision that must structure our perceptions of her work. H.D. emerges from the dissensions of our era as a holistic artist, for whom the psychic and the somatic are in touch. To know her is to confirm what she knew as 'the other-side of everything', which includes all that lies beyond patriarchal religion, beyond racialism and beyond the 'heterosexual presumption.'

Since the feminist presses have been offering the possibility of writing directly for other women, I've experienced a modest but persistent freeing from the self-censorship we have all engaged in, though my training in personal discretion and the citation of established authority still runs deep. When Sue Roe invited me to write about H.D. in the context of this book, I was both excited and daunted by the opportunity to identify myself openly as a reader of specific gender, sexuality, education and experience. I was also aghast at the banalities that a 'straight' account of these conjunctions brought forth. I resolved to follow Emily Dickinson's clew and 'tell it slant'. The multifaceted use of quotation that resulted may seem to some a classic instance of modernist evasion, but it has been enabling for me. I realise that there are suppressions, silences and empty echoes here; but there are also showings, recognitions and subject-rhymes. (In order to avoid footnotes, I have identified the authors by name only in the text, giving details of their works at the end. Where there is no name, it is my writing).

Once I had found a medium in which my mind could move freely, the piece almost 'wrote itself.' Perhaps what H.D. calls the UNC. (Unconscious) was at work here, excavating earlier levels, saying more than one meant or thought one knew. The next stage was happily a collective one: sharing the writing with friends who would comment honestly, and amending it in the light of their reactions. The French feminist Hélène Cixous has spoken of 'the labour of un-forgetting, of un-silencing, of un-earthing, of un-blinding and un-deafening oneself.' From before this specific project, many friends have shared that labour with me: Linda Anderson, Julia Ball, John Broadbent, Ruth First, Penny Florence, Cynthia Fuller, David Fuller, Jeanne Blanchenay Houghton, Ben Knights, Wendy Mulford, David Punter, Winifred Rushforth, Sandi Russell, Nicole Ward Jouve, Sarah Whittaker, Liz Yorke. Sue Roe believed this writing could come to birth, Rachel Blau DuPlessis was its *sage-femme* and Flick Allen performed the Caesarian operation.

By comparison, scholarly writing has often been more lonely, more difficult (though not more demanding) and less real to me. It is part of my job to read essays by other people — whether those of undergraduates or professional critics. I am concerned at the contradictory relationship between the kinds of discourse in which poetry is written, and the kinds of discourse in which it is written about. In my mind's eye, the prose paragraph has come to resemble a monolith: a stone blocking the 'cave of making', obstructing the reader's movement between the secondary text and the primary text that is under discussion. To equate sequential logic with the convincing 'thrust' of phallocentric criticism might be to oversimplify, but I've been drawn for some time to the subversive wordplay and multiple activity of *l'écriture féminine*. I also wanted, here, to create a text in which physical space has its part in the play of meanings, just as our bodies do in what Kristéva calls the 'semiotic process'. Hence the lavish layout, which invites the reader to consider the rhythm of each double-page unit as part of the movement of the whole piece. Even the space after the last words should be active in this, lest they suggest too easy a closure.

Diana Collecott
Durham, January 1986

In her mother's . . . in her mother's
house, after long absence, the girl . . .
the young woman strokes the bed cover,
dis-/ a displaced caress. She has s-/
struggled with her mother, refused her,
refused to apologise. Cries/represses
tears. Strokes the bedcover saying,
sotto voce: 'I was inside her. She. She
bore me. If I deny her, I deny myself.'

WHY *SHE?*

I say I: I am going to say I.
(Nicole Ward Jouve)

What is 'i'? The primal scratch —
the mark made by the child on the body
of the mother: 'I want to get in . . .
I want to get out!'
(Juliet Mitchell)

Learning to write. Mummy guides the pen.
When I can do it myself — I laugh.
(It was a sense of presence).

We have crawled back into the womb;
you command?
be born again,
be born,
be born;

      H.D., 'Magician'

SHE IS *I*.

    The last part of the lecture concerned
    the archi-trace as erasure: erasure of the
    present and thus of the subject, of that
    which is proper to the subject and of his
    proper name. The concept of a (conscious
    or unconscious) subject necessarily refers
    to the concept of substance — and thus of
    presence — out of which it is born.
          (Jacques Derrida)

I laugh, holding the pen, making
meaning on the page, spell my name
('Diana could read by the time she was four'
— the maternal boast). Later the
laughter goes with a delight in the
intelligible: she directs me into
reading, teaches me to hear poetry
and to speak it.

JOUISSANCE

> Laughter is the evidence that the instant
> *took place:* the space that supports it
> signifies time. Located elsewhere, distant,
> permissive, always already past: such is
> the *chora* that the mother is called upon
> to produce with the child so that a
> semiotic disposition might exist.
>
> (Julia Kristéva)

chora = a receptacle . . .
(according to Plato: 'an invisible
and formless being which receives
all things and in a mysterious way
partakes of the intelligible, and
is most incomprehensible')

= J'OUIS SENS

> First, Giovanni wanted to surpass his father,
> within the very space of the lost-unrepresentable
> -forbidden jouissance of a hidden mother, seducing
> the child through lack of being.
> But then, and most importantly, Giovanni could
> share in this both maternal and paternal jouissance:
> He aspired to become the very space where father
> and mother meet. . . .
> Our long biographical and historical, sacred
> and figural journey has shown that for Bellini,
> motherhood is nothing more than such a luminous
> spatialization, the ultimate language of a jouissance
> at the far limit of repression, whence bodies,
> identities and signs are begotten.
>
> (Julia Kristéva)

Motherhood —

I saw the first pear
as it fell —
. . . .
and I fell prostrate
crying:

H.D., 'Orchard'

My mother chose motherhood; the books
were unwritten, or written too late . . .

EITHER/OR:

the PROBLEM!

> As for my next book, I am going to hold
> myself from writing till I have it impending
> in me: grown heavy in my mind
> like a ripe pear; pendant, gravid,
> asking to be cut or it will fall . . .
>   (Virginia Woolf)

> My brother is considerably taller. I am
> five and he is seven, or I am three and
> he is five. It is summer. The grass is
> somewhat dry, a few leaves crackle under
> our feet. They have fallen from a pear
> tree that has large russet pears. The pears
> have been gathered. (*Pears? Pairs?*) . . .
>   H.D., *Tribute to Freud*

NOT BOTH

> My body knows it will never bear children.
> What can I say to my body now,
> this used violin?
> Every night it cries out strenuously
> from its secret cave.
>
> Old body, old friend,
> Why are you so unforgiving?
>
> Why are you so stiff and resistant
> clenched around empty space?
>
>   Jane Cooper 'Waiting'

The child cries in frustration at all
she cannot do — yet.

The woman bleeds for the last time —
almost to death. She needs a blood transfusion
before they will perform a hysterectomy /
/ take out her uterus / remove her womb

I WANT A FUSION

Now there is a space where her
womb was

          receptacle?
'Not a big organ, the size of a
grapefruit perhaps' (the surgeon's
knowing smile): 'women always
imagine that the uterus is large.'

Nonetheless, the contractions
were overwhelming — though
they brought nothing to birth

Three lines remained with her from
their 'O' level study of *King Lear:*
  'Oh how this mother swells up toward my heart!
  Hysterica passio, down thou climbing sorrow . . .'
and
  'Never, never, never, never, never.'
(She had herself used the latter in
teaching as an example of trochaic
pentameter . . .)

ma pauvre chère amie . . . ce sont
     les larmes d'une déçue . . .

(I have forgotten the French for
'womb' — a Freudian slip? The
dictionary supplies a Latinate word
of the masculine gender: *uterus.*
Ah, *un uterus déçu . . .*)

OR TRANSFUSION OF MY MOTHER'S ART
                              H.D.

but using a new kind of writing, a rhythm for
the first time associative, personal, ruminative
and atemporal, she has gotten . . . to another
kind of inspiration. One might well apply
Kristévan terms about the *chora* — the release
of an imagined primal space from the body of
the mother . . .
                    (Rachel DuPlessis on H.D.)

Unlike H.D., I do not know Greek. I
do not know whether *chora* can be related
to *choros* and to the rhythms
of the moving body, the speaking voice.
I am content for the moment that in my
mind both *chora* and *matrix* relate to
the imaginary space in which the womb
had moved. And now they make, what?
A space for the dance, for laughter,
thought or song —

Rhythm,
a sequence of linked instants,
is immanent to the *chora*
prior to
any signified spaciousness:
henceforth, *chora*
                and rhythm,
space and time
coexist.
                (Julia Kristéva)

for you are abstract,
making no mistake,
slurring no word
in the rhythm you make,
the poem,
writ in the air.

      H.D., 'The Dancer'

One may write music and music but who will
dance to it? The dance escapes but the
music, the music — projects a dance over
itself which the feet follow lazily if
at all. So a dance is a thing in itself.
It is the music that dances but if there
are words then there are two dancers, the
words pirouetting with the music.
                (W. C. Williams)

The heterosexual presumption? I, too,
fell for the Jungian dream: a formal
ballroom, black and white, Lord Yang
and Lady Yin dancing together. Did my
'Unconscious' bully me into matrimony
(a dignified and commodious sacrament)
— at 21? The groom in black, the bride
in white: *animus* + *anima*. And all the
time my conscious mind insisting that
I was supplying a perfect example of
Sartrean 'bad faith'. Sleepwalking with
one's eyes open . . .

At university, D. H. Lawrence was thrust
down our throats. Never mind that three-
quarters of Eng. Lit. undergraduates were
women. We went down on him. How many
never woke from *that* dream of fulfilment? I
must owe to Lawrence — or was it to
Frieda? — the brute courage to leave husband
for lover. Looking for Mr. Right: the
Woman's Own recipe for schizophrenia
(patient husband, rejected and dejected, seeks
Jungian analyst — for me). So that, in the
end, you only feel whole when you are alone

The association of man and woman
In daunsinge, signifying matrimonie —
A dignified and commodious sacrament.
Two and two, necessarye coniunction . . .

T. S. Eliot, 'East Coker'

See, they return; ah, see the tentative
Movements, and the slow feet,
The trouble in the pace and the uncertain
Wavering!
See, they return, one, and by one,
With fear, as half-awakened;
As if the snow should hesitate
And murmur in the wind,
                    and half-turn back; . . .

Ezra Pound, 'The Return'

TWO AND TWO . . .

HERSELF, indeed! A meaningless hieroglyph. The text of H.D.'s *Her*, written in the 'twenties, remained unpublished until the 'eighties (this is the 'sixties, remember?). But I forget, there was *Bid Me to Live* — so named by H.D.'s male mentor. *Her* title was *Madrigal. He* preferred the plea in Herrick's poem ('. . . *or bid me love, and I will give/ A loving heart to thee . . .*') that she had chosen as epigraph. It recalled her youthful romance with Aldington, which is only one line in the novel's counterpoint. Eventually published in 1961, noticed only for its portrait of Lawrence as Rico, and damned by *my* male mentor, in an authoritative review, for its 'vibrant subjectivity.'

Yet for me H.D.'s war novel brought
another reality into view: a sickening
swing of the camera through 180° from
the interminable trenches — mud and
maleness — to the lone woman in a
London room intermittently invaded by
the world. *Hidden from History:* a breakthrough
like Shiela Rowbotham's, talking
to a seminar in the seventies not about
dating, but 'dating'; hard to
recognise, to act on, at the time.

Written actuality is subjective: even
the first papyrus was once a blank.
(Helen McNeil)

156

SEE THEY RETURN —

. . . to the sightless realm where darkness is married to dark
and Persephone herself is but a voice, as a bride,
a gloom invisible enfolded in the deeper dark
of the arms of Pluto as he ravishes her once again
and pierces her once more with his passion of the utter dark
among the splendour of black-blue torches, shedding
    fathomless darkness on the nuptials.

                  D. H. Lawrence, 'Bavarian Gentians'

Whenever a woman goes to write a novel she
first chooses herself as heroine . . . *women
are incapable of the indirect method.*
    Richard Aldington, *The Egoist* (1914)

Orpheus with his lute made trees,
And the mountain-tops that freeze,
Bow themselves when he did sing . . .

Shakespeare and Fletcher, *King Henry VIII*

I recited that as a child. When,
as a woman, I heard the voice of
Eurydice, the wood moved within me.
('And here am I, and wood within this wood').

Rico to Julia: 'I don't like the second half of the Orpheus
sequence as well as the first. Stick to the woman
speaking. How can you know what Orpheus feels? It's
your part to be woman, the woman vibration.
Eurydice should be enough . . .'

H.D., *Bid Me to Live*

Eurydice

So you have swept me back,
I who could have walked with the live souls
above the earth,
I who could have slept among live flowers
at last;

so for your arrogance
and your ruthlessness
I am swept back
where dead lichens drip
dead cinders upon moss of ash;

. . . .

here only flame upon flame
and black among the red sparks,
streaks of black and light
grown colourless;

why did you turn back,
that hell should be reinhabited
of myself thus
swept into nothingness?

. . . .

A Double Matrix: Re-Reading H.D.

So for your arrogance
and your ruthlessness
I have lost the earth
and the flowers of the earth,
and the live souls above the earth,
and you who passed across the light
and reached
ruthless;

you who have your own light,
who are to yourself a presence,
who need no presence;

yet for all your arrogance
and your glance,
I tell you this:

such loss is no loss . . .

hell is no worse than your earth
above the earth,
hell is no worse, . . .

my hell is no worse than yours
though you pass among the flowers and speak
with the spirits above earth.

. . . .

At least I have the flowers of myself,
and my thoughts, no god
can take that;
I have the fervour of myself as a presence
and my own spirit for light;

and my spirit with its loss
knows this;
though small against the black,
small against the formless rocks,
hell must break before I am lost;

before I am lost,
hell must open like a red rose
for the dead to pass.

                    H.D.

The British Museum, 1967: I found this poem
in the yellowing pages of *The Egoist* of fifty
years before. Its 'vibrant subjectivity' shocked me:
where was the decorum one had come
to expect of the 'Perfect Imagiste'? Little wonder
that Pound did not praise the poem in his essays,
nor Pearson reprint it in the *Selected Poems of
H.D.* (1957). Again we would wait – for the posthumous
Collected Poems of 1983 (did Eliot or Pound wait
for a 'Collected' until they were dead?) By then,
the *New Freewoman* had been long under the earth, but
the name still vibrated in that margin of consciousness that
I excluded as a postgraduate pursuing, in the pages of
The Egoist, the least trace of Eliot and Pound. The
same margin would bleed into the text when I later read
Aldington's testimony that, when H.D. was assistant
editor of *The Egoist*, 'Ezra and Eliot pushed her
ruthlessly aside', or her own cry from the heart:
'I can't think that I *must* be Pound-Eliot.'

The 'double bind' of the woman academic —
who does not menstruate until she has her
doctorate.

To be a woman poet in our society is a double
bind situation, one of conflict and strain.
For the words 'woman' and 'poet' denote
opposite and contradictory qualities and roles.

(Suzanne Juhasz)

Must the multiple nature of female desire and
language be understood as the fragmentary,
scattered remains of a raped or denied sexuality?
The rejection, the exclusion of a female
imaginary . . . places woman in a position where
she can experience herself only fragmentarily . . .
in the little structured margins of a dominant
ideology, this mirror entrusted by the (masculine)
'subject' with the task of reflecting or
redoubling himself.

(Luce Irigaray)

Myself then, imperfect, in a room of my own,
gathering the scattered limbs of a thesis . . .
'Congratulations: You've broken through the
Last barrier of male privilege!' *Unhunhhh*.
Writing a C.V. is painful: one is over-conscious
of spaces: how to account for the 'lost' years
of marriage — no children to show for it.
Marital status? Divorced. 'Oho, a divorc*ee*'.
Ph.D., 1972: *William Carlos Williams and the Need
for a Specifically American Poetic*, catalogued,
of course, under my married name, which came
last. It was with a kind of secret shame that
I had signed on, in the B.M. Reading Room, under
the name I grew up with: at least this would be
my own province, booklined against bank-managers
and professors who insisted to the contrary
('But of course now you are married you will
take your husband's name'; *I x take thee y . . .*)
The B.M. Reading Room: submerged in an undersea
womb of one's own . . .

I did not know how to differentiate
between volcanic desire,
anemones like embers
and purple fire
of violets
like red heat,
and the cold
silver
of her feet:

. . . .

there is a purple flower
between her marble, her birch-tree white
thighs,
or there is a red flower,

there is a rose flower
parted wide,
as her limbs fling wide in dance
ecstatic
Aphrodite,
there is a frail lavender flower
hidden in grass;

O God, what is it,
this flower
that in itself had power over the whole earth?
for she needs no man,
herself
is that dart and pulse of the male,
hands, feet, thighs,
herself perfect.

H.D., 'The Master'

WHERE ARE THE POETESSES? . . .

If you take the moon in your hands
and turn it round
(heavy, slightly tarnished platter)
you're there

if you pull dry sea-weed from the sand
and turn it round
and wonder at the under-side's bright amber
your eyes

look out as they did here,
(you don't remember)
when my soul turned round,

perceiving the other-side of everything . . .

H.D., 'Sigil'

I LOOK EVERYWHERE FOR GRANDMOTHERS,
AND SEE NONE . . .

(Elizabeth Barrett Browning)

Aldington, Richard, Mrs. (H.D.)
D., H. *See* Doolittle, Hilda
Doolittle, Hilda (Mrs. Richard Aldington)
H.D., *see* Aldington, Mrs. Richard
See . . . see . . . see . . .

> In a sense, it seems I am drowning; already
> half-drowned to the ordinary dimensions of
> space and time, I know that I must drown,
> as it were, completely in order to come out
> on the other side of things (like Alice with
> her looking-glass or Perseus with his mirror)
> I must drown completely and come out on the
> other side, or rise to the surface after the
> third time down, not dead to this life but with
> a new set of values, my treasure dredged from
> the depth. I must be born again or break utterly.
>
> H.D., *Tribute to Freud*

Try again. Abandon Lawrentian phallicism
for Poundian formalism. *Objectivity and
again objectivy!* Well, it got you a job,
didn't it? Yes — the position of honorary
male. One (one?) can refuse privilege. It
flutters the dovecot when one does, but
fresh stereotypes settle like snow.

YOU ARE A POEM,

The tutorial essay shaded into the academic
article, published under two names: my
father's and my husband's. Until the late
seventies, everything I wrote was really
written for my doctoral supervisor:

> wandering about the body's writings
> *le corps nous mène jusqu'aux autres*
> in each to defeat the invigilator.
> imagine no kindly scoutmaster.
> he/I enters even here between us.

(Wendy Mulford)

What happened to my body meanwhile?
Was it running alongside to catch up with
the bilingual talking head, asking its own
questions, breathlessly, as it came? That
sturdy autonomous child, myself, was certainly
in the offing, refusing to be side-stepped or
ignored, laughing joyously, insisting on its
presence in the text. ('Diana was always
foursquare' — my mother's voice again). The
answers, then, came less directly from H.D.
than from Adrienne Rich —

THOUGH YOUR POEM'S NAUGHT
                    (E.P. to H.D.)

THE PROFESSOR, MOSES, AMEN-RA ETC. . . .
ROLLED INTO ONE
                              (H.D. on Freud)

But in fact we were always like this,
rootless, dismembered: knowing it makes the difference.
Birth stripped our birthright from us,
tore us from a woman, from women, from ourselves
so early on
and the whole chorus throbbing at our ears
like midges, told us nothing, nothing
of origins, nothing we needed
to know, nothing that could re-member us.

Only: that it is unnatural,
the homesickness for a woman, for ourselves . . .

        Adrienne Rich, 'Trandscendental Étude'

or Olga Broumas —
> *This/is the woman I woke from sleep,*

but before them was H.D. —

> This is Gaia, this is the beginning. This
> is the end. Under every shrine to Jupiter,
> to Zeus-pater, or Theus-pater or God-the-
> father . . . there is an earlier altar. There
> is, beneath the carved superstructure of
> every temple to God-the-father, the dark
> cave or grotto or inner hall or *cella* to
> Mary, Mère, Mut, mutter, pray for us.
>
> <div align="right">H.D., <i>The Gift</i></div>

Tribute to Freud was as baffling and
exciting as my first reading of the
Waste Land. Shantih: 'The Peace which
passeth understanding'. *J'ouis sens.*
It was like being a child again, tracing
the story, reading the 'Writing on the Wall'
with H.D. (for the Freud title was not hers).
Playing with meanings like the old game of
Heads, Bodies and Legs — the head, at last,
cautiously coming together with the body.
Living with different levels of narration and
interpretation (Freud's *The Interpretation of
Dreams* might be a model), dwelling on signs
and images, savouring *her* scepticism at *his*
answers . . .

the woman that woke/me sleeping.
                    Olga Broumas, 'Sleeping Beauty'

it is true that we play puss-in-a-corner, find
one angle and another or see things from different
corners or sides of a room. Yes, we play
hide-and-seek, hunt-the-slipper, and hunt-the-
thimble and patiently and meticulously patch
together odds and ends of our picture-puzzle.
We spell words upside down and backward and
crosswise, for our crossword puzzle, and then
again we run away and hide in the cellar or
the attic or in our mother's clothes-closet.
                              H.D., 'Advent'

'But you feminists — women of your generation —
you are destroying marriage, destroying the family
. . . Everything I lived for — '

'Women. Yes, we are important to each other. Yet
I love my father and my brothers. Nothing is taken
from you.'

after Daddy's death, the gentle rites
of recall, going over old photographs:
she nestles in her father's lap /
I remember the warmth of his arms

beyond all other, the Child,
the child in the father,
the child in the mother,

the child-mother, yourself;

H.D., *Helen in Egypt*

Works Cited in the Text

Olga Broumas, *Beginning with O.* (Yale University Press, New Haven and London, 1977).

E. B. Browning, *The Letters*, Vol. I, ed. Frederick G. Kenyon. (Macmillan, New York, 1899).

Diana Collecott, 'Remembering Oneself: the reputation and later poetry of H.D.', *Critical Quarterly*, 27 (1985), 7–22; Introduction to H.D.'s *The Gift* (Virago, London, 1984), pp. ix–xviii.

Jane Cooper, *Scaffolding: New and Selected Poems* (Anvil Press, London, 1984).

Jacques Derrida, 'Freud and the Scene of Writing' in *Writing and Difference* (University of Chicago Press, Chicago, 1978).

Rachel Blau DuPlessis, *H.D.* (Harvester Press, Brighton, 1986).

T. S. Eliot, *The Complete Poems and Plays* (Faber and Faber, London, 1969).

H.D., *Bid Me to Live*, with a new Introduction by Helen McNeil (Virago, London, 1984).
Collected Poems, 1912–1944, ed. Louis L. Martz (Carcanet, Manchester, 1984).
The Gift, with a new Introduction by Diana Collecott (Virago, London, 1984).
Her, with a new Introduction by Helen McNeil (Virago, London, 1984).
Helen in Egypt (Carcanet, Manchester, 1985).
Tribute to Freud (including 'Writing on the Wall' and 'Advent') (Carcanet, Manchester, 1985).

Luce Irigaray, *Ce sexe qui n'en est pas un* (Minuit, Paris, 1977). Translation from *New French Feminisms*, ed. Elaine Marks and Isabelle de Courtivron (Harvester Press, Brighton, 1981).

Nicole Ward Jouve, 'Of mud and other matter' in Jenny Taylor ed., *Notebooks, Memoirs, Archives: Reading and Re-Reading Doris Lessing* (Routledge & Kegan Paul, London, 1982).

Suzanne Juhasz, *Naked and Fiery Forms: Modern American Poetry by Women* (Octagon Books, New York, 1978).

Julia Kristéva, 'Place Names' and 'Motherhood According to Giovanni Bellini' in *Desire in Language* (Basil Blackwell, Oxford, 1982).

D. H. Lawrence, *The Complete Poems*, ed. V. de Sola Pinto and F. Warren Roberts (Penguin Books, Harmondsworth, Middx., 1977).

Juliet Mitchell, 'The Letter "i" '; paper to the Southampton Conference on Sexual Difference, July 1985. See Robert Young ed., *Sexual Difference, The Oxford Literary Review*, 8 (1986) p. 184.

Wendy Mulford, *The ABC of Writing* (Torque Press, Southampton, 1985).

Ezra Pound, *Selected Poems, 1908–1959* (Faber and Faber, London, 1975).

Adrienne Rich, *The Fact of a Doorframe: Poems Selected and New, 1950–1984*. (W. W. Norton, New York, 1984).

William Shakespeare, *The Complete Works*, ed. Peter Alexander (Collins, London, 1951).

William Carlos Williams, *Kora in Hell: Improvisations* (1920) in Webster Schott ed., *Imaginations* (New Directions, New York, 1970).

Virginia Woolf, *The Diary*, ed. Anne Olivier Bell, Vol. III (1928) (Hogarth Press, London 1980).

7

From 'Coded Mannequin' to Bird Woman: Angela Carter's Magic Flight

Paulina Palmer

To the memory of my mother,
Miriam D. Palmer

In the concluding pages of Angela Carter's *Nights at the Circus* a serio-comic incident occurs in which the central protagonist Fevvers, Cockney Venus and bird woman, gives an enthusiastic if cliché-ridden speech heralding the new age of women's liberation. She looks forward to the era when 'all the women will have wings, the same as I . . . The dolls' house doors will open, the brothels will spill forth their prisoners, the cages, gilded or otherwise, all over the world, in every land, will let forth their inmates singing together the dawn chorus of the new, the transformed — '.[1] Fevvers' flight of fancy remains incomplete, since her words are sharply interrupted by a cynical comment voiced by her foster mother Lizzie: 'It's going to be more complicated than that. . . . You improve your analysis, girl, and *then* we'll discuss it'. (p. 286) The episode is an important one, not just in terms of the novel in which it appears but in terms of Carter's fiction as a whole. The conversation between Fevvers and Lizzie illustrates a key area of tension in Carter's writing, by juxtaposing two antithetical impulses which inform it. While, on the one hand, a reference to celebratory and utopian elements is introduced, on the other, there is an equally strong emphasis on the analytic and the 'demythologising'.[2] In certain passages, such as the one quoted above, the two impulses interact. However, each is of interest in its own right and may, in fact, be identified with a particular stage of Carter's fiction. In her 'early' texts (those published prior to 1978), it is the analytic and 'demythologising' impulse which is to the fore. These include *The Magic Toyshop* (1967), *Heroes and Villains* (1969) and *The Passion*

179

of New Eve (1977). The themes which occupy her at this stage are: gender and its construction, the cultural production of femininity, male power under patriarchy, and the myths and institutions which serve to maintain it. The image which she frequently adopts to represent woman's role in society (man's too, on occasion) is the *puppet*. As well as carrying Hoffmannesque associations of the fantastic,[3] the image has connotations of the 'coded mannequin',[4] the metaphor employed by Hélène Cixous to represent the robotic state to which human beings are reduced by a process of psychic repression. The focus on the celebratory and utopian is something of a new departure in Carter's fiction. It does not fully emerge until the texts published in the late 1970s and 1980s, *The Bloody Chamber* (1979) and *Nights at the Circus* (1984). Here she treats themes relating to liberation and change, in the organisation of personal life and the social formation. Acts of resistance against patriarchy are represented. The deconstruction of femininity and masculinity is explored and, in keeping with the shifts in contemporary feminist thought,[5] the perspective becomes increasingly woman-centred. A re-evaluation of female experience takes place and the emergence of a female counter-culture is celebrated. The image of the puppet is no longer central to the text. It is replaced by the images of Fevvers' miraculous wings which, she observes, make her body 'the abode of limitless freedom' (p.41), and the egg from which she claims to have been hatched. These images represent ideas of liberation and rebirth; they evoke, in Cixous' words, 'the possibility of radical transformations of behaviour, mentalities, roles, and political economy'.[6]

While both the stages of Carter's fiction I have outlined above relate to areas of feminist inquiry, my own preference, I admit, is for her more recent works. I welcome the introduction of themes relating to female specificity and to social and psychic change. They are in consonance with my own point of view and political interests, ones which may be generally defined as 'radical feminist'. The texts she published prior to 1978 were marred, in my opinion, by an element of distortion. This led me to read them in the manner associated with the critic Pierre Machery, very conscious of 'absences', 'omissions' and 'silences'.[7] It seemed to me, and to the friends and students with whom I discussed these texts, that Carter, while presenting a brilliantly accurate analysis of the oppressive effects of patriarchal structures, ran the risk of making these structures appear even more closed and impenetrable than, in actual fact, they are. In discounting the possibility of change and marginalising themes relating to female commonality and collectivity, she resembled certain sociologists, the kind criticised by Liz Stanley and Sue Wise in their book *Breaking Out*.[8] So concerned are these sociologists to analyse the processes and effects of gender-role socialisation, that they ignore or disparage as examples of 'malsocialisation' those people — feminists, lesbians and men with a 'redefined' masculinity — who challenge or, to a certain degree, elude their influence.[9] The contribution made by utopian elements to political writing (socialist and/or feminist) is a controversial issue. Critics often dismiss such elements as escapist or simplistic. Carter's *The Magic Toyshop* has, in fact, been praised, for the avoidance of them.[10] However, I endorse the view, expressed by Terry Lovell, that 'successful political struggles always depend on their ability to connect with utopias — with the belief and hope that things might be better.'[11] And it is important to recognise that, resistant though the psyche is to change, modifications do sometimes occur in the formation of femininity and masculinity. The liberation movements of the 1960s and 1970s have had a profoundly radicalising effect on the lives of many of us. The consequence is, we do not inevitably remain fixed in the roles of 'sleeping beauties' or 'frozen boys'.[12] There are other reasons too, besides personal ones, why I welcome the new developments in Carter's fiction. They give scope for interesting innovations in its intellectual content and style. Motifs and passages of symbolic narrative relating to psychoanalytic materials are a constant factor in her writing. They link it to the topic of the re-evaluation of psychoanalytic theory, one which occupies a central, though contentious place, on the current feminist agenda.[13] However, marked differences are apparent in the uses she makes of these motifs. In the early texts she employed them to represent the self-perpetuating and closed nature of patriarchal structures and institutions. In recent texts, on the contrary, she uses them for more optimistic purposes: to depict the pressures exerted by the unconscious, manifested in psychic fragmentation, fantasy and dream, with the possibility these offer for change. Attention is drawn to the opening up of areas of identity that were closed and to the formation of alternative structures, psychic and social. A similar shift is evident in the intermingling of fantasy and realism, known as 'magic realism', which is Carter's favourite mode. In the early texts she exploited this mode to evoke the individual's experience of anxiety, estrangement and isolation (the kind of emotions discussed by Freud in his essay on 'The Uncanny').[14] In the texts published recently, however, she uses it as a vehicle for the expression of emotions which have a liberating effect. These include pleasure and wonder.

Up to now I have concentrated on defining the differences between Carter's early texts and her more recent works. However, connections also exist between the two, ones which have a bearing on the topic of sexual politics. From a feminist point of view, Carter's chief achievement in *The Passion of New Eve*, *The Magic Toyshop* and *Heroes and Villains*, is to problematise both woman's position in the family unit and the relations between the sexes which form the hub of family life. By foregrounding the contradictions discernible in these relations and in heterosexual sexual practice, she draws attention to the fissures and gaps existing in the structures and institutions of patriarchy. She thus prepares the way for the emphasis on change and transformation, as well as the introduction of themes relating to female specificity, which are the centre of interest in *The Bloody Chamber* and *Nights at the Circus*. My project here is to explore some of the connections between the two stages of her writing. I also aim to consider *en route* a few of the fascinating issues and questions, relevant to feminist readers and writers, which her fictional and theoretical works raise.

Carter's recognition of the part played by the family in reproducing structures of male dominance and female subordination is indicated by the variety of different familial forms she represents in her fiction. In *The Passion of New Eve* the polygamous tyrant Zero brutally dominates a harem of wives; in *Heroes and Villains* Jewel and Donally contend together for leadership of the tribe; and in *The Magic Toyshop* despotic Uncle Philip rules the 'private micro-world'[15] of the Western family unit. While *The Passion of New Eve*, as Carter points out,[16] takes as its central theme the cultural production of femininity, the latter two novels focus on one of the roles conventionally allocated to woman in a patriarchal culture — *object of exchange*. The interaction between the protagonists is organised to illustrate the fact that 'male domination is rooted in a struggle for recognition between men in which women are mere objects or tokens: the prize'.[17] *The Magic Toyshop* is a text of particular interest to the feminist reader. It illustrates Carter's skilful use of the device of intertextuality to analyse femininity and female subordination as cultural constructs. In it, she reworks episodes and motifs from not just one text but three. These are the biblical story of the Garden of Eden, E. T. A. Hoffmann's tale *The Sandman* and Freud's account of the psychic structures relating to the family unit (the primal scene, the Oedipal configuration and the castration myth). Thus her novel becomes, in the words of Barthes, 'a multi-dimensional space in which a variety of writings, none of them original, blend and clash.'[18] The deliberately subversive reworking of the three texts which she achieves accords with the deconstructive approach to fiction which she endorses in the essay 'Notes From the Front Line'; here, she concludes that:

> reading is just as creative an activity as writing and most intellectual development depends upon new readings of old texts. I am all for putting new wine in old bottles, especially if the pressure of the new wine makes the old bottles explode.[19]

Carter's reworking of the three texts mentioned above highlights the part played by myth and culture in the construction of the subject. Culture, she suggests, assumes primacy over subjectivity. The hero Melanie finds herself trapped, against her will, in conventional family roles and structures. While in bed with her lover Finn, with her little sister Victoria playing in the room, she has a sudden disquieting sense that she and Finn 'might have been married for years and Victoria their baby.'[20] Involuntarily, she finds herself slotted into the roles of wife and mother. In a similar manner Finn, occupying the place usually taken by Uncle Philip at the breakfast table, is greeted by Victoria as 'Daddy'. (p. 183) In rebelling against his uncle's authority, he discovers himself usurping his position. Throughout the narrative, images of mutilation and castration (Melanie's fantasy of the severed hand, and Finn's bee-stung eye) advertise to the reader the elements of violence at the heart of the patriarchal family unit. They also highlight the violent nature of the myths which perpetuate its existence.

Carter's reworking of all three texts is skilfully contrived. However, it is her reinterpretation of motifs from Hoffmann's tale *The Sandman* [21] that deconstructs the patriarchal social hierarchy most effectively. Freud, in his psychoanalytic analysis of the tale, foregrounds male experience. He interprets it as symbolic of male fears of castration and marginalises the motif of the female puppet Olympia. [22] Carter, on the contrary, makes the puppet central. She treats the relations between puppet-master and puppet as symbolic of the control exerted by a patriarchal culture on women and the roles available to them. The roles to which Melanie is introduced, in her uncle's toy theatre or in other episodes of the novel, include wood-nymph, bride and victim of rape. In representing them, Carter pinpoints the ambiguities in woman's position. She foregrounds the contradiction between the romantic images of femininity reproduced in culture and art, and the facts of sexual violence. She also creates a lively interplay between art and nature, theatrical representation and 'real life', in typical 'magical mannerist' fashion. [23]

Another subversive feature discernible in Carter's reworking of motifs from Hoffmann is the way she allows certain cracks and fissures to become visible in patriarchal structures and roles. Her treatment of the motif of the *double* is notably ambiguous. On the one hand, it advertises the apparently immutable nature of patriarchal roles, by illustrating the primacy which culture and myth exert over subjectivity. On several occasions in the novel, the artificial double is presented as equalling in importance or even claiming precedence over the real-life original. The portrait of the bull terrier, Melanie thinks, stands guard over the house while the actual dog is absent. (p. 60) And Uncle Philip tends to prefer the company of his puppets, which are obedient to his will, to his flesh and blood relatives who challenge it. (pp. 132, 167) On the other hand, the motif simultaneously carries opposite implications, evoking ideas of liberation and change. Carter's introduction of it suggests the concept of the split subject. This challenges the notion of unified character, pointing to the existence of multiple identities and the possibility of change they contain.[24]

Carter's treatment of the motif of the *eye*, another one she inherits from Hoffmann, is similarly ambiguous in meaning. Her description of the peephole which Finn constructs in the wall of his room in order to spy on Melanie while she is undressing, introduces the theme of voyeurism. It draws attention to the power exerted by the male gaze. The gaze is a practical means for men to impose control on women, as well as a symbol of sexual domination.[25] However, the fact that Melanie responds with indignation to the intrusion on her privacy and retaliates by using the peephole to spy on Finn back (p. 109), complicates the meaning of the image. On peering in it, she catches sight of him walking on his hands. This results in a momentary instance of role-reversal. She becomes the observer and he the observed. She represents the norm while he, in his odd position, becomes the freak and 'spectacle'. These are roles which, in a patriarchal society, are generally reserved for women. Thus, in her treatment of both motifs Carter indirectly reveals that, despite appearances to the contrary, the roles adopted by men and women are, in fact, flexible. They are open to change.

Carter's analysis of the roles allocated to woman in the family unit, discussed above, is accompanied by the problematisation both of relations between the sexes and of heterosexual sexual practice. Probing beneath the ideology of romantic love and familial affection, she discloses the contradictions which exist in these relations. She also reveals the element of violence in male-defined models of sexual pleasure. The connection between sex and violence is a theme which confronts writers of fiction with notable difficulties, and Carter's treatment of it is by no means free from ambiguity. It raises questions of vital concern to feminist readers and writers. Is it possible to represent a female protagonist as a victim of sexual harassment or violence while, at the same time, portraying her as an autonomous individual? Can a writer represent a male protagonist as perpetrating acts of violence without either glamorising him or depicting him as an inhuman monster? What is the distinction between representations of violent sex which constitute a serious inquiry into the topic, and ones which have to be classed as pornographic?

In problematising relations between the sexes and presenting them as an arena of political struggle, Carter is generally in accord with the interests of contemporary feminism. One of the achievements of the Women's Movement, in its analysis of sexual politics, has been to distinguish sexual desire from reproduction. It has challenged the assumption, promoted by sexologists, that 'heterosexuality is natural and that the most natural form of heterosexual activity is coitus, i.e. penetration of the vagina by the penis'.[26] Feminists have drawn attention to the fact that sex, both in the sense of 'sexual preference' and 'sexual practice', is socially constructed. They have highlighted not only the frequent occurrence of acts of violence in heterosexual relations, but also the disturbing fact that the models of sexual practice promoted by a patriarchal culture are inherently violent. The myth of the 'natural' aggression of the male and the passivity of the female, and the notion that pain and submission are essential components of female sexual pleasure, illustrate the existence of this model. They also help to perpetuate it.

Carter's treatment of relations between the sexes in her writing forms an important and, in some cases, controversial contribution to the feminist analysis of the topic outlined above. In her theoretical work *The Sadeian Woman* she analyses the construction of sexual desire and gender. She also foregrounds the significance of pain and victimisation in symbolic myths of femininity, while emphasising, disquietingly, its cultural consequences:

> Female castration is an imaginary fact that pervades the whole of men's attitude towards women and our attitude to ourselves, that transforms women from human beings into wounded creatures who were born to bleed.[27]

In her fiction she places a similar emphasis on pain and victimisation. She explores the part played by sexuality in securing woman's subordination, revealing heterosexual sexual practice to be instrumental in maintaining male supremacy. In *The Magic Toyshop*, attention is drawn to the contrast between Melanie's romantic fantasies about 'the lover made up out of books and poems she had dreamed of all summer' and her predatory lover Finn, his 'insolent, off-hand, terrifying maleness, filling the room with its reek.' (p. 45) In social terms, he is represented as her inferior and, when he forces his attention on her, she feels 'bitterly offended'. (p. 46) Carter challenges romantic convention by describing the episode of the couple's first kiss as a sexual assault:

> Finn inserted his tongue between her lips, searching tentatively for her own tongue inside her mouth. The moment consumed her. She choked and struggled, beating her fists against him, convulsed with horror at this sensual and intimate connection, this rude encroachment on her physical privacy, this humiliation. (p. 106)

In describing Melanie as gradually resigning herself to the prospect of sex and marriage with Finn, Carter analyses the contradictions in her emotional response. On the one hand, Melanie resents Finn's insolence and familiarity. On the other, she feels gratitude towards him for his attempt to protect her from her Uncle Philip's bullying. As is typical of woman in a patriarchal society, she is pressured to seek refuge from one man in the arms of another.

In *Heroes and Villains* attention is again focused on the social differences between the male and female protagonists. Jewel is a member of a 'barbarian' tribe. He is ill-educated and prone to irrational fears and fits of violence. Marianne, on the contrary, is the daughter of a professor. She is well-educated, controlled and articulate. However, the social and educational advantages she enjoys are almost entirely cancelled out by the disadvantages of gender. Her relationship with Jewel, whom eventually she marries, is, in terms of power, ambivalent from the start. Finding him lying helpless and wounded after a raid on her home town, she succours him with food. His response is not to show gratitude but to smear her with war-paint and claim her as his hostage. The ideology of male dominance and female submission, Carter implies, is strong enough to obscure the actual facts of the situation. Thus, Marianne discovers, to her surprise, that 'she had wanted to rescue him but found she was accepting his offer to rescue her'.[28] Jewel's treatment of her quickly lapses into physical violence. Having persuaded her to steal a lorry and drive him to freedom, he hits her to make her drive faster. Subsequently, he introduces her into the tribe to which he belongs. When she tries to escape, he follows her to her hiding place in the forest and rapes her.

In making the female heroes of both novels victims of sexual harassment or rape, Carter encounters certain obvious problems. She runs the risk of depriving the hero of sexual and intellectual autonomy, and reducing her to the state of helpless victim. She also runs the risk of tainting her fiction with the attitudes associated with popular genres which exploit the topic of sex and violence for the purpose of titillation, reproducing the chauvinistic cliché that female pleasure is dependent on submission and victimisation.[29] Carter succeeds in surmounting both these risks. She achieves this by foregrounding the contradiction between the female hero's intellectual autonomy and independent spirit, and her vulnerability to physical attack, one which the male protagonist exploits. Melanie and Marianne are portrayed as courageous and resourceful individuals. They respond to the 'terrible violation of privacy'[30] which the sexual encounters to which they are subjected involve, not with tears or masochistic pleasure but with anger and indignation.

Just as Carter succeeds in crediting her female protagonists with a strong degree of autonomy, so too she manages to make her male protagonists convincingly drawn humanbeings, without in any way condoning the acts of violence they commit. Her representation of them, trapped in codes of aggression and competition, comes remarkably close to the memorable definition of masculinity coined by Frankie Rickford: Rickford suggests that:

> masculinity may be a state of frozen terror and the urgency of men's sexual desire, a desperation to bury themselves in a warm body to escape from it for a few seconds.[31]

Jewel's acts of violence, for example, appear to be motivated by a determination to dominate Marianne, which is bred of fear. He gives as his reason for the rape the fact that he is 'very frightened' of her. (p. 56) He expresses surprise at the discovery that she does not 'sprout sharp teeth in her private parts' (pp. 49, 59), a piece of propaganda promulgated by the tribe to which he belongs. (p. 59) Any sign of her vulnerability fills him with pleasure, since he interprets it as proof of his capacity to subjugate her. His triumphant remark, 'I've nailed you on necessity, you poor bitch' (p. 56), when his act of rape forces her into marriage with him, indicates the urgency of the power struggle in which he feels himself to be engaged. Carter's reference to the picture of Eve tempting Adam with a perfidious smile, which he wears tattooed on his back (p. 85), has the effect of placing this struggle in the context of misogynistic culture. It lifts it from a narrowly personal plane to a political and ideological one.

An important question raised by Carter's treatment of the interrelation between sex and violence in her fiction is: how does one distinguish between a text which constitutes a serious consideration of the topic and one that is an exercise in pornography? The question is complicated by the fact that, as critics have pointed out, the meaning of a visual image or fictional episode is frequently ambiguous. Even though a text generally carries a 'preferred reading',[32] it is, in part, open to the different interpretations which the observer or reader chooses to impose on it. Thus, an episode which one reader may interpret as a serious investigation into the female victim's response to the experience of violent sex, may strike another as pornographic. The austerely functional style of writing in *Heroes and Villains* allows little room for ambiguity. Few readers would be likely to interpret the account of Marianne's rape, in which Carter emphasises the victim's indignation and anger, as in any way titillating. However, the sensuous and rhetorically ornate style of the stories in *The Bloody Chamber* does, I feel, allow room for ambiguity. Certain features of the title-story in the volume, such as the female protagonist's admission that she finds her husband's objectification and violent treatment sexually stimulating, the visually explicit reference to the pornographic pictures he owns, and the description of the choker of rubies as a 'bloody bandage' and his act of defloration as an 'impalement',[33] form a whole which verges dangerously close to pornography. Alternatively, it may be a pastiche of it. It has been suggested that whether or not an episode is to be read as pornographic depends, in part, on the narrator's point of view.[34] In the story *The Bloody Chamber* the point of view is the complex, and at times contradictory, one of the female victim. This, combined with the strongly feminist dénouement to the tale, possibly saves it from toppling over the edge. This is not the case with another of Carter's texts, *The Infernal Desire Machines of Dr Hoffman* (1972). Here the point of view is chauvinistically male. The sexual atrocities represented in this novel (and some of them are very brutal indeed)[35] are described by a male narrator. His response is one not of anger, but of detached curiosity. The fact that, in the final pages, the atrocities are revealed to be illusions, contrived by the evil Dr Hoffman and illustrating (parodying perhaps?) misognystic male fantasies, does not, in my opinion, justify their inclusion in the text. In 'Notes from the Front Line' Carter admits that in her youth she suffered from what she calls 'a degree of colonialisation of the mind', which caused her to possess 'an element of the male impersonator'.[36] Certain episodes in the novel appear to illustrate, in an unpleasant and disturbing manner, this aspect of her cultural conditioning.

While problematising relations between men and women by revealing the inequalities and element of violence they contain, Carter at the same time emphasises the ambivalent and contradictory nature of women's relations with one another. In this she agrees with certain feminist theorists who emphasise the divisions which a patriarchal culture creates between women. They point out that since women occupy the position of subordinates they are likely to identify with the interests of the dominant group (men). They thus may be incapable of giving one another any strong degree of loyalty or support.[37] This is the case with the majority of female protagonists in Carter's early texts. Although in *The Passion of New Eve* she does, in fact, touch on the theme of female community, her approach to the group of matriarchal guerilla fighters which she introduces, is, on the whole, satirical. In *The Magic Toyshop* and *Heroes and Villains*, the female protagonists are separated by conventional rifts and divisions. Mrs Rundle, the nanny in the former novel, is prevented from playing a part in the upbringing of her charges on the death of their parents by the fact that, as she herself remarks, she is not 'family'. (p. 94) She assumes it to be right and proper that they remain in the care of their Uncle Philip, despot though he is. Mrs Green, Jewel's foster mother in the latter book, behaves towards Marianne in a manner which is notably unsupportive. Identifying with the interests of the men of the tribe, on whose good will she depends for survival and status, she gives Marianne the advice with which women have been fobbed off for centuries: she counsels her 'to reconcile herself to everything from rape to mortality'. (p. 59) While sympathising emotionally with Marianne's situation as victim of male violence, she makes no practical effort to protect her from attack. As Marianne recognises, Mrs Green's attitude towards her is 'ambivalent'. (p. 49) The adjective is a crucial one. It pinpoints the attribute which Carter, in her early texts, represents as typical of relations between women: the *contradictions* they reveal. And, though the theme of female relations is by no means central to *The Magic Toyshop* or *Heroes and Villains*, each does contain an episode, one of symbolic significance and emotional tension, which concentrates on exploring these contradictions.

In *The Magic Toyshop* the episode in question takes the form of a spontaneous act of generosity performed by one woman towards another. Melanie, pitying her Aunt Margaret's oppressed and cheerless plight as the wife of Uncle Philip, decides, in a sudden fit of warmth, to give her one of her own dresses. Carter's account of the event places emphasis on the symptoms of hesitancy and unease revealed by the two women, Melanie in handing over the dress and Margaret in accepting it. Melanie helps Margaret put it on and, finding it to be a perfect fit, feels an uncomfortable sense of identification with her. She helps Margaret arrange her hair and, at this point in the text, Carter cunningly introduces a reference to Hollywood film conventions:

Melanie felt like a sympathetic friend in a Hollywood film who has finally persuaded the plain stenographer to take off her glasses and have herself a facial. (p. 189)

The passage quoted above foregrounds the contradictions in the encounter between the two women. It indirectly reminds the reader that, in a patriarchal society, contact between women is frequently ambiguous. They help to arrange each other's hair and make each other beautiful not for their own pleasure and satisfaction, but in order to attract a man.

Not content with the gift of the dress, Melanie also insists on giving Margaret her most prized possession, the pearls which she inherited from her deceased mother. When Margaret refuses to accept the pearls as a gift but agrees merely to borrow them, Melanie reacts to the situation as follows:

> Melanie shrugged. She wanted to give them away outright and have done with it, even if her mother watched somewhere in the room from a frame. She felt young and tough and brave, giving away her relics. And the pearls nestled so sweetly, cuddling up to her aunt's flesh, which had the same sheen on it as they. She hoped her aunt would grow so attached to the pearls during the day that she would think they had always been her own. (p. 189)

The passage above is extremely complex in significance. The reference to the framed photo of Melanie's mother in the room draws attention to Melanie's orphan state. It also emphasises her courageous defiance of patriarchal codes of property-inheritance; instead of keeping the pearls to pass on to her own future daughter, she insists on giving them away. Attention is also focused on Melanie's sudden recognition of the sensuous attraction of Margaret's appearance. Elements of the erotic and the maternal unexpectedly surface in the text. The description of the pearls 'nestling sweetly' and 'cuddling up to her aunt's flesh', hints at Melanie's strong sense of identification with the jewels. With her own mother dead, she unconsciously sees Margaret as a surrogate mother. She would like to emulate the position of the pearls, nestling and cuddling up to Margaret's body. She hopes that Margaret will, in time, grow so attached to her that she will think of her as her own child. Melanie's affection for Margaret is intensified by Carter's subsequent comment that she loves her, experiencing 'the love, warm and understanding, inside her'. (p. 195)

The episode in *Heroes and Villains* which explores the ambiguous nature of relations between women reveals even stronger contradictions. Marianne, the female hero, is ordered by her husband Jewel to kiss his cousin Annie, with the aim, as he explains, of proving to her that she is 'flesh and blood'. (p. 103) Throughout the novel Carter emphasises the feelings of distrust and animosity which separate Marianne from the female members of the tribe. On account of her social and educational advantages, Marianne feels no affinity with the uneducated tribal women, while they, in turn, suspect her of wielding malevolent supernatural powers. She carries out Jewel's order unwillingly. She is scared of picking up an infection from Annie's sick baby and fears Annie will stab her with a knife. And she regards the act as 'another intolerable ordeal', invented by Jewel to humiliate her. It is, of course, ironic that the kiss, and the intimate contact between the two women which it signifies, does not occur voluntarily but is performed at the command of a man. However, in the act of kissing Annie, Marianne's attitude towards her suddenly changes. Moved by a fit of compassion, she bursts into tears — and the following poignant scene takes place:

> Her tears splashed on Annie's cheek. Annie touched them with her finger and then licked her finger to see if they were salt enough. Marianne slid down to her knees, sobbing as if her heart was breaking. Annie pushed the girl away and turned her back on her with a sigh. (p. 104)

Annie's gesture of touching and tasting Marianne's tears, as well as being a means to test and establish the fact of her humanity, represents a physical act of 'communication' between the two women. It is one which is symbolically appropriate. Since, in a patriarchal culture, women seldom enjoy direct access to economic power, the only gift they have to bestow on one another is tears, images of suffering and pity. The episode terminates on a note of ambiguity. Though rejecting any further contact with Marianne, Annie nonetheless emits a sigh of regret.

An interesting feature of the two episodes discussed above is that they constitute isolated incidents in the novels in which they appear. The theme of the complexity of relations between women which they treat is in no way developed in either novel. Carter's failure to develop it may indicate her recognition of the problematic aspect which such relations assume in a patriarchal culture. Alternatively, it may reflect her own personal feelings of ambivalence towards the topic of woman-identification, as well as the strongly heterosexist cultural climate prevalent in the 1960s, when both novels were published. This was the period of the 'Swinging Sixties', the so-called 'Sexual Revolution'. During these years, as those of us who lived through them are aware, the bias towards 'compulsory heterosexuality'[38] was oppressively pronounced. The 'permissive sexuality' in fashion at the time revealed strict limits. Sexual pleasure and erotic fulfilment were defined as exclusively phallocentric.[39] Themes relating to female specificity such as friendship and relationships between women, female community and lesbian sexuality were, in general, either ignored or marginalised. Any attempt on the part of women to give them primacy, either in literature or life, was censured as morally deviant. Women who identified as lesbian were forced to endure social ostracism or found their relationships and views distorted by public prejudice.[40] That Carter was, to a degree, influenced by these heterosexist attitudes is apparent from her theoretical work, *The Sadeian Woman*, where, unfortunately, she reproduces them. This fact mars an otherwise brilliant book. A critique of the limitations of 'feminism and psychoanalysis', voiced by Elizabeth Wilson, is indirectly relevant to the perspectives which Carter adopts in the book; Wilson complains that:

> the way feminists have used psychoanalytic theory to analyse sexual desire has had nothing to say about lesbianism and in most cases has been unable to deal with the stark reality of rape and violence towards women in a way that expresses an appropriate degree of indignation . . .[41]

Although in *The Sadeian Woman* Carter illuminatingly explores the connections between Sade's misogynistic fantasies and current myths about femininity, the attitude she adopts to the atrocities which he depicts in his fiction raises problems for the feminist reader. It is one of detached interest and intellectual curiosity, not indignation. This kind of attitude has, in fact, been criticised by feminist theorists. Mary Daly, for example, rebukes those scholars who, by means of their 'indifference and detachment',[42] minimise and indirectly condone the sadistic practices which have been inflicted on women throughout history. Another serious flaw in *The Sadeian Woman* is Carter's misrepresentation of lesbian sexuality. She restricts her consideration of the topic to a discussion of the lurid sex-life of Sade's monstrous female creations Juliette, Durand and Clairwil, and omits reference to its contemporary actuality. By taking this course, Carter (no doubt unwittingly) gives the reader the impression that lesbian sex exists only as a figment of the pornographic male imagination and is synonymous with the brutal and depraved. Comments which she makes in her essay 'Notes from the Front Line', where she unthinkingly equates the term 'sex' with 'hetero sex' and ignores the existence of lesbianism, reveal a similar prejudice.[43] They illustrate the way feminist writers and scholars, as Adrienne Rich points out in her influential essay,[44] may indirectly promote the conscription of women into heterosexuality by marginalising or misrepresenting lesbian existence, or even by erasing it from discourse. It is not, in fact, until Carter's recently published texts that this heterosexist bias disappears and is replaced by a positive representation of relationships between women.

When we turn to these texts we find that they combine, in a manner unprecedented in Carter's work, an analysis of the oppressive nature of patriarchal structures with a treatment of themes relating to psychic change and female specificity. The fairy-tale format which she utilises in the collection of short stories, *The Bloody Chamber*, is not one noted for its feminist perspective. On the contrary, as Karen E. Rowe observes in her study of the topic, 'fairy-tales perpetuate the patriarchal *status quo* by making femal subordination seem a romantically desirable, indeed an inescapable fate'.[45] However, in *The Bloody Chamber* Carter succeeds in transcending the ideological limitations which fairy-tales generally reveal. While the fairy-tale format of the stories enables her to treat women's conventional role as object of exchange, the motif of magical metamorphosis which it includes gives her the opportunity to explore the theme of psychic transformation, liberating her protagonists from conventional gender roles. The metamorphosis of beast into human, performed by certain of the male protagonists in the stories, appears to signify the female hero's acceptance of the validity of sexual desire. In certain instances, it also signifies the transformation of masculinity. Thus, Mr Lyon loses his power of aggression and becomes fully human (p. 51), while the wolf in *The Company of Wolves* discovers that he possesses a capacity for tenderness. (p. 118) The majority of the stories in the collection conform to the conventional fairy-tale model in treating relations between men and women. However, the title story breaks the mould by exploring a relationship between mother and daughter, giving it a very unusual 'twist'. From the point of view of the shift that occurs in Carter's fiction from a preoccupation with patriarchal cultural forms to the introduction of a woman-centred perspective, the story represents something of an intermediate stage. Whereas the first half focuses on the daughter's sexual infatuation with the sadistic Bluebeard and with his attempt to accommodate her into his pornographic fantasy life, the latter treats the themes of female community and sisterhood. In focusing attention on these themes, Carter introduces two delightful and ingeniously contrived examples of role reversal. She allocates the role of rescuer of the young bride who is about to be murdered by Bluebeard not to a male hero but, unexpectedly, to the bride's mother. The description of the latter riding up to perform her act of 'furious justice', with 'her hat seized by the wind . . . so that her hair was her white mane, her black lisle legs exposed to the thigh' (pp. 39–40), is serio-comic. It looks forward, in tone, to the description of the army of female lovers in *Nights at the Circus*. And, while celebrating the figure of the mother as liberator, Carter neatly deflates the authority of Bluebeard by transforming him, metaphorically, into a puppet. Whereas in the earlier text *The Magic Toyshop* the male protagonists initiate and dominate the action while the female ones are reduced to the role of 'coded mannequin',[46] in *The Bloody Chamber* the roles are inverted. The instance of role reversal is prophetic. It heralds the challenging of stereotypes of femininity, as well as the focus on female community, which are exhilarating features of *Nights at the Circus*.

Nights at the Circus has been rightly acclaimed by critics as 'a glorious enchantment', 'a spell-binding achievement'.[47] Like several other of Carter's fictions, it represents a skilfully contrived exercise in intertextuality. Shakespeare, Milton, Poe, Ibsen and Joyce are some of the writers to whom she alludes, with the effect of creating a polyphonic interplay of European cultural attitudes and moments.[48] The voices of these writers interact in, to cite the Russian critic Mikhail Bakhtin, a medley of 'paradoxically reconstructed quotations'.[49] This medley unites the serious and the comic, the high and low. It subverts any single, unified utterance, in typical carnivalistic manner. The 'carnivalistic', as Bakhtin points out in his discussion, is not a particular kind of genre but a 'flexible form of artistic vision'.[50] Reference to his analysis of this vision is instrumental in illuminating certain significant facets of Carter's novel. It also indicates the way carnivalistic perspectives may be adapted as a vehicle for the treatment of important feminist themes, including an analysis of patriarchal culture and the representation of female community. The imagery and terminology which Carter employs in the novel accord with the spirit of carnival. Ma Nelson, the Madame of the brothel where Fevvers spends her childhood, is described as 'The Mistress of the Revels' (p. 49); Buffo, the chief clown, is 'the Lord of Misrule' (p. 117); and God is represented as 'the great ringmaster in the sky'. (p. 120) Other features of the novel which are in consonance with Bakhtin's analysis include: the mingling of sacred and profane materials; the introduction of utopian elements, such as the reference to taming tigers with music; and the emphasis Carter places on the relativity of experience. The latter is apparent in the variety of different versions of reality which the protagonists accept. A juxtaposition is achieved between the attitudes and ideologies of figures as disparate as Colonel Kearney (a capitalistic entrepreneur), the escaped convict (a believer in the innate goodness of humanity) and the Shaman (who is ignorant of history and geography). In Bakhtin's words, the carnival spirit 'proclaims the jolly relativity of everything';[51] it 'offers the chance to have a new outlook on the world, to realize the relative nature of all that exists, and to enter a completely new order of things'.[52]

Carter's interest in exploring 'a completely new order of things', psychic and social, is apparent from the motifs on which the novel is structured. She exploits the image which Bakhtin terms 'the grotesque body, the body in the act of becoming'.[53] Her description of Buffo the clown deconstructing himself in the circus ring, wearing 'his insides on his outside' (p. 116), agrees with Bakhtin's account of the way 'carnival objects are turned inside out', in a manner symbolic of 'the destruction of the old and the birth of the new world' which carnival celebrates.[54] However, unlike Bakhtin, Carter takes the unusual step of giving a feminist critique of certain carnivalistic images and values. Instead of regarding the beatings and thrashings associated with carnivalistic mirth[55] as manifestations of playful exuberance, she uses them to represent the violence which is rife in a maledominated culture. The brutal slapstick in which the clowns engage verges on the murderous. Their dances take the form of 'cheerless arabesques as of the damned'. (p. 243) There is nothing playful about the behaviour of the ape-man who is represented as 'beating his woman as though she were a carpet'. (p. 115) In fact, in the course of the narrative, the circus ring, with its hierarchy of male performers and 'carnival-like proceedings' (p. 146), becomes an effective symbol of the patriarchal social order. It is associated with a spirit of competition, a preoccupation with financial profit and an oppressive treatment of subordinates, including women and animals.

Characteristic of carnivalistic perspectives is the focus placed on abnormal states of mind, including mental breakdown, split personality and dreams. These phenomena, as Bakhtin comments, may give the individual an insight into 'the dialogical attitude of man to himself'; they 'contribute to the destruction of his integrity and finalizedness', by revealing the possibility of him becoming 'a different person'.[56] These phrases are relevant to Carter's novel, since they give a strikingly accurate description of the process of mental breakdown and subsequent reconstruction of masculinity experienced by Walser, the journalist who accompanies the circus troupe to Russia. He joins the troupe with the aim of discovering whether or not Fevvers' wings are fake, and is subsequently chosen by her as her 'New Man, fitting mate for the New Woman'. (p. 281) Unlike Buffo the clown who deconstructs himself physically, Walser achieves the task mentally. He is not the only member of the troupe to move towards a state of redefined masculinity. The ape-man also renounces his machismo and starts to learn gentleness.

As I mentioned at the start of this essay, the most powerful image of liberation and transformation in the novel is Fevvers herself and her magnificent wings. The image of the winged bird-woman which she represents is, however, more complex in significance than it appears. It is 'transparent' in the sense that a number of contradictory meanings are constructed on it. Though it is predominantly an image of liberation, the male protagonists impose on it stereotypical interpretations of femininity, invented by a patriarchal culture. 'Angel of death' 'queen of ambiguities', 'spectacle' and 'freak' are some of the conventional feminine roles which they attribute to Fevvers in the novel. The egg from which she claims to have been hatched is an image which is similarly ambiguous. On the one hand, it represents psychic rebirth. On the other, it provides a vehicle for Lizzie to theorise about the oppressive nature of reproduction and child-care under patriarchy. Suspecting Fevvers of becoming interested in marriage and domesticity, she rebukes her with the words: 'I've raised you to fly up to the heavens, not to brood over a clutch of eggs.' (p. 282)

The motifs of liberation and change around which Carter structures the novel apply not only to the individual but also to the community and the group. A central theme in the text is the conventional patriarchal representation of woman in terms of polarities, a device which results in her being depicted either by symbols of transcendence (goddess and angel) or by symbols of the sub-human (nature and animals).[57] In order to highlight the latter, Carter constructs a witty parallel between the subordinate position of the troupe of performing apes in the circus and the position of the women performers. Both are forced to endure frequent indignities and brutalities. Moreover, at a similar stage of the narrative, both rebel against their captors and succeed in liberating themselves from the tyranny of the circus.

In achieving freedom from male-dominated institutions, the female protagonists are represented as challenging, to a degree, patriarchal divisions and roles. In keeping with the feminist slogan 'the personal is political', Fevvers and her foster-mother Lizzie are revealed, in the course of the narrative, to be political comrades, as well as friends. The brothel where Fevvers spends her adolescence becomes, during the day in the absence of male clients, a miniature women's centre, humming with feminist activity. And the female inmates and warders of Countess P's horrific asylum join together to form 'an army of lovers'. (p. 217) Having successfully vanquished their oppressor, they escape, committing themselves to the project of creating a female Utopia in the taiga. On walking out into the Siberian wilderness, they discover that 'the white world around them looked newly made, a blank sheet of fresh paper on which they could inscribe whatever future they wished'. (p. 218) The image evokes connotations of prelapsarian (and pre-patriarchal) existence. It also relates to Carter's description of Walser's mind becoming 'a perfect blank' (p. 222), in preparation for the subsequent reconstruction of his masculinity. Carter's treatment of the women's journey is celebratory, emphasising the theme of female community. She describes how they 'set off hand in hand, and soon started to sing, for joy'. (p. 218)

The novel contains a number of episodes focusing on woman-identification and female collectivity, themes which, in her earlier texts, Carter either marginalised or ignored. The most notable is the representation of the lesbian relationship between Mignon, the wife of the ape-man, and the Princess of Abyssinia. The relationship between the two women is presented in utopian terms. It is associated with the Orpheus-like capacity to tame wild beasts (in this case, tigers) with music, which the women possess. Carter describes music as 'their language, in which they'd found their way to one another'. (p. 168) Commenting on the emotional unity which they have achieved, she portrays them as 'beings who seemed, as a pair, to transcend their individualities'. (pp. 202–3) Taken together, these phrases may be related to Cixous' treatment of the motif of music as an image representing concepts of personal communication, as well as the transformation of the subject and the subversion of the individual ego. Cixous describes music as 'the mistress of correspondences'. She compares the way 'the subject flounders in the exploded multiplicity of its states, spreading out into every possible contradiction transegoistically',[58] to the polyphony constructed by musical notes. Carter's decision to represent the relationship between Mignon and the Princess in terms of music, her description of the emotional transformation which the relationship involves and her suggestion that it prefigures a new feminist era, generally accord with Cixous' treatment of the image.

The novel concludes aptly on a note of carnivalistic mirth. In the penultimate paragraph, Fevvers' peal of loud laughter is described as uniting her in spirit with the whole cosmos, giving rise to a gust of universal merriment:

> The spiralling tornado of Fevvers' laughter began to twist and shudder across the entire globe, as if a spontaneous response to the giant comedy that endlessly unfolded beneath it, until everything that lived and breathed, everywhere, was laughing. (p. 295)

However, the function of Fevvers' laughter is more than merely festive. As well as irreverently mocking the existing political order, it is socially and psychically liberating. Bakhtin's discussion of the subversive potential of laughter helps to explicate its various levels of meaning. He points out that laughter signifies 'the defeat of power, of earthly kings and of all that oppresses and restricts. . . . It liberates not only from external censorship but, first of all, from the great interior censor.'[59]

In treating, in *Nights at the Circus*, themes of liberation and change in personal relationships and the social formation, Carter focuses attention on topics which, though absent from or marginalised in her earlier texts, were indirectly heralded in them by means of her analysis of the contradictions and element of violence in patriarchal social structures and institutions. She completes the movement from the representation of woman as 'coded mannequin', trapped in conventional feminine roles and positions, to the representation of her as 'bird-woman', courageously exploring new realms, both personal and political. I look forward to seeing where her future flights of fiction will lead her.

Notes

1. *Nights at the Circus* (Chatto and Windus, Hogarth, London, 1984), p. 285. All subsequent page references are to this edition and will be included in the text.
2. Angela Carter, 'Notes from the Front Line' in Michelene Wandor (ed.), *On Gender and Writing* (Pandora, London, 1983), p. 71.
3. On the relation between E. T. A. Hoffmann and fantasy, see Rosemary Jackson, *Fantasy: The Literature of Subversion* (Methuen, London, 1981), pp. 43–4, 66–7.
4. Hélène Cixous, *Sorties*, trans. Ann Liddle, in Elaine Marks and Isabelle de Courtivron (eds.), *New French Feminisms* (Harvester Press, Brighton, 1981), p. 97.
5. A survey of these developments is given by Hester Eisenstein, *Contemporary Feminist Thought* (Allen and Unwin, London, 1984), pp. 45–96.
6. Cixous, *Sorties, ed. cit.*, p. 96.
7. *A Theory of Literary Production*, trans. Geoffrey Wall (Routledge & Kegan Paul, London, 1978).
8. *Breaking Out: Feminist Consciousness and Feminist Research* (Routledge & Kegan Paul, London, 1983), pp. 94–7.
9. *Ibid.*, p. 97.
10. See the critique by Gina Wisker, 'Woman Writer, Woman Reader, Male Institution: The Experience of a Contemporary Women's Writing Seminar', *Journal of Literature Teaching Politics* 3 (1984), 28.
11. 'Writing Like a Woman: A Question of Politics' in Francis Barker *et al.* (eds.), *The Politics of Theory: Essex Sociology of Literature Conference* (University of Essex, Colchester, 1983), p. 24.
12. Frankie Rickford, 'No More Sleeping Beauties and Frozen Boys' in Eileen Phillips (ed.), *The Left and the Erotic* (Lawrence and Wishart, London, 1983), pp. 139–47.
13. For a clarification of trends in 'feminism and psychoanalysis' see Jacqueline Rose, 'Femininity and its Discontents', *Feminist Review* 14 (1983), 5–21.
14. *The Standard Edition of the Complete Psychological Works of Sigmund Freud*, trans. James Strachey (Hogarth, London, 1953–73), Vol. XVII.
15. Mark Poster, *Critical Theory of the Family* (Pluto Press, London, 1978), p. 170. A useful introduction to feminist perspectives on the family is Lynne Segal (ed.), *What is to be done about the Family?* (Penguin Books, Harmondsworth, Middx., 1983).
16. 'Magical Mannerist: John Haffenden talks to Angela Carter', *Literary Review* 77 (November 1984), 36.
17. Jessica Benjamin, 'Master and Slave: The Fantasy of Erotic Domination' in Ann Snitow *et al.* (eds.), *Desire: The Politics of Sexuality* (Virago, London, 1984), p. 300.
18. *Image, Music, Text* (Hill and Wang, New York, 1977), p. 146.

Quoted by Jonathan Culler in *On Deconstruction: Theory and Criticism after Structuralism* (Routledge & Kegan Paul, London, 1983), p. 33.
19. 'Notes from the Front Line', *ed. cit.*, p. 69.
20. *The Magic Toyshop* (1967 edn; Virago, London, 1981), p. 177. All subsequent page references are to the 1981 edition and will be included in the text.
21. *Tales of Hoffmann*, trans. R. J. Hollingdale (Penguin Books, Harmondsworth, Middx., 1982), pp. 85–125.
22. 'The Uncanny', *ed. cit.* A relevant critique is given by Cixous, 'La fiction et ses fantômes: Une Lecture de *l'Unheimliche* de Freud', *Poetique* 10 (1972), 199–216.
23. 'Magical Mannerist', *loc. cit.* 34–8.
24. See Cixous, 'The Character of Character', trans. Keith Cohen, *New Literary History* 5 (1974), 383–402. Other relevant discussions include Catherine Belsey, *Critical Practice* (Methuen, London, 1980), pp. 56–85; and Julia Kristéva, *Desire in Language: A Semiotic Approach to Literature and Art*, trans. Thomas Gora *et al.* (Blackwell, Oxford, 1981), pp. 125–209.
25. See E. Ann Kaplan, 'Is the Gaze Male?' in Ann Snitow *et al.* (eds.), *op. cit.*, pp. 321–38.
26. Margaret Jackson, 'Sexology and the Universalisation of Male Sexuality' in L. Coveney *et al.* (eds.), *The Sexuality Papers: Male Sexuality and the Social Control of Women* (Hutchinson, in association with the Explorations in Feminism Collective, London, 1984), p. 71.
27. *The Sadeian Woman: An Exercise in Cultural History* (Virago, London, 1979), p. 23.
28. *Heroes and Villains* (1969 edn; Penguin Books, Harmondsworth, Middx., 1981), p. 18. All subsequent references are to the 1981 edition and will be included in the text.
29. Beatrice Faust discusses the genre 'Sweet Savagery' in *Woman, Sex and Pornography* (Penguin Books, Harmondsworth, Middx., 1981), pp. 137–46.
30. *Heroes and Villains*, *ed. cit.*, p. 90.
31. 'No More Sleeping Beauties and Frozen Boys', *ed. cit.*, p. 142.
32. Annette Kuhn, *Women's Pictures: Feminism and Cinema* (Routledge & Kegan Paul, London, 1982), p. 15. See also Michèle Barrett, 'Feminism and the Definition of Cultural Politics' in Rosalind Brunt and Caroline Rowan (eds.), *Feminism, Culture and Politics* (Lawrence and Wishart, London, 1982), pp. 37–58.
33. *The Bloody Chamber and Other Stories* (1979 edn; Penguin Books, Harmondsworth, Middx., 1981), pp. 7–41. All subsequent page references will be to the 1981 edition and will be included in the text.
34. See Annette Kuhn, *op. cit.*, pp. 112–14; and B. Ruby Rich, 'Anti-Porn: Soft Issue, Hard World', *Feminist Review* 13 (1983), 59–60.
35. *The Infernal Desire Machines of Dr Hoffman* (1972 edn, Penguin Books, Harmondsworth, Middx., 1982), pp. 43–6, 132–4, 158–62. All subsequent page references will be to the 1982 edition and will be included in the text.

36. 'Notes from the Front Line' *ed. cit.*, p. 71. The success of *The Infernal Desire Machines of Dr Hoffman* in pleasing a male entertainment market is illustrated by Tom Robbins' comment, 'Angela Carter is one of my favourite drugs', quoted on the cover of the 1982 edition.

37. See Jean Baker Miller, *Towards a New Psychology of Women* (Penguin Books, Harmondsworth, Middx., 1978), pp. 3–14; and Ann Oakley, *Subject Women* (Martin Robertson, Oxford, 1981), pp. 265–73.

38. Adrienne Rich, *Compulsory Heterosexuality and Lesbian Existence* (Onlywomen Press, London, 1981), pp. 4–5.

39. For reference to the sexual values of the 1960s see Dana Densmore 'Independence from the Sexual Revolution' in *Radical Feminism*, ed. Anne Koedt *et al.* (Quadrangle Books, New York, 1973), pp. 107–19.

40. See Elizabeth Wilson's moving personal account of lesbian existence in the 1960s in 'Gayness and Liberalism', *Conditions of Illusion: Papers from the Women's Movement* (Feminist Books, London, 1984), pp. 110–28.

41. 'A New Romanticism?' in Eileen Phillips (ed.), *The Left and the Erotic, op. cit.*, p. 50. Wilson's remark is not entirely accurate since authors such as Rosalind Coward and several French feminist writers, notably Luce Irigaray, have related psychoanalytic theory to lesbian sexuality, sometimes with a strong political emphasis. Feminist discussions of Freud's case-study *Dora* also make connections between the two areas. For an example of the latter, see Maria Ramas, 'Freud's Dora, Dora's Hysteria' in *Sex and Class in Women's History*, ed. Judith L. Newton *et al.* (Routledge & Kegan Paul, 1983), pp. 72–113.

42. *Gyn/Ecology: The Metaethics of Radical Feminism* (Women's Press, London, 1979), p. 143.

43. *Ed. cit.*, p. 73.

44. *Compulsory Heterosexuality, op.* cit., pp. 4–9.

45. 'Feminism and Fairy Tales', *Women's Studies* 6 (1978–9), 237.

46. Cixous, *Sorties, ed. cit.*, p. 97.

47. Gillian Greenwood, 'Flying Circus', *The Literary Review* (October 1984), 43.

48. Carter also alludes to art conventions, especially surrealistic ones. Her description of Fevvers' feathered headdress and robe (p. 14) recalls Max Ernst's *The Robing of the Bride*, and her representation of the way the tigers 'scattered their appearance upon the glass' of the mirrors in the train crash (p. 206) may be related to René Magritte's *Découverte* and *Le Faux Miroir*.

49. *Problems of Dostoevsky's Poetics*, trans. R. W. Rotsel (Ardis, U.S.A., 1973), p. 89.

50. *Ibid.*, p. 139.

51. *Ibid.*, p. 103.

52. *Rabelais and His World*, trans. Helene Iswolsky (M.I.T. Press, Massachusetts, 1968), p. 34.

53. *Ibid.*, p. 317.
54. *Ibid.*, pp. 410–11.
55. *Ibid.*, pp. 200–7.
56. *Problems of Dostoevsky's Poetics, ed. cit.*, pp. 96, 122.
57. For a detailed discussion of these symbols and their significance, see Sandra M. Gilbert and Susan Gubar, *The Madwoman in the Attic: The Woman Writer and the Nineteenth-century Literary Imagination* (Yale University Press, Newhaven, 1979), pp. 18–20.
58. 'The Character of Character', *loc. cit.*, 396, 398.
59. *Rabelais and His World, ed. cit.*, pp. 92, 94.

8

The Poetry of Sylvia Plath

Barbara Hardy

When I first read the poetry of Sylvia Plath, probably in 1960, when *The Colossus* was published, I thought of her as a fine poet, not as a woman poet. Trying now to think most particularly of her as a woman writer, and to contemplate my own response, as that of a woman writer, I find my concern solicited by her transformation of the themes, structures and language of sexuality.

I was, and continue to be, impressed by Sylvia Plath's imaginative ability to override separatist interests, as she used her artistic energy to speak for both sexes. As with all imaginative effort by members of minority groups who break out of their category, I find her persistent movement away from the particular concern with sexual politics marked and unusual. Before the revival of the Women's Movement in the late 1960s, this poet concentrated the intelligence and passions on a woman's problems, and then, with a creative leap beyond questions of gender, on personal problems which concern everyone, like parental and filial relations, marriage, and sterility, as well as larger political issues like commercialism, materialism, war. The narrative, drama and rhetoric of Sylvia Plath's poetry show a salient tendency to use the subject and language of a woman's experience as metaphor or metonymy. What happens to the articulation of a woman's experience is what the poet described as happening to all personal or private experience in relation to the public or political life. In a famous passage, she describes her sense of what Coleridge defined as the imaginative capacity to reconcile the 'opposite or discordant qualities', 'of the general, with the concrete; the idea, with the image; the individual, with the representative'.[1]

> I think my poems come immediately out of the sensuous and emotional experiences I have, but I must say I cannot sympathize with these cries from the heart that are informed by nothing except a needle or a knife or whatever it is. I believe that one should be able to control and manipulate experiences, even the most terrifying — like madness, being tortured, this kind of experience — and one should be able to manipulate these experiences with an informed and intelligent mind. I think that personal experience shouldn't be a kind of shut box and mirror-looking narcissistic experience. I believe it should be generally relevant, to such things as Hiroshima and Dachau, and so on.[2]

Her sense of a woman's special suffering (already a generalised version of private experience) rapidly becomes subsumed or consumed in a larger language and vision. Or almost always. There are a few poems which are or seem to be bounded by the woman's experience.

The Colossus contains an apparently simple woman's poem about pregnancy, 'Metaphors'. I first thought it a frivolous string of fancies violently broken by a final melodramatic image in 'the train there's no getting off', and later concurred with Helen Vendler's judgment that the poet is pretending 'a buoyant sense of physicality, and playing herself false.'[3] She admits that the last line is 'grim', and calls 'the rest' 'pure silliness'. But I have revised my opinion. It is true that the poem's beginning is simple-minded, posing a 'riddle' too easy to answer, and going on to use metaphors that are crashingly obvious, like 'elephant', 'ponderous house', 'melon strolling on two tendrils', rising loaf, money in fat purse. But I wonder now whether the poem is not aware of its own inadequacy of comparison? The initial fancifulness is revised. The poem modulates from obvious comparisons to less obvious ones, from funny images to less funny ones. It resembles Shakespeare's sonnet, 'Farewell, thou art too dear for my possessing', where the choice of legal and commercial metaphors degrades, by association, the tenor for which they form the vehicle, and suddenly stops, to give way to a richer imagery in the final couplet. In 'Metaphors' obviousness and amusement break down together in the seventh line, 'I'm a means, a stage, a cow in calf', which introduces a sense of abstraction, and lowered humanity. The images move from the pleasures of 'red fruit, ivory, fine timbers!' to pain, if only that of a bad bellyache, in 'eaten a bag of green apples'. The last line, 'Boarded the train there's no getting off', moves us out of the series of fanciful but rational and lucid items. There are no trains one cannot get off; the exercise of comparison through reasoned resemblance breaks down. I now read this poem as encompassing a movement from physical pride and pleasure, through a sense of apprehended pathology, into a sense of shocking passivity and instrumentality. Naturalistic metaphors shift to surrealist fantasy. The new image and the move to a new image-set take us into the experience of fear and loss. The poem's literary title is a deceptively mild invitation to contemplate a startling range of metaphorical reference and function.

Men's poems about pregnancy take the occupational risk of being patronising. Dylan Thomas's 'If my head hurt a hair's foot', talks about pain in childbirth, but in a way which transmutes physicality into abstraction:

If my head hurt a hair's foot
Pack back the downed bone. If the unpricked ball of my
   breath
Bump on a spout let the bubbles jump out.
Sooner drop with the worm of the ropes round my throat
Than bully love in the clouted scene.

There is rough decorum in the use of masculine puns, innuendoes, and images, but no imagined sense of the woman's response in equivalently sensuous terms, only the drama of heroic maternity, the brave and defiant insistence that the child thrust its 'iron head'. The poem's concluding regret that birth will initiate a process of dying has nothing to do with imagining the feeling of childbed. I do not want to suggest that Thomas's poem is in any sense unsuccessful; it is a good and characteristic poem about birth as entrance to death. I use it as an example of a poem about childbirth written from the man's point of view, a useful contrast with Sylvia Plath's poem because of its heroics. The language of 'Metaphors' is imagistic, its form that of specious inventory and abrupt transmutation. The poem imagines an apprehension which transforms the sense of physical enhancement. Although the poem invites us to consider the function of metaphorical association, I don't suggest that the rhetorical subject does more than act as an intellectual sub-text to the passional sense of alarm and not-knowing. The poem embodies a particular experience of pregnancy. In 'You're', which appeared in *Ariel*, the same structural device of stringing metaphors like beads describes not a pregnancy but an embryo. It is not a peculiarly maternal poem, but moves away from the proprietary suggestiveness of 'my little loaf', which assimilates woman-as-cook to woman-as-oven, to become more generously parental in a single shift to first-person-plural, 'our travelled prawn', as the idea of a journey justly refusing to exclude the man's share in the making. This is a more trivial poem, simply expressing a simple mood of euphoria, with no darkening, and I mention it in order to emphasise the emotional complexity of 'Metaphors'.

The second poem dealing exclusively with maternal emotions is *Three Women: A Poem for Three Voices*, written for radio. Each of the very similar three voices utters a different version of experience in the maternity ward: happy fertility, unhappy sterility, unhappy fertility. (The uncompleted term is obvious, and historically indicative; one would expect it to be dealt with in a poem written now.) The poem contains a clearly directed aggression towards men. Invective is generalised, mythologised and politicised as an attack on the man-made, man-governed society.

The third woman, whose pregnancy is unwanted, attacks men, partly through the image of doctors, as they move through the 'bigness' of pregnant women, smiling 'like fools', and 'to blame for what I am'. The last accusation is dramatically particularised, but the other images precisely represent that physically strong sense of woman-man contrast which must strike many women in male-ruled hospitals. The images are mild, and carry with them no sense of a patronising medical presence, merely of a feeble and guilty one. The first woman, the happily fertile mother, is entirely concerned with her love for the child. This is generated simply and sensuously:

What did my fingers do before they held him?
What did my heart do, with its love?
I have never seen a thing so clear.
His lids are like the lilac-flower
And soft as a moth, his breath.

And with a sense of solicitude, 'How long can I be a wall around my green property?' and exposure. Sylvia Plath's Gothic imagination is flexible enough to express unbearable, because unlimited, tenderness, fear, and fondness:

It is a terrible thing
To be so open: it is as if my heart
Put on a face and walked into the world.

The grotesque image achieves the same effect, through markedly different means, as some of the utterly simple questions. The poet joins two ways of uttering love; extremes of language meet, registering feeling through extremity, and also through the collision of opposites. The question 'What did my heart do . . . ?' is interesting in its total exclusion of anything but parental love. There is only obsessive and concentrated maternity.

But despite the drama of exclusiveness, the image and story of the sterile woman is used to utter and swell aggression against the male society. Hostility is compounded in a dynamic act of myth-making, in which the world of manmade machines, and institutions of business, religion and politics join rational imagery to the wild metonymy of the flat male body. The woman's colleagues in the office 'were so flat!'. She feels that their 'cardboard' quality is infectious. To flatness and cardboardliness is added the sterility of abstraction and intellect:

That flat, flat, flatness from which ideas, destructions,
Bulldozers, guillotines, white chambers of shrieks proceed,
Endlessly proceed — and the cold angels, the abstractions.

The poetry works both through generalisation and logic, but also through particuliarity and fantasy. The horridly apposite and particular imagery of flattening machines (bulldozers and guillotines) joins the abstraction of ideas. The mechanical world spawns its dead and deadly examples. The typewriter keys are images of reduction, 'black' and 'alphabetical'; their abstractness is compounded by what they type out, orders for 'parts' 'parts, bits, cogs' and figures, 'the shining multiples'. The feeling becomes more political, again through modulation, association, and blurring. The sterile woman rehearses the intimate details of her therapy, 'I have stitched life into me like a rare organ' and 'I have tried to be blind in love', and her affection for the husband, briefly and affectionately imaged as the 'dead blind sweet one' through whom she tried not to look for the face of the child. The particulars of narrative generate the image of the unimageable unborn child, in language whose impressions of calm and elevation are accurate but also ironic. Two modes work in double harness:

> I did not look. But still the face was there,
> The face of the unborn one that loved its perfections,
> The face of the dead one that could only be perfect
> In its easy peace. Could only keep holy so.

Out of this pained and hard speculation, which has emerged smoothly from the narrative of ordinary living, language swerves into an impassioned indictment, the more powerful for occurring as a displacement. Structural shift articulates feeling abruptly, wildly, and without rational argument:

> And then were other faces. The faces of nations,
> Governments, parliaments, societies,
> The faceless faces of important men.

We come back to the obsession with roundness and flatness, the old insistence on the male jealousy of everything not flat, then a new mythical rendering of Father and Son, who design a flat, holy, clean and sterile heaven. This is a new polemical version of purgatory, in which the conventional woman's activity of washing-day provides the metaphor for a spiritual refinement worked-out and worked by the familiar masculine gods:

> Let us flatten and launder the grossness from these souls.

There is irony in the transmission of female labour (literal) to male power (symbolic). The metaphorical act is a rhetorical version of refinement. The fantasy is fully responsive to both meanings of 'sterile'. In local detail and structural motion, the poem finds a form for the feelings of an intense, erotic but clearly politicised, attack on man and his powers. Intelligence and control discover a drama, a language and an imagined environment which permit and limit such aggression. To put it this way makes it sound narrowly diplomatic, which of course it isn't. I want to praise not only the rationality of this poetry, which cuts deep and strong channels for wild, sick, intense passions, but the ability to utter, limit, and expand animus. In the literature of feminist polemic, aggression towards men is commonly let rip. The organised passions of Sylvia Plath's dramatic lyrics richly and subtly use and modify the deliberated and propagandist crude languages and naive structures.[4] They include, break, and extend feminist passions.

Another exclusively woman's experience is that of sister-hood, a subject rarely treated by Sylvia Plath, whose poetry about other women tends to be aggressive and hostile. 'The Babysitters' is a deceptively rambling and anecdotal poem of reminiscence about youth, set in an interestingly domestic and anti-domestic environment. The babysitters play out the role of reluctant mother-surrogates, as they cope with kids' fads ('the seven-year-old wouldn't go out unless his jersey stripes/Matched the stripes of his socks') and superfluous work ('my fingers red/With triangular scorchmarks from ironing tiny ruching and puffed sleeves'). The narrator can't cook and is depressed by babies, but she and her friend can escape into freedom, on 'Children's Island'. As the speaker looks back, the imagery of Alice is invoked with a difference; 'What keyhole have we slipped through . . . ?' suggests the entry to wonderland, but is corrected to propose enclosure. The ease of 'slipped' is shifted to the failure of 'slipped through' after this second question, 'what door has shut?' The memory of the two floating free girls is made strange in ironic miniature, like Alice's garden, through one of the poet's favourite images, that of the doll; the passivity and flimsiness of object and plaything associations are increased by the epithet in 'two cork dolls'. The poem's last line widely but cryptically asserts, 'Everything has happened.' Nothing is definite or defined, but the poem suggests, through an absence of specification, that what has happened is womanhood. The girls can no longer play games when 'the big people' are out because they have become big people. They can no longer resentfully but impermanently serve the women's world as mere babysitters. The question 'O what has come over us, my sister!' is answered through a silence, which makes a loud sound in this garrulous narrative. The poem expatiates in order to shut up. The address to a sister and familiar whose experience can be used to particularise and generalise through warm wry feeling is unusual, perhaps unique, in Sylvia Plath's published poetry.

Most of her portraits of women are hostile, though the hostility is never simple. Mythological characters and caricatures, mostly of older women, the mother, aunt, and Dame Kindness, attack the conservatism, lies and dangers of the woman's traditional community. But aggression is often mingled with reluctant intimacy and affection. Aspects of 'womanliness' are appreciated, if with distaste. In 'The Disquieting Muses' mother-love bakes black magic into gingerbread, but the speaker doesn't claim to have total comprehension of the protective mother, who may or may not have seen the Muses, and who may or may not have tried to exorcise them. And since they are disquieting Muses, the poem doesn't commit itself on the question of the rights and wrongs of such exorcism. What is clear is the complex satiric portrait, in motherly failure, of rites and conventions of nurture:

> In the hurricane, when father's twelve
> Study windows bellied in
> Like bubbles about to break, you fed
> My brother and me cookies and ovaltine . . .

And:

> Mother, you sent me to piano lessons
> And praised my arabesques and trills
> Although each teacher found my touch
> Oddly wooden in spite of scales. . . .
> I learned, I learned, I learned elsewhere,
> From muses unhired by you, dear mother.

216

What is clear, too is the act of valediction, as the mother is floated off into unreality, 'On a green balloon bright with a million/Flowers and bluebirds that never were', leaving the daughter to the inheritance of the disquieting kingdom whose company will be borne in silence, for better or worse.

The mother figure is created in order to define and understand a tradition of neat, comforting fantasy, to define and blame its dangerously tamed stories and images. The incantatory refrain of 'Mother, mother', echoing the ballad 'Edward, Edward', utters reproach. The world of home comforts and feminine accomplishment is identified as generator of the stony company it has invited by exclusion. The inspiration and affection of these Muses probably needs to be cold, uncompanionable, unnerving.

These images of a woman's world are defined and created in order to define and create its opposite, through logic, irony and sardonic humour. The mythological figure in the poem 'Kindness', a revised twee version of Dame Kind or Nature, also possesses a deadly natural touch. She is conservatively domestic in her consolations and deprivations, and appears as a presiding woman, attending and encouraging the functions of wife and mother, unable to stop the 'blood-jet' poetry. (That image of haemorrhage is a brilliant choice for the drama of woman as old wife and nurse.) In the comic violent poem 'The Tour', another role-model is satirically created, and forcefully affronted, in a dreadful disruptive parody of the world of household goods and gods. The aunt rebukes free sluttishness, 'in slippers and housedress with no lipstick!' and 'the tour' startlingly sends up the cosy house-proud display. Domestic objects become malignant, in ways familiar but strange: the frost box looks like a cat because of its normal constituents, 'fluffy stuff', but makes 'millions of needly glass cakes'. (This reversal of nourishment is like Mrs Jo's pins-and-needles bread in *Great Expectations*.) The bad mother is the bad housekeeper, feeding not for health but for sickness, 'migraine or the bellyache'. The central heating system explodes, dooming the lady of the house to hairlessness and near suffocation. The pool is a pretty blue but predatory: in a surreal parody of domestic routine it returns several maids and a plumber 'steamed and pressed and stiff as shirts'. Hospitality is refused, as innocent but acid 'lemon tea', is joined by 'earwig biscuits'. The satiric portrait of the midwife-monster is then made to menace the normal order, 'She can bring the dead to life/With her wiggly fingers for a very small fee.' Here and elsewhere, friendly talk is dreadfully babied, 'Here's your specs' and 'Toddle off home to tea'.

Through wildness, caricature and speed these poems attack woman as the conventional keeper of convention. Without using rational modes of argument and analysis, they exploit devices of association to take the attack beyond sexist subversions. At almost every point in the poetry, the woman's tradition becomes a metonymy for the consumer society — its possessiveness, its materialism, its competitions. The collision between the older conservative women and a younger rebel no doubt has biographical roots, but my concern here is to point out not private origins but public expansions.

Other women characters appear in the narrative lyrics, not directly associated with a historical clash of value and feeling, but carrying strong social significance. In 'Face Lift' reifications are prominent; 'like chalk on a blackboard', 'Tapped like a cask', 'Old sock-face, sagged on a darning egg'. Revoltingly realised is a dissociation of psyche from soma, prominent in the last example. The hostility towards men is gentle but clear. Technology has made operations easy and sociable: 'They've changed all that' and 'Fizzy with sedatives and unusually talkative', but the child's operation is linked with that of the older woman by the figure of the man: in the first case, 'Jovian voices of surgeons' and in the second, quietly, 'a kind man/Fists my fingers for me'. Again, the poem uses loud modes of caricature and exaggeration with reticence and tiny nuance. The social implications come in casually, through images of an expensively leisured woman, 'in long skirts on my husband's sofa, my fingers/Buried in the lambswool of the dead poodle;/I hadn't a cat yet'. The face-lifted lady is an unsympathetic character with whom we must come to sympathise: such blandness is imputed to her that it appeals on behalf of her victimisation. Through the revulsion we acknowledge the social origins of these hygienic, clever, and approved cosmetic distortions. The poem begins with the ironic benign tone, 'You bring me good news from the clinic' and ends with a compounded (doubled) image of perverted age:

> Mother to myself, I wake swaddled in gauze,
> Pink and smooth as a baby.

This is, implicitly, a drama of sterility, but that sterility is more than biological. The poem is about more than man's exploitation of woman.

This sly irony mimics and exaggerates cruel or bland tones to create a radically repelled reader. 'Face Lift' resembles Auden's Brechtian ballad, 'Miss Gee', in which a calloused sensibility is impersonated to produce a counter-reaction. A similar technique is used in Sylvia Plath's 'Gigolo'. The central character looks like a simple-minded, anti-male caricature, but explodes into social condemnation. Once more, there are terrifying suggestions of sterility, 'There one is safe/There are no family photographs', abuse, 'my way of turning/Bitches to ripples of silver', and deadening thing-images, 'Pocket watch', 'my engine', 'the tattle of my gold joints', and 'mill a litter of breasts like jellyfish'. In the last image the reduction to thing is combined with a reduction to animal, and both associations are made more featureless and fragmented by the synecdoche: three powerful rhetorical figures twist together. The mechanical man is Narcissus, trailing moral meanings as he gazes, 'All the fall of water an eye/Over whose pool I tenderly/Lean and see me'. But the rhetoric of dismemberment insists on social denaturing. The flip style has a modishness just right for the caricature of man and of society. Once more, violence is used with quiet aplomb. Once more, both men and women are reduced and instrumentalised.

The title of 'The Applicant' implies a commercial subject. Its procedure is to propose and confuse sexual themes. The poem begins with an ambivalent sexual object, as the applicant, addressed as 'person', is asked if she/he has rubber breasts or a rubber crotch. Most of the actions in the poem refer to womanly help and healing, such as curing headaches, sewing, cooking, closing dead eyes, and talking ('Talk, talk, talk'), but some of them are not domestic. The 'hand' and the 'living doll' do woman-things, but the middle image, the 'suit', has different significances:

> How about this suit . . .
>
> Black and stiff, but not a bad fit.
> Will you marry it?
> It is waterproof, shatterproof, proof
> Against fire and bombs through the roof.
> Believe me, they'll bury you in it.

The hand and doll are also (more lucidly) offered in marriage. To marry a hand is metonymy, to marry a suit is a metaphor. Sylvia Plath frequently uses the image of marriage for union or junction, and in this swerving structure of imagery, the categories shift, making it impossible for us to read the poem as a simple allegory of the male applicant, the female provision, and the mutual degradation of marriage. It is more integrally read, I believe, as a poem about political salesmanship and passive consumers. Anything and everything is on offer by the commercial persuaders; the argument about the bomb-proof suit uses absurdity to enlarge social meanings. The poem's form is not developmental. Its expansion and dislocation of categories occur in the middle. It begins with a strong, if not exclusive, suggestion of matrimonial service, is then concerned with a different provision, then ends with a return to coherent imagery of marriage. This structural twist makes the chief character (the applicant) change sex. The form is disturbingly disruptive, the disruption insisting that marriage is only one aspect of social constriction and commercial transaction. The placing of the thematic and emotional expansion creates a pointed disorder.

Sylvia Plath's two most famous poems, 'Lady Lazarus' and 'Daddy' also transcend their ostensible or initial subject-matter, more conspicuously and climactically than 'The Applicant'. Here, too, Sylvia Plath uses grotesque and fierce exaggeration, of character, action, and language. A narrative of personal relationship is most shockingly dislocated. Sylvia Plath describes 'Daddy'[5] as a story about a girl with an Electra-complex. The father figure, like the Doctor in 'Lady Lazarus', is a Nazi, the personal image is degraded, the political image made psychically intimate. Each poem works through an intensification of images of masculine authority. The doctor is a convenient social type of male dominance, as well as one with a special interest for Sylvia Plath. The doctor also fuses well with the figure of the Nazi experimenter, assimilated to the biographical figure of Sylvia Plath's German father. Both poems use a political story as a channel for sexual hostility. The hostility is an unnerving blend of ancient and modern, public and private mythologies. Both poems use the figure of displacement found in 'The Applicant'. The poem quietly introduces the metaphor of the bomb, as part of the hard sell, the advertiser's promise of profit, and in so doing disturbs and breaks the image of marriage, to open out larger devastations and falsehoods. In 'Lady Lazarus', the politicisation of the act of suicide, which is introduced and developed as a personal story, is introduced through three similes:

> . . . my skin
> Bright as a Nazi lampshade,
> My right foot
> A paperweight,
> My face a featureless, fine
> Jew linen.

The poem then reverts to the personal narrative, but eventually the Doctor is made Germanic through the address, 'Herr Doktor' and Herr Enemy', and at the end, 'Herr God, Herr Lucifer'. We move out of personal distress into the holocaust, then out of political incrimination of the Nazis, into the incrimination of Christianity.

This kind of displacement seems to be a favourite figure in Sylvia Plath's poetry. She used it to turn image into action, simplicity into complexity, privacy into politics. The device of making an image become part of action is no novelty: George Eliot makes Daniel Deronda think in tropes of voyages and departures which anticipate events and in 'The Love Song of J. Alfred Prufrock', T. S. Eliot plants the image of an 'overwhelming question' in a simile describing winding streets, but later on uses it literally. Sylvia Plath tends to use such figures of transformation in which imagistic explication or decoration become part of the primary action, to promote the private concern to a public status, to enlarge the theatre of passion. She sometimes transforms action permanently, but sometimes preserves the enlarged metaphor or simile as a threatening act of comparison, within a parenthesis, but transgressing boundaries. 'Poppies in October' tells a story, and sets a scene, in which poppies bloom in late season, 'a love gift/Utterly unasked for', astoundingly out of context, an illumination, a grace. The poem begins by comparing the brilliance of the poppies, grandly but acceptably, to the sun, 'Even the sun-clouds this morning cannot manage such skirts', and the image stays in its place, making its minor contribution, as a trope, to the landscape and the story. But it is followed by a second point of comparison, which behaves differently:

> Even the sun-clouds this morning cannot manage such skirts.
> Nor the woman in the ambulance
> whose red heart blooms through her coat so astoundingly . . .

The poem proceeds, without returning to the woman and her heart, as if the image could be left behind with that of the sun-clouds. But it cannot. The poem has been flooded with associations of blood and sickness which 'have nothing to do' with the setting or the story or the feelings, which remain discordant, unexplained, a vehicle more arresting than their tenor. There is a tapping of feeling too strong to stay subordinate. Background tries to become foreground. A sub-text refuses to stay in its place. But of course the image has everything 'to do' with the story, creating a depth beneath its surface of amazement, joy and praise. The poem continues with its narratives and feelings, apparently unabashed, but has been opened, exposed, broken. The poet discovers a way of selecting while admitting the passional whole from which she has made the selection, thus preserving concentration and truth to wholeness.

Despite current fictions, there are many critics like myself, brought up in the climate of the old New Criticism, who are not ideologically committed to a belief in the self-contained poem or the self-contained analysis. I have so far been discussing Sylvia Plath's treatment of men and women within individual poems, but my view of the poet is more than a series of responses to separate works of art and my reading of the politicised theme of personal relations is both local and general, concentrated and diffuse. Some of the poet's widenings of theme become more, and differently, apparent when we read the poetry intertextually, and such widenings force us beyond the boundaries of single texts. There is a large number of poems in which images of marriage are used fairly consistently for unpleasant unions and junctions, creating a sub-text which is cumulative and intertextual. These pejorative marriage metaphors have two effects. Within individual poems, they introduce a subtextual disturbance. 'Poppies in July' plays on the visual resemblance between a wrinkled red poppy-petal and a mouth, next makes the mouth not just red but 'bloodied', then wishes that 'my mouth could marry a hurt like that!', and last adds the antithetical wish, also deriving from poppy-essence, for an opiate to numb pain and turn blood to colourlessness. The marriage metaphor adds both an incongruity and a congruity to the idea of embracing — accepting and loving — a pain. In the poem 'In Plaster' the union of body and plaster cast is finally imaged as 'a kind of marriage' and the comparison reflects back on earlier descriptions of dependence, construction, incompatibility, frigidity, inequality, caring, activity and passivity. But the cast has been figured as 'She' from the beginning. The image of marriage revises and strengthens these earlier implications, but its appearance makes it plain that the allegory of marriage is not there from the beginning. The poem is opened up with a new and ironic gloss, at the end. Like many of her poems, it may tempt readers to allegorical interpretation, but the power of this poem, I propose, lies in an avoidance of allegory, a tension between the particular and the general. The entry of the marriage metaphor, which is carefully held at speculative and noncommitted arm's-length by 'it was a kind', should be seen as a late entry. Allegorists should try reading the poem with the marriage image appearing at the beginning, instead of the image of a twin, 'shaped just the way I was' which initiates the gender of both 'characters' as female; and they should try deleting the qualification of vehicle in 'it was a kind'. These images are carefully worded, and carefully timed, retarded and self-conscious associates in the process of connotative accretion.

Another instance of sexual image comes at the end of 'Parliament Hill Fields'; 'The old dregs, the old difficulties take me to wife', and another in 'Insomniac', where night-howling cats are said to be 'like women, or damaged instruments'. In these two instances, the image of marriage, and of women, is used as a vehicle, its larger associations restricted to connotations of difficulty and pain. Even an exception turns out to obey the rule: in 'Winter Trees' the marriage metaphor does not appear as pejorative, but working through the associations of ring, to denote growth:

> Memories growing, ring on ring,
> A series of weddings.

This image, another of Sylvia Plath's forms of tenor-vehicle ambiguity (the rings on the trees are images of memory, and the memories images for tree-aging) gives way to the familiarly pejorative sexual association,

> Knowing neither abortions nor bitchery,
> Truer than women

which joins with many aggressive impulses towards women in the work.

In all these poems, the sexual rhetoric tends to be loaded with animus. The metaphors or similes are usually subordinated to the subject and feeling of the poem, but reach out beyond it to cohere with each other, forming an intertextual pattern. This eventually provides the critic with a set of image-associations carrying significance and information, like Shakespeare's image-clusters. But these subordinated poetic images also do something else, perhaps with particular facility because of the porous obscurity of much of this poetry. The intertextuality doesn't simply create, beyond the individual poems, a biographically interesting set of materials and references which inform or encourage speculation about experience and attitudes. It also feeds back into the poetry, disturbing the relationship of vehicle and tenor, making many poems not primarily concerned with the themes of sexuality and domesticity spill over into other regions.

It is true that a thorough acquaintance with any writer ends in a double possession of works in themselves and of works as part of the whole career. In looking at the novels of George Eliot, for instance, we can appreciate their individual preoccupations and come to accumulate autobiographical obsessions. The reader may also introduce, consciously or unconsciously, a new historical reading-emphasis, like that which is impelling me, in this essay, to select a certain theme. If a radical feminist reader looks, with a political purpose, for attacks on men, or defences of women, she will find them in the aggressions of the political poems, in recurrent imagery of men as black and flat, in the pejorative references of the marriage metaphors. But if a reader is not a hard-line feminist but concerned to argue the victimisation of both man and woman, in an area conceived to be larger than that of sexual politics, such poems can be shown to have an enlarged significance. The reader who looks for larger political references in the sexual themes and language will discover them to be metonymies and metaphors, often possessing an interesting two-way action. It would be specious of me, however, to pretend that I don't think the feminist readings are not fully responsive to the expanse and depth of Sylvia Plath's generative passions and meanings.

Notes

1. Coleridge, *Biographia Literaria: or Biographical Sketches of My Literary Life and Opinions* (1817) Chapter 13.
2. Quoted by A. Alvarez, 'Sylvia Plath', *The Art of Sylvia Plath*, ed. Charles Newman (Faber and Faber, 1970).
3. Helen Vendler, *Part of Nature, Part of Us* (Harvard University Press, Cambridge, Mass., 1980).
4. For instance, 'Rape', by Adrienne Rich, a fine poet whose feminist polemic is sometimes richly imaginative, sometimes polemically stereotyped. To hear her read is to realise that the human voice can add particularity and passion to language which seems thinly propagandist on the page, an unnerving experience for women who feel strongly about women and men as victims of patriarchy.
5. From the note to 'New Poems', a reading prepared for BBC but not broadcast; quoted in A. Alvarez, *loc. cit.*

9

'The Shadow of Light':
The Symbolic Underworld of Jean Rhys

Sue Roe

'Please try not to be so sad. Can't you think that it is the price of feeling anything at all, or living, or acting or being yourself even — it's the shadow of light as it were, this black melancholy — or — the other way round.'*

I

'It was a vague and shadowy fear . . .'[1]

How might it be possible to evaluate the work of Jean Rhys? To read as a woman, even to read as a feminist, the work of a writer who deeply and firmly believed that 'a woman without a man is nothing',[2] whose female characters appear to revel in dependency and depression, for whom there is always a kind of artistic justice in being abandoned by a man; a writer whose *tour de force*, *Wide Sargasso Sea*, charts the psychological journey of a white Creole girl from feelings of loss, alienation and victimisation, through fatal passion into madness?

The chronic submissiveness, the almost constitutional sadness, of Jean Rhys's heroines is such that readers of her writing have often found it difficult to evaluate, even, after a while, difficult to tolerate. Phyllis Rose, reading Rhys's autobiography for the first time, found herself experiencing again her reservations about the fiction: 'that it is narrow, complaining, its heroines tiresomely self-pitying and

* From a letter from Jean Rhys to Selma Vaz Dias, 9 January 1961, published in *Jean Rhys: Letters, 1931–1966*, selected and edited by Francis Wyndham and Diana Melly (Deutsch, London, 1984), p. 200.

vain . . .'[3]: the black melancholy emanates, then, from the spirit, or the constitution, of the writer herself. P. A. Packer, a man reading Jean Rhys's writing, reads her work as autonomous art rather than the product of an individual female sensibility. He admires this work, and takes it seriously, but is neverthless increasingly exercised, like Rose, on the subject of the heroines' characteristic displays of helplessness and irresponsibility. He takes a pragmatic line, which has a somewhat jarring effect, given the particular atmosphere and ambiance of Rhys's fictions, but his objections are, essentially, feminist ones, and his reservations must be taken into account. He quotes Anna, of *Voyage in the Dark*, thinking about clothes — ' "All right, I'll do anything for good clothes. Anything — anything for clothes" ' — commenting,

> Perhaps this is a perfectly natural desire for a young girl but it is also perfectly reasonable to expect her to realize that the money to pay for such things will not just fall into her lap.[4]

It *is*, of course, a perfectly reasonable expectation, but it focuses quite sharply the difficulty of thinking of the Jean Rhys heroine in the light of such reasoning. Putting his objection another way, Packer highlights the *positioning* of the heroine within the framework of the novel, thereby happening upon one reason for this difficulty. This time, Packer comments on the spectacle of Anna, observing her landlady:

> 'The landlady was washing the steps. She plunged her hands into a pail of filthy water, wrung out the cloth and started to rub again.' [*VID*, p. 24] One cannot imagine any of the heroines of these books doing that.
>
> (Packer, p. 256)

One cannot — the idea is absurd — and the incongruity and inappropriateness of moral responsibility, or practical solution, in a Jean Rhys novel, draws vivid attention to the fact that if one *could* imagine Anna washing the steps — or otherwise taking her life into her own hands — the entire psychological balance of these novels would be thrown into disarray, or, to put it another way, there would not be any story. For the positioning of Jean Rhys' heroines — as Anna is positioned here — on the fringes of their own stories, as helpless, impotent observers of their own fates, is important not only stylistically and structurally but as the entire focus and basis of Rhys's subject-matter. These are not novels about redressing balances, re-establishing patterns, realigning moral and economic forces. They are, on the contrary, about the *effects*, particularly on the female consciousness, of imbalance, unhappiness, fear of failure, fear of success. Rhys's writing represents a particular kind of psychological quest, which is dependent for its entire force and resonance on the motionlessness, the de-motivation, of her heroines. The novels are not designed to accommodate the notion that there are external actions which may be taken to alleviate internal distress, or that there is a direct relationship between moral and economic responsibility. Her heroines, by the time the reader encounters them, are no longer capable of making such connections. This incapacity is fundamental to their plight. It may seem, on the face of it — as it does to P. A. Packer — that it is 'their poverty which seems to be the root cause of their hardship' (p. 255), but whatever the Jean Rhys heroine has always lost, it is never made simply of money. We need to penetrate Jean Rhys's all too readily acclaimed style, to look beneath the polished surfaces of her plots, to understand what this poverty is made of.

Jean Rhys herself suffered great loss, and her loss permeates, suffuses and sustains her writing — her writing practice, and her fictions. There is paradox in this, but there is paradox at every turn both in Rhys's work, and in the making of it. Carole Angier, whose sensitive book on Jean Rhys charts the parallel developments of her life and work, has discovered that there was a real-life model for Walter, the 'perfect' lover of *Voyage in the Dark*, a handsome Englishman named Lancelot Hugh Smith, with whom the young chorus girl, Ella Gray (Rhys's first pseudonym) fell helplessly and hopelessly in love. He had, Angier relates, all the qualities of a hero:

> He was kind, he was elegant, he made her laugh; he bought her lovely clothes, and listened to her talk of home. He made her feel less shy. He was father, friend and lover in one — he was

perfection, and she thought him a god. It seemed as if, in this first affair, she had gone straight to the heart of her dream.[5]

This dream had to end, though, not through reasons of justice or morality, but because it was a fiction. Or, as Angier puts it, 'not because chorus girls couldn't marry rich respectable men — they did; but because it was a contradictory, impossible dream'. There was darkness, melancholy, in the character of Lancelot Hugh Smith as well as in that of 'Ella Gray', which made him able to mirror her own uncertainty, but which was also disconcerting, for both of them. Angier's interpretation of what happened focuses the difficulty, for 'Ella Gray', and later for the writer, Jean Rhys, of living with a dream, and then having to live without it:

> She longed for someone entirely secure, yet entirely sensitive; someone utterly respectable and safe, yet able to understand her lonely, fearful, rebellious nature. Against all expectation, Lancelot really was this dream. But being so made him less, not more, able to love her and stay with her. His respectability rejected her, as she'd been afraid it would — and so did the very things that drew him to her, his own hidden loneliness and fear. Lancelot couldn't bear to see people in pain or need; he didn't even want to think about them ('My dear, don't harrow me. I don't want to hear'). As soon as he felt the real depths of Ella's need, he must have wanted to bolt.
>
> (Angier, p. 35)

Interestingly, the force which pushes to the surface of this story — the model for all the stories Jean Rhys was later to write — is the tenacity of Rhys's own melancholy, her own, deeply rooted black despair, the familiarity of loss ('His respectability rejected her, as she'd been afraid it would'), which is bigger, stronger, even than the dream of love and happiness which she also held on to firmly, right up to the end of her life. To David Plante, who in her late years was patiently trying to carve a path through her spasmodic and muddled recollections in order to retrieve and piece together her autobiography — the unfinished *Smile Please* — she protested,

You don't understand. You never understood. I want out. I

never wanted to be a writer. Never. I couldn't help it. All I wanted was to be happy.[6]

Nevertheless, she wrote: about, throughout, in the face of, an unhappiness which both dogged and drove her. She told Plante,

nothing ever justifies what you have to do to write, to go on writing. But you do, you must, go on. You hear a voice that says, 'Write this', and you must write it to stop the voice.
(Plante, p. 38)

She wrote 'to stop the voice' — the black, bleak voice of loss, melancholy, despair, but she also wrote to *release* it. Her story, 'Let Them Call It Jazz', expresses the importance, the power, the potential potency of voice even in the face of the most dire and hopeless circumstances imaginable. The black girl in the story, hauled off to prison for disturbing the peace, hears the voice of a woman singing from the punishment cells, to 'tell the girls cheerio and never say die',[7] and is pulled up by it, out of her own despair into another level of feeling and belief in herself. Even the experience of hearing it played at a party, much later, reinterpreted, quite wrongly, as a jazz tune, cannot allay its power and status as the voice of one strong woman speaking to other women: men can call it whatever they like, says the woman to herself: 'That won't make no difference to the song I heard',[8] its potency, its secrecy, its power to articulate a particular kind of solidarity between women.

Jean Rhys valued this voice, her access to this particular, rather primeval world, or way of feeling, but she went on resisting it. Writing — the search to find and sustain this voice — was, for her, obsessional: a compulsion, and a gift. Though she cared about style, endlessly paring and shaping and re-drafting each novel, the impulse to write was wholly instinctive, seeming to issue from a part of the mind which was incapable of formulating ideas. David Plante, who, having access to her mind in its most confused states, came to know her, arguably, as intimately as anyone, is convinced of this. He notes that,

To have argued with Jean about her opinions would have been

mad: she simply would not have understood if one had said, 'But Jean, don't you wonder *why* you say that about women?' In terms of psychology (she said she had never read Adler, Jung or Freud, didn't know what they were about, and didn't want to know) . . . , she never asked why her main female characters acted as they did: they just did, as she did. There is about them a great dark space in which they do not ask themselves, removing themselves from themselves to see themselves in the world in which they live: Why do I suffer?

(Plante, p. 40)

In keeping with this attitude, she would have had no truck with the notion that, for a woman reading Jean Rhys's writing, specific questions, particular foci of attention, might present themselves. In this regard, Plante describes the wearying procedure of reading out her letters to her:

If the letters enclosed reviews, she asked the title and the first line, then said, 'Tear it up.' When the title was 'The Dark Underworld of Women' or 'The Woes of Women' or had 'women' in it in any way, she'd grab the review from me and tear it up herself and throw it in the basket, laughing, and say, 'No, I've had enough of *that*!'

(Plante, p. 39)

It was as though it were necessary to fiercely defend the place within Jean Rhys from which the source of her writing — her voice — issued; as though she demonstrates, always — and this permeates the novels themselves — a deep reluctance to fathom feelings so deeply rooted that to retrieve them, to make them coherent, accessible, would be somehow to defuse them, so that their power and potency as the unconscious source of her creative expression would be diminished. This must be true of many writers, but it concerns us when we read Jean Rhys's writing because it is a reluctance which is profoundly present in her fiction. It works together with her strong and finely balanced sense of poise, or style, to create rhythms and imagery of patterning and dismantling, advance and retreat, which are the keys to her deepest subject-matter.

II

'H.J., I want to be happy. Oh, I want it so badly. . . . I don't want anything black or miserable or complicated any more.'

(*Q*, pp. 60–1)

Her heroines, like Jean Rhys herself, have insights from which they are desperate to defend themselves. This mechanism of resistance becomes indistinguishable from their general depression, or malaise: as draining of energy, and as debilitating. One way of maintaining this line of most, and least, resistance, is by soliciting a man — a hero — who will play the role of protector. Almost any man is eligible for this role, even, for example, Stephan, the rather shady, shadowy character whom Marya, the heroine of Rhys's first novel, *Quartet*, has married; until, that is, his role of impostor is detected by the authorities, and he is removed to prison. His absence leaves Marya desolate and dejected:

> She spent the foggy day in endless, aimless walking, for it seemed to her that if she moved quickly enough she would escape the fear that hunted her. It was a vague and shadowy fear of something cruel and stupid that had caught her and would never let her go. She had always known that it was there — hidden under the more or less pleasant surface of things. Always. Ever since she was a child. (p. 28)

The life she has led with Stephan has been a dramatisation of her most deeply realised conception of her own, autonomous place in the scheme of things. He gives a surface demonstration of life led obliquely, in the shadows, of the vague, portentous fear, which is a feature of Marya's sense of her own history, so that, paradoxically, his presence represents something persuasive and protective and there is a level on which they are deeply, precariously compatible. This is, however, something which it is impossible to articulate: there is a muteness between them which helps them to both sustain and, essentially, ignore, the fundamental evasiveness on which their relationship is built:

> He never explained his doings. He was a secretive person, she considered. Sometimes, without warning or explanation, he

would go away for two or three days and, left alone in the hotel, she dreaded, not desertion, but some vague, dimly-apprehended catastrophe. But nothing happened. It was a fantastic life, but it kept on its legs so to speak.

(Q, p. 20)

He was 'secretive and a liar', but he adored her, and drama-tised his adoration: 'She was the petted cherished child, the desired mistress, the worshipped, perfumed goddess'. (p. 20) But in order to sustain his own version of this dream he is driven to forgery, deception and petty theft, as a result of which he us ultimately forced to abandon her.

Loss drives Marya — in this she is characteristic of Jean Rhys's heroines — into the arms of another man, who in turn can offer solace, shelter, pretence, and the continuation of the dream of happiness. In *Quartet* the other man is Heidler — 'H.J.' — who is large, paternal, and quietly perverted: again, he is compatible with Marya in the sense that he seeks the most direct, most disingenuous route to 'happiness', side-stepping the defeat and depression which really drive him, and which eventually surface. He shields Marya effectively, for a while, from the dangerous and terrifying solitude imposed on her by her husband's arrest, but ultimately his loyalty to his wife proves stronger than his whimsical attachment to this frail, adoring girl who had seemed to offer him, among other things, the reinstatement of his fast diminishing youth. Stronger, too, than his 'love' for Marya, is his sense of the proprieties, and his brute male egotism. Eventually, Marya tells his wife, Lois, that she feels she ought to leave the menagerie. Naturally, says Lois, . . .

'H.J. imagines that he's in love with you — for the minute.' She went on in a reflective voice: 'Of course, mind you, he wants things badly when he does want them. He's a whole hogger.'
   'So am I', Marya told her. 'That's just why I must go off.'
   The other made an impatient and expressive gesture, as if to say: 'D'you suppose that I care what you are, or think or feel? I'm talking about the man, the male, the important person, the only person who matters.'

(Q, p. 64)

Unequivocal as this might seem, it *is* an insight which is

avoidable, in Heidler's presence. He is capable of screening his destructive power over the three of them, by turning it in upon itself, so that the boundaries between sheer egotism and the capacity to shield Marya from herself become confused:

> 'Hullo, H.J.,' she said, and sat up quickly. He was too formidable standing over her. 'Listen. I've been telling Lois that I want to go — I think I'd better.'
> 'Oh, I think I'd better. I think I'd better,' she kept on saying in a little, pitiful voice; but when he took her in his arms she thought: 'How gentle he is. I was lost before I knew him. All my life before I knew him was like being lost on a cold, dark night.'. . . .
> He whispered: 'I love you, I love you. What did you say?'
> 'That you don't understand.'
> 'Oh, yes, I do, my dear,' said Heidler. 'Oh, yes, I do.'
> (Q, pp. 65–6)

He shields her from the cold, dark night of her inability to act on her own perceptions, her incapacity to distinguish between love and the screening device he offers, so that being with Heidler becomes not unlike being stranded with herself and her own confusions, except that Heidler's presence is infinitely soothing, by very virtue of the fact that he seems to *authorise* incapacity . . .

> sometimes she could feel sure that her life was a dream — that all life was a dream. 'It's a dream,' she would think; 'it isn't real' — and be strangely comforted.
> (Q, p. 96)

By this stage in Rhys's first novel, her heroine is already more or less anaesthetised. Being with Heidler induces a state of lethargy close to unconsciousness, which is typical of Rhys's heroines' relationships with their men. Marya becomes,

> so languid as to be almost incapable of movement. A profound conviction of the unreality of everything possessed her. She thought: 'I wonder if taking opium is like this?'
> (Q, p. 65)

This is, of course, the outcome of obsessive dependency, but it is also, on a fundamental level, desirable. The purpose of the Jean Rhys hero is always to obliterate. The decadence of these novels is in their recurring theme of sex not so much as prostitution (prostitution demands strategy and organisation, of which the Jean Rhys heroine is incapable) but as a drug, which will dull their senses, take them into some other realm of consciousness, and enable them to forget. This is what Anna, of *Voyage in the Dark* hopes for, from her Mr Jeffries:

> I sat down on the bed and listened, then I lay down. The bed was soft; the pillow was as cold as ice. I felt as if I had gone out of myself, as if I were in a dream.
> Soon he'll come in again and kiss me, but differently. He'll be different and so I'll be different. It'll be different. I thought, 'It'll be different, different. It must be different.'

> (*VID*, p. 21)

The love drug is not dependable, however. While it is capable of screening despair, it can also release it, since the relationship between sexuality and the unconscious — and, specifically, between sexuality and loss — can be highlighted as starkly by disingenuous love as by more genuine, more deeply rooted styles of communication. The business of attributing love with the power to shield and screen and protect is ultimately dangerous: even while the hero screens the heroine from her deepest fears, he simultaneously releases these, as Anna discovers through her relationship with Walter:

> I wanted to pretend it was like the night before, but it wasn't any use. Being afraid is cold like ice, and it's like when you can't breathe. 'Afraid of what?' I thought.

> (*VID*, p. 76)

If this dependency, this confusion, is love, then love is paradoxical, painful, and smacks of madness, Marya reflects:

> If this was love — this perpetual aching longing, this wound that bled persistently and very slowly. And the devouring hope. And the fear. That was the worst. The fear she lived with — that the little she had would be taken from her.

Love was a terrible thing. You poisoned it and stabbed at it and knocked it down into the mud — well down — and it got up and staggered on, bleeding and muddy and awful. Like — like Rasputin. Marya began to laugh.

(Q, pp. 95–6)

The truth is, of course, that this is not love. The horror and absurdity of arbitrary and destructive power are enmeshed, here, with the confusion between fear and dependency, as the sudden, hysterical naming of Rasputin reveals, but the inability to recognise an insight and to name it for what it is still persists while the hero goes on protecting and pretending. Heidler is no more 'in love' with Marya than she is with him, but he is in love with the *idea* of her, and of his liaison with her. Ultimately, he cannot sustain the fantasy which she, in turn, constructs around him. But the compulsion to play this game, confused as it becomes with Marya's dread of being abandoned with her own loss (another area she cannot name) is inescapable, so that, in time, Marya comes to depend on Heidler to protect her from the very feelings he releases in her — to depend on Heidler, that is, to protect her from her fear of Heidler:

> She watched the handle of the door turning very gently, very slowly. And during the few moments that passed from the time she heard the board creak to the time she saw Heidler and said, 'Oh, it's you then, it's you,' she was in a frenzy of senseless fright. Fright of a child shut up in a dark room. Fright of an animal caught in a trap.
> 'What is it? What is it, then?' whispered Heidler. 'My darling! There, there, there!'

(Q, p. 71)

This strategy of advance and retreat, this pattern which emerges, of different and enmeshing styles of abandonment, comes to dominate the heroine to the extent that, eventually, the only form of survival is total retreat: from the relationship; from the feelings it evokes; from herself. Ultimately, loss has to be enacted, dramatised: hence the sense one has, on reading a novel by Jean Rhys, that the heroine's abandonment by her lover is somehow artistically appropriate or accurate. The solitude of the Jean Rhys heroine is fundamental, so that her desertion makes artistic as well as psychological sense. But, just as the fear which is an aspect of her solitude seems to have a hidden source somewhere way, way back into the past ('She had always known it was there. Always. Ever since she was a child'), her feelings of abandonment, black melancholy or despair are thrown into relief by solitude, and seem to be linked with the process of remembering. Here is Anna, for example, left alone to reflect on the nature of her relationship with Walter Jeffries:

> That was when it was sad, when you lay awake at night and remembered things. That was when it was sad, when you stood by the bed and undressed, thinking, 'When he kisses me, shivers run up my back. I am hopeless, resigned, utterly happy. Is that me? I am bad, not good any longer, bad. That has no meaning, absolutely none. Just words. But something about the darkness of the streets has a meaning.'
>
> (*VID*, p. 49)

'The darkness of the streets' — this black melancholy, which permeates, becomes all-embracing — has a source, and a meaning. The profound relationship between sexuality and loss somehow focuses the lurking presence of history, the importance of the past, not through the recollection, at this juncture, of precise incidents, but through the incidental recognition of the potency of recollection as *process*. There might, then, be a way of naming the typical despair, the black melancholy, of the Jean Rhys heroine, which has to do with tracing the narrative backwards as well as forwards, and with recognising that, for her, recollection becomes as powerful a force as the forgetting enabled by submissiveness and dependency. Thrown back on their own resources, the heroines of Jean Rhys's oeuvre are given, increasingly, to the habit of remembering, which Rhys herself developed in *Voyage in the Dark*, and exploited to its limits in *Good Morning Midnight*. The narrative of recollection is woven together with the more polished, stylised narrative of events, enabling the heroines to experience a collision of time schemes which enables the emergence of a particular symbolic imagery. The insights contained in the novels, the voice which is eventually most plangently released, in *Wide*

Sargasso Sea, are developed by means of this symbolic narrative, which the heroines experience as a kind of interior chant even while they display all the muteness, the inarticulacy, of despair. It is this symbolic narrative which is the important legacy of the heroines' unsatisfactory lovers. Paradoxically, even as the heroes abandon and desert and refuse to save them, they release in them resources which, as Jean Rhys's oeuvre develops, eventually enable the depiction of a grande passion of which one of the main features is that both the heroine and the hero describe it: *Wide Sargasso Sea* depicts a passion through which both male and female voices are released. This symbolic narrative, upon which the final, conclusive novel came to be based, is released through the previous heroines' experiences of loss and recollection. What, exactly, is the nature of this loss? What have the heroines forgotten? What are they enabled, in the course of their respective narratives, to remember?

III

You are walking along a road peacefully. You trip. You fall into blackness. That's the past.

(GMM, p. 144)

In Jean Rhys's second novel, *After Leaving Mr Mackenzie* this second, interior narrative has already begun to be released. It is by far the blackest and bleakest of Rhys's novels, depicting a heroine, Julia Martin, whose bohemian morality and behaviour are starkly contrasted with the activities and feelings of her poor relations, and the extreme emotional poverty of both styles of life is exposed. The contrasts throw into relief the emotional brutality of which this heroine is capable, and the novel is dogged by an uncomfortable pathos which pulls at the reader's sympathies: it is less easy to sympathise with Julia herself, juxtaposed as she is with her poor relations, than with any of Rhys's other heroines.

Julia is also shown in a contiguous relationship, with Mr Horsfield, who rescues her from the solitude she faces after leaving Mr Mackenzie, and who hovers benignly and coyly slips her discreetly folded five pound notes. He too, the narrative assures us, has had his share of troubles, and Jean

Rhys takes care to give us, at strategic points in the narrative, Mr Horsfield's side of the story. But this, like the merciless contrast between Julia and her family, does not entirely work; in Mr Horsfield's case, because his version is always so similar to Julia's that in giving Mr Horsfield his interior monologue I cannot help feeling that Rhys was actually still writing about Julia. Here is Mr Horsfield, for example, at the end of the affair, behaving distinctly like a Jean Rhys heroine:

> He shut the door and sighed. It was as if he had altogether shut out the thought of Julia. The atmosphere of his house enveloped him — quiet and not without dignity, part of a world of lowered voices, and of passions, like Japanese dwarf trees, suppressed for many generations. A familiar world.
>
> (*ALMM*, p. 127)

Technically, it is easy to see what Jean Rhys was doing: by placing her heroine within the context of a group of others who also have reflections, who also have points of view which are profound in their implications, the full measure of Julia's position as outsider might be taken. But Jean Rhys does not write most effectively about 'the outsider'. In fact the most important outcome of this technical experiment is that this context gives Julia an opportunity to be both abandoned and enraged, and her rage acts as a releasing mechanism which detaches her on some profound level, if not superficially, from this group of contrasting characters, and enables her to think backwards as well as forwards.

It is a novel about loss, compounded by loss: this time, abandonment by a lover is followed by bereavement. After leaving Mr Mackenzie, Julia leaves Paris to return to London, where her mother is dying, and thus, though the narrative for the most part moves conventionally forward in a linear sequence of events, Julia herself is shown going back: to her native London, to her family, and, very graphically and starkly, to the body of her mother.

The body of Julia Martin's mother is central to this text. It, and a picture in Julia's room, which is described in detail at the beginning of the novel, are the only things Julia really looks at. Both of these depict still life — *nature morte* —

though the oil painting, depicting 'a half empty bottle of red wine, a knife, and a piece of Gruyère cheese' (p. 8) depresses Julia, whilst the body of her dying mother, similarly graphically described, is 'still beautiful, as an animal would be in old age.' (p. 70) The mother's face against the white frilled pillow is reminiscent of the picture in that 'Every object in the picture was slightly distorted and full of obscure meaning' (p. 8):

> Dark-skinned, with high cheek bones and an aquiline nose. Her white hair, which was still long and thick, was combed into two plaits, which lay outside the sheet. One side of her face was dragged downwards. Her eyes were shut. She was breathing noisily, puffing out one corner of her mouth with each breath.
>
> (*ALMM*, p. 70)

The contrast between this and the 'sunken face, bound in white linen' (p. 89) which is the face of Julia's mother after death, is immense. The dead face is frightening — horribly so — not only because it is inanimate but because it has the effect of propelling Julia out of the present back into a childhood which on some level she still inhabits, but which she is nevertheless unable to retrieve. The procession to the crematorium focuses, for Julia, a sensation which has been hovering beneath the surface throughout the narrative, and the revelation released by grief is the embryo of an entire narrative level which Jean Rhys will carry over into her subsequent novels:

> Everybody walked in a short procession up to the chapel of the Crematorium, where a clergyman with very bright blue eyes was waiting. That was . . . a painful dream, because she was obsessed with the feeling that she was so close to seeing the thing that was behind all this talking and posturing, and that the talking and the posturing were there to prevent her from seeing it. Now it's time to get up; now it's time to kneel down; now it's time to stand up.
>
> But all the time she stood, knelt, and listened she was tortured because her brain was making a huge effort to grapple with nothingness. And the effort hurt; yet it was almost successful. In another minute she would know. And then a dam inside her head burst, and she leant her head on her arms and sobbed.
>
> (*ALMM*, p. 94)

The feeling of emptiness, nothingness, which is a feature of loss, is here released as voice. At this juncture, this voice can express only despair, depression, in the abstract: the 'nothingness' of grief. Like the oil painting, the voice of grief is 'slightly distorted and full of obscure meaning', but it is meaning which cannot be articulated.

It comes to be experienced — though still mutely — as a split: a division between depression and release, which seem contradictory:

> She was crying now because she remembered that her life had been a long succession of humiliations and mistakes and pains and ridiculous efforts. Everybody's life was like that. At the same time, in a miraculous manner, some essence of her was shooting upwards like a flame. She was great. She was a defiant flame shooting upwards not to plead but to threaten. Then the flame sank down again, useless, having reached nothing.
>
> (*ALMM*, pp. 94–5)

But though this 'flame' — her conviction of the value of her own grief — sinks down again, as though some essential insight is about to materialise, but is then extinguished, there *is*, at this juncture, some capacity being released in Julia, which though it remains to her obscure, is released again in a scenario which offers a key to the reader.

After her mother's death, Julia goes on experiencing this apparent split between depression and revelation:

> [She] felt well and rested, not unhappy, but her mind was strangely empty. It was an empty room, through which vague memories stalked like giants.
>
> (*ALMM*, p. 114)

'It was an empty room', this mind, because it contained loss, but still, 'memories stalked like giants': the articulation of grief, if not of the meaning or the implications of loss, has released the capacity to remember, and recollection invites the mind to take part in a new process, inhabits the empty spaces with a new imagery, initiates a new, interior narrative in which the 'meaning' of this novel is contained, in an imagery of shadow and light.

In the section of *After Leaving Mr Mackenzie* entitled

'Childhood', the insight is given before the process of recollection through which Julia has access to it:

> When you are a child you are yourself and you know and see everything prophetically. And then suddenly something happens and you stop being yourself; you become what others force you to be. You lose your wisdom and your soul.
>
> (*ALMM*, p. 115)

Though it is not altogether clear, it seems that Julia herself, rather than the narrator, is thinking here. Certainly, the notion that with her childhood — or, more specifically, here, her separation from her mother — Julia has also paradoxically lost her sense of her own independence, is fundamental to her characterisation.

Though separation enables independence, the *shock* of separation sometimes renders autonomy impossible; blurs the boundaries between subject and object so that the objective world — represented, for example, in the oil painting — takes on threatening, imposing resonances. Shock polarises; but beneath the surface it actually *blurs* distinctions, causing confusion and incapacity. This is the major insight arrived at in *After Leaving Mr Mackenzie*, which Jean Rhys carries over into her subsequent novels, *Voyage in the Dark* and *Good Morning Midnight* — the two novels in which past and present are intertwined, sometimes indistinguishable, and their implications inextricable.

But this is not an insight available to the heroines themselves. They act on this knowledge, but they do not recognise it as such. It is made available to the reader through the heroine's recollection, which in *After Leaving Mr Mackenzie* is condensed into a single scenario. In the 'Childhood' section of the novel, Julia asks herself, 'How far back could you remember?' (p. 115): the narrative is in the second person, as though the remembering self is separate from the present self (Julia has experienced this sense of separation earlier in the narrative, when exposed to the morality of her family: 'She felt as though her real self had taken cover, as though she had retired somewhere far off and was crouching warily, like an animal, watching her body in the armchair arguing with Uncle Griffiths' (p. 59)):

You were walking along a long path, shadowed for some distance by trees. But at the end of the path was an open space and the glare of white sunlight. You were catching butterflies . . . taking hold low down or the wings would break in your hand . . .

'You're a cruel, horrid child, and I'm surprised at you.' . . .

That was the first time you were afraid of nothing — that day when you were catching butterflies — when you had reached the patch of sunlight. You were not afraid in the shadow, but you were afraid in the sun.

The sunlight was still, desolate, and arid. And you knew that something huge was just behind you. You ran . . . panting, your heart thumping, much too frightened to cry.

But when you got home you cried. You cried for a long time; and you never told anybody why.

The last time you were happy about nothing; the first time you were afraid about nothing. Which came first?

(*ALMM*, pp. 115–16)

The shadows offer pleasure: this is your path, these are your butterflies; the openness of the path, its issue into space, is soothing, it means you are not trapped, abandoned, in the shadows. But the space is not empty, it is occupied. A voice issues from it. It blames you; it tells you that you are guilty. Your pleasure is someone else's pain. This knowledge is experienced as imposition, interference. If the space is not empty but inhabited, what is the meaning of the shadow? Whatever occupies the space penetrated by sunlight is strong, potent: it has the power to encroach on you, to reinterpret your pleasure, to make it malign. There is something huge just behind you: the knowledge that when light is thrown on your behaviour it is open to reinterpretation on the part of others — your mother, for example, who has now abandoned you. In the light of all this, the happiness, the innocence, of childhood, is impossible to retrieve: 'you stop being yourself; you become what others force you to be. You lose your wisdom and your soul.' (p. 115)

The process of recollection, then, is releasing, offering access to the articulation of feelings of happiness and fear, guilt and dread, but for the heroines of these novels it is always confusing. Which came first — the end of happiness or the beginning of fear? Sexuality or loss? A philosophical problem ensues: which is 'real' — the present or the past?

Anna, of *Voyage in the Dark*, remembers in an imagery which is initiated by, and often indistinguishable from, the imagery of the present. England reminds her ceaselessly of her contrasting childhood in the Caribbean, so that,

> Sometimes it was as if I were back there and as if England were a dream. At other times England was the real thing and out there was the dream, but I could never fit them together.
>
> (*VID*, pp. 7–8)

Sunday, particularly, reminds her of the rituals of the past, and the stilted language of the English-speaking Caribbean:

> 'To the memory of Doctor Charles Le Mesurier, the Poor of this Island were Grateful for his Benevolence, the Rich Rewarded his Industry and Skill.' That gave you a peaceful and melancholy feeling. The poor do this and the rich do that, the world is so-and-so and nothing can change it. For ever and for ever turning and nothing, nothing can change it.
>
> (*VID*, p. 37)

There might, then, be a way of imposing order within the novels, a way of putting things in black and white, which depends not simply on the depiction of contrasting mental landscapes, but through which Jean Rhys might make use of *specific* landscapes — the contrasting geographical and mental landscapes of Europe and the Caribbean. This might, moreover, present other ways of developing the releasing technique of recollection. With her third novel, *Voyage in the Dark*, Rhys began to draw on her recollections of her *own* childhood landscape, to infiltrate the scenarios of her own past, to thread through her writing aspects of her own history.

IV

Being black is warm and gay, being white is cold and sad.
(*VID*, p. 27)

Black people sing. Their voices are strong and beautiful, plangent and full of potency. Their appropriation of the English language, in their songs, has a portentous accuracy to which the evasive English seem not to have access. Anna

Morgan's black companion, Francine, used to sing to her of sadness and regret, and the words of her only English song transcend dislocations of time and place:

> She used to sing:
>   Adieu, sweetheart, adieu,
>   Salt beef and sardines too,
>   And all good times I leave behind,
>   Adieu, sweetheart, adieu.
> That was her only English song.
>   — It was when I looked back from the boat and saw the lights of the town bobbing up and down that was the first time I really knew I was going. Uncle Bob said well you're off now and I turned my head so that nobody would see me crying — it ran down my face and splashed into the sea like the rain was splashing — Adieu sweetheart adieu — And I watched the lights heaving up and down —
>
> (*VID*, pp. 27–8)

Voyage in the Dark is about displacement; the loss integral to leaving home; about things being over; about termination. As this narrative of loss develops, it is woven through with Anna's memories of her Caribbean childhood, which acts as a soothing mechanism, based on recollection, but which enables her to forget. While she remembers the past, she can forget the present: the process of recollection acts as a way of masking loss. The visual and aural effects of this mechanism of mental and sensual contrast are powerful, and the narrative of the novel's conclusion, in which the scenarios of abortion and masquerade — the carnival of masks — are juxtaposed, is moving and dramatic.

This very powerful collision of past and present, in which the effects of recollection have as much capacity to break Anna as the effects of abortion, shows her in a condition of dramatic collapse, as though being propelled towards the very end of her mental, physical and emotional resources. In the first completed version of the novel, which the publishers asked Rhys to revise, Anna died aborting her child, and in the existing version the imagery of dying is still strong:

> The horse went forward with an exaggerated swaying lilting motion like a rocking-horse — I felt very sick — I heard the

concertina music playing behind me all the time and the noise
of the people's feet dancing — the street was in a greenish
shadow — I saw the rows of small houses — . . . — and then
the savannah — . . . — and then that turning where the shadow
is always the same shape — shadows are ghosts you look at them
and you don't see them — you look at everything and you don't
see it only sometimes you see it like now I see — a cold moon
looking down on a place where nobody is a place full of stones
where nobody is

I thought I'm going to fall nothing can save me now but still
I clung desperately with my knees feeling very sick.

'I fell,' I said. 'I fell for a hell of a long time then.'

'That's right,' Laurie said. 'When [the doctor] comes tell him
that.'

(*VID*, p. 158)

Abortions were of course risky in the 1930s, when *Voyage
in the Dark* is set, but there is a very powerful sense, in the
final section of this novel, that Anna is terminating more
than the child of a casual affair. This abortive birth releases
a particular, chanting voice which plangently relates the
impossibility of living in the present in the shadow of the
past; the impossibility of expressing emotion which is too
deeply felt to be articulable; the ghostliness of sustained
depression; the paralysis and incapacity which ultimately
result from trying consistently to forget. Like the black
woman who is found crying in the corridor and whose desolate story is related in *Good Morning Midnight* (pp. 79–81),
Anna is here 'at the end of everything'.

Though Jean Rhys was to sustain her technique of
juxtaposing past and present, loss and recollection,
throughout the novel which followed *Voyage in the Dark,
Good Morning Midnight*, she could not sustain the rich,
strong voice which she achieves in *Voyage in the Dark*. She
takes a consciousness of loss to its limits, in *Voyage in the
Dark*, so that in *Good Morning Midnight* the voice becomes
colder, bleaker, more cynical. At the end of this, her fourth
novel, she shows the heroine, Sasha Jensen, rejecting the
pathetic gigolo who has hung around throughout the story,
only to finally admit to her room a rather sinister gentleman
in a white dressing gown who lives in the adjoining room.
If the gigolo, who looked, in the end, as though even he

might be capable of easing loss and despair with passion, has
turned out to be cold and frightening and alien and alienating,
then White Dressing Gown, who looks as though he is all
these things, might turn out to be passionate and consoling.
Who knows. Who cares.[9]

The ending of *Good Morning Midnight* contains a brief,
seemingly incidental scenario which indicates the extent to
which Rhys's fourth heroine really is at the end of this
desolate process of remembering and forgetting, and it calls
up in addition — for the first and only time, in *Good
Morning Midnight* — the question of black and white
contrasts in such a way that Rhys's own passage from this
novel to *Wide Sargasso Sea* is suggested. Sasha and the gigolo
are on their way back to her room:

> In the taxi I say: 'Whistle that tune, will you? The one you said
> is the march of the Legion.'
> He whistles it very softly. And I watch the streets through the
> window. À l'Hôtel de l'Espérance. . . .
>
> *
>
> I am in a little whitewashed room. The sun is hot outside. A
> man is standing with his back to me, whistling that tune and
> cleaning his shoes. I am wearing a black dress, very short, and
> heel-less slippers. My legs are bare. I am watching for the
> expression on the man's face when he turns round. Now he ill-
> treats me, now he betrays me. He often brings home other
> women and I have to wait on them, and I don't like that. But
> as long as he is alive and near me I am not unhappy. If he were
> to die I should kill myself.
> My film-mind. . . . ('For God's sake watch out for your film-
> mind. . . .')
>
> (*GMM*, p. 147)

In her film-mind, Sasha suddenly, arbitrarily conjures up
for herself a vision of herself as a black woman — presumably
based on the story of the black woman, told earlier in *Good
Morning Midnight*, whose life has been one humiliating
exploitation after another. This is a salient little scenario,
which contrasts very starkly with the memories of the Caribbean related in *Voyage in the Dark*, which are all focused on

Anna's memories of being among the black women, and feeling at home with them. As a child, Anna remember,

> I was happy because Francine was there, and I watched her hand waving the fan backwards and forwards and the beads of sweat that rolled from underneath her handkerchief. Being black is warm and gay, being white is cold and sad.
>
> (VID, p. 27)

Jean Rhys herself wanted to believe this, right up to the end of her life. She was still protesting, during her late years, that the black people of her youth had not been treated badly by the English; she still wanted to remember them as her friends. In *Smile Please* she recalls 'a negro girl called Francine' with whom she was 'great friends' (p. 51), and could always remember, she tells David Plante, being kissed, once, in a café, by a Nigerian . . .

> and I understood, a little. I understand why they are attractive. It goes very deep. They danced, danced in the sunlight, and how I envied them.
>
> (Plante, p. 22)

'Black girls . . . seemed to be perfectly free.' (p. 51) The young Gwen Williams (Rhys's name by birth) would watch them through the jalousies on their way to mass, dressed in dramatic, colourful dresses with sweeping trains, and want to be black: 'They were more alive, more a part of the place than we were'. (p. 50) The black men were proud and dignified. She remembers, she tells David Plante . . .

> a black man in Dominica walking through the yard. My father and I were on the back steps of the house. My father made me give loaves of French bread — . . . — and sixpence to poor black men who came to us. No women ever came. I recall this black man walking away from us the loaf under his arm, and his dignity. His dignity and his unconquerable mind.
>
> (Plante, p. 19)

By contrast, white men seem devious, evasive, silently manipulative. Rhys's first memory, of her sixth birthday, focuses all this; it is, moreover, her first recollection of abandonment, desertion. In her honour, her brothers and sister staged a private production of *Red Riding Hood:*

> I was wearing the new white dress, a birthday present, and a wreath of frangipani. . . . The [wreath] I was wearing had been given to me first thing in the morning and there I was crowned, bursting with pride and importance, safe, protected, sitting in a large armchair, my father on one side, my mother on the other,. . . .
>
> Suddenly my eldest brother, who was playing an honest wood-cutter, if there is such a character, said in a bored voice, 'I'm not going on with this nonsense', and walked off the stage.
>
> (*SP*, p. 23)

Black men are honourable, dignified: they have a place, a home, even if it is elsewhere. Their minds are 'unconquerable', whilst the minds of white men are fickle, undependable. Their decisions are arbitrary, their use of language, even their actions, cannot be trusted. They are devious. On some deep level they seem not to belong: they are not of a piece with their surroundings, in the way that black people are.

Shock polarises; so does nostalgia. Being white is being disingenuous, sparing with affection; at once intrusive and fundamentally disengaged. Being black is fluid and yet rooted, generous and dignified, at once autonomous and interacting. Jean Rhys's own recollections of her Caribbean past, like Anna Morgan's, release a voice of sadness and regret, a warm engagement with ingenuous feeling; but, at the same time, they present black and white contrasts: being black is warm and gay, being white is cold and sad.

The insight released by the narrative of contrasting past and present in *Good Morning Midnight*, however, cuts through this juxtaposition. The artifice of narrative; the *imagination* of Sasha Jensen, for whom the capacity of sentimentality is completely burnt out, reveals another scenario, an image of black despair. The scene she conjures up is an image of emotional exploitation in which Sasha herself plays the part of a black woman. In the scene she envisages, being black is no longer warm and gay. Being a black woman, in some scenarios, might actually be no warmer or gayer than being a white woman. In some circumstances, it might even be worse. She remembers the black woman, found on the landing, whose voice had expressed complete despair, the termination of all hope, and she imagines herself in her position: 'He often brings home other women and I have to wait on them, and I don't like that. But as long as he is alive and near me I am not unhappy. If he were to die I should kill myself.' (*GMM*, p. 147)

This theme — of passion in the face of exploitation; the potential destructiveness of passion — is Jean Rhys's theme in *Wide Sargasso Sea*. It is a novel which issues out of a body of writing about loss and grief, desire and disappointment which, having its basis in a narrative technique based on a process of recollection, can itself discard this, because Jean Rhys's creative voice is now sufficiently powerful to express loss, passion and despair, in a linear narrative. It is as though by exploiting to the limits of her capacity her ability to express loss and grief, Rhys could then, in *Wide Sargasso Sea*, explore the full range of her imagination. As the letters relating to its progress reveal, this final novel was for Rhys a work of creative inspiration. In it she explores the potent and arresting *paradoxes* inherent in conditions of happiness and fear; grief and madness; passion and madness. It is a story which powerfully reveals the effects upon the mind of the kinds of exploitation historically inherent in gender difference. It tells of passion, and its capacity to affect mental states. It discovers what can happen when desire is met with coldness. In order to tell these things, Rhys developed an entirely new and plangent voice. *Wide Sargasso Sea* is the product of her 'film-mind'.

V

It should have been all a dream I know with start and finish present day. Or not?

(*Letters*, p. 216)

Wide Sargasso Sea, Jean Rhys told Francis Wyndham, 'should have been a dream — not a drama.'[10] Initially, it was to have been a madwoman's story, an experiment Rhys had begun several years previously, and then discarded. The mood of the book — its tone of voice — was to have resembled that of the original ending of *Voyage in the Dark*:

'time and place abolished, past and present the same', but then she remembered that 'everybody [had] said it was "confused and confusing — impossible to understand etc." ',[11] so she decided to start again, writing it 'as a story, a romance, but keeping the dream feeling and working up to the madness.'[12]

Though *Wide Sargasso Sea* is written in a linear narrative which moves relentlessly, powerfully forwards, it does nevertheless have a dream quality. From the beginning, it is as though there are strange forces at work within this story which drive the characters forcefully towards the final dénouement, and disaster. The symbolic imagery which Rhys had used at isolated moments in *After Leaving Mr Mackenzie* and *Voyage in the Dark* — the imagery of ghosts, and shadows, and light — permeates *Wide Sargasso Sea*. The excesses of light and landscape, the sudden, mysterious sunsets, penetrate the mind and emotions of Mr Rochester and, we are made to feel, perhaps turn his head; the cold, cardboard feeling of England is an appropriate setting for Antoinette's final incarceration.

In this powerful, prowling landscape, hemmed in by the dumb watchfulness of its people, it seems natural to be in perpetual search of shelter. You are hiding from the landscape, in which the power of the sun itself could easily kill you. It is beautiful and dangerous; powerful and obsessive and destructive, like Rochester's desire for Antoinette; this desire, and this landscape, are capable of destroying Rochester, too, but he is determined not to be conquered. He knows enough about power to know that it is manipulative, disingenuous:

> It was a beautiful place — wild, untouched, above all untouched, with an alien, disturbing, secret loveliness. And it kept its secret. I'd find myself thinking, 'What I see is nothing — I want what it *hides* — that is not nothing.'
>
> (*WSS*, p. 73)

The landscape of the Caribbean, and Antoinette herself — for Mr Rochester the two are indistinguishable — do have a secret, and in a very real sense it is the same secret. It is a secret contained in all Jean Rhys's novels, powerfully dramatised in this, her final full-length work, a secret to do with the relationship between love and fear, desire and dread, passion and destruction, history and the unconscious. The fundamental secret of this network of relationships is that you cannot penetrate it and remain entirely in control; you cannot love, or even desire, without being changed by forces you do not, at the time, entirely understand. But Mr Rochester, who is used to power, used to being in control, cannot know this.

Antoinette does know it. It is a knowledge which seems to be contained in the powerful, dream-like landscape she has grown up in. She knows it very deeply and unconsciously; it is knowledge which surfaces in her dreams, even as a very small child:

> I dreamed that I was walking in the forest. Not alone. Someone who hated me was with me, out of sight. I could hear heavy footsteps coming closer and though I struggled and screamed I could not move. I woke crying. The covering sheet was on the floor and my mother was looking down at me.
>
> (*WSS*, p. 23)

Rhys has used this imagery of the forest before, in the early memory described in *After Leaving Mr Mackenzie*, where it heralded the loss and guilt of separation. It has the same connotations here, but as a dream it takes on an additional resonance, a portentous quality in keeping with the mood or voice of *Wide Sargasso Sea*. Just before her marriage, Antoinette has the dream again. This time she is dressed in white, walking with difficulty, following the man who accompanies her:

> I follow him, sick with fear but I make no effort to save myself; if anyone were to try to save me, I would refuse. This must happen. Now we have reached the forest. We are under the tall dark trees and there is no wind. 'Here?' He turns and looks at me, his face black with hatred, and when I see this I begin to cry. He smiles slyly. 'Not here, not yet,' he says, and I follow him, weeping. Now I do not try to hold up my dress, it trails in the dirt, my beautiful dress. We are no longer in the forest but in an enclosed garden surrounded by a stone wall and the trees are different trees. I do not know them. There are steps

leading upwards. It is too dark to see the wall or the steps, but I know they are there and I think, 'It will be when I go up these steps. At the top.' I stumble over my dress and cannot get up. I touch a tree and my arms hold on to it. 'Here, here.' But I think I will not go any further. The tree sways and jerks as if it is trying to throw me off. Still I cling and the seconds pass and each one is a thousand years. 'Here, in here', a strange voice said, and the tree stopped swaying and jerking.

(*WSS*, p. 50)

There is both premonition and recollection in this. The knowledge that this man will take her right to the summit of her passions and that this will ultimately destroy her is strong; so, too, obliquely, is the identification with the insidious power of place. The man's face is 'black with hatred': her own skirt trails in the dirt, as the black women's do. It is a matter of pride to them: 'they don't care about getting a dress dirty because it shows it isn't the only dress they have' (p. 71), but Antoinette, in her dream, only has one dress, just as she only had one dress when the Luttrell family visited Coulibri, prior to her mother's marrying Mr Mason. (p. 22) There was only one chance for her mother to climb out of the poverty of her widowhood in Coulibri, and she took it. But Mr Mason, through his ignorance of the black people and their capacity to contain rage and resentment, had let them burn Coulibri. The English understand nothing about this landscape; the dream is a dream of Hell (p. 51); but Antoinette marries Mr Rochester, because he can release her from all this: he can take her to England. Or to Heaven.

The dream is a dream of death, or of release, and the mind of Antoinette roams ceaselessly over these two landscapes. Mr Rochester is aware of this, of course: she is always either sleepy or imagining. When she is sleepy she speaks of death and her voice is troubling, portentous:

at night how different, even her voice was changed. Always this talk of death. (Is she trying to tell me that is the secret of this place? That there is no other way? She knows. She knows.) . . .

'If I could die. Now, when I am happy. Would you do that?

You wouldn't have to kill me. Say die and I will die. You don't believe me? Then try, say die and watch me die.'

'Die then! Die!' I watched her die many times. In my way, not in hers. In sunlight, in shadow, by moonlight, by candlelight. . . . Very soon she was as eager for what's called loving as I was — more lost and drowned afterwards.'

(*WSS*, pp. 76–7)

He is maddened by her, impassioned by her, rather than in love with her. She evades him, always. She would question him about England and he would tell her the answers, but 'nothing [he] said made much difference. Her mind was already made up' (p. 78), and her ideas about England are based on fiction:

Some romantic novel, a stray remark never forgotten, a sketch, a picture, a song, a waltz, some note of music, and her ideas were fixed.

(*WSS*, p. 78)

This inability to penetrate her mind obsesses him; makes him more, not less, passionate: 'One afternoon the sight of a dress which she'd left lying on her bedroom floor made me breathless and savage with desire. When I was exhausted I turned away from her and slept, still without a word or caress'. (p. 78) But the power of this kind of desire is of a piece with the landscape: the more obsessed with her he becomes, the stronger the power of *place* becomes for him, so that he, like she, becomes drowned in its light and shadow, its destructive powers.

It is this awe-inspiring respect for the Caribbean landscape which informs the powerful paradoxical forces that sustain *Wide Sargasso Sea* and which makes the book feel like a tremendous homage to the West Indies, while Rhys is at the same time writing powerfully about the destructive forces which drive its people. Rhys drafted and re-drafted the novel, striking every time at Mr Rochester — 'Dreadful man, but I tried to be fair and all that, and give some *reason* for his acting like he did.'[13] The truth is, of course, that Mr Rochester marries Antoinette for her dowry and gradually destroys her by believing the local stories about the madness in her family. He is frightened by these stories, and his fear

257

makes him cold. By giving him a love potion to draw him back to her, Antoinette destroys not only him but herself, but Antoinette's mental destruction has happened already, in her childhood, when the local people burned her house, and her black friend, Tia, betrayed and injured her.

For a long time, Jean Rhys's Mr Rochester was a cruel and wealthy man:[14] with such a hero, the book would not 'click into place', despite Rhys's guiding idea: to present a sympathetic white Creole heroine, whose mental history would justify her eventual madness. Significantly, the landscape itself — and Jean Rhys's immersion in it, as she relentlessly wrote and rewrote this novel, eventually released the clue which pulled the writing up out of its basis in an idea of exploitation and infused the paradoxes which inform the published text. Rhys wrote a poem — as she was in the habit of doing, for recreation or to create a breathing space — which seemed strangely to speak in a tone of voice which communicated to her the novel's complexity of meaning. It is a poem — a song, really, all Rhys's poems are songs — about a man madly in love with a Creole girl who disappears 'after the obeah nights'. It is entitled 'Obeah Night', and it reminded Rhys, suddenly, of a conjunction of forces recognised by the Obeah, or Voodoo, practices traditional to the Caribbean Islands. At the same time, Rhys's editor, Diana Athill, fortuitously suggested 'a few weeks of happiness for the unfortunate couple'[15] before Mr Rochester starts receiving letters telling him of his wife's madness. The conjunction released a powerful and important memory for Rhys:

As soon as I wrote that bit I realised that he must have fallen for her — and violently too. The black people have or had a good word for it — 'she *magic* with him' or 'he *magic* with her'. Because you see, that is what it is — magic, intoxication. Not 'love' at all. There is too the magic of the place, . . . — it can be a very disturbing kind of beauty.

(*Letters*, p. 262)

Passion issues from an imaginary place — from desire, and dream, and recollection. The power of this novel is in Rhys's instinctive depiction of a landscape which exactly echoes the psychological resonances of the relationship for which it acts as a setting. The power of Mr Rochester is that he — in a way that Rhys did *not* specifically plan — is so subject to this conjunction of meanings which he cannot grasp, that he, along with Antoinette, is destroyed by the conjunction of geographical and psychological landscapes, which has him in its thrall. At the end, he has lost as much as Antoinette has lost:

> I hated the mountains and the hills, the rivers and the rain. I hated the sunsets of whatever colour, I hated its beauty and its magic and the secret I would never know. I hated its indifference and the cruelty which was part of its loveliness. Above all I hated her. For she belonged to the magic and the loveliness. She had left me thirsty and all my life would be thirst and longing for what I had lost before I found it.
>
> (*WSS*, p. 141)

Mr Rochester makes a kind of escape — he retreats to England, and incarcerates his wife. But we know from the servant Leah's account that 'his stay in the West Indies has changed him out of all knowledge. He has grey in his hair and misery in his eyes' (p. 145). By contrast, there is a profound, if symbolic, sense in which Antoinette triumphs. She triumphs by dreaming for the third time, and, this time, by meeting herself in her dream, and by knowing what she must do. The final dream, of setting cardboard England alight, takes her right back to the beginning. In it, she retrieves all the symbolism, not only of Coulibri, the house of her childhood, but also that of all the interior, symbolic narratives of Rhys's earlier novels of loss. She conquers loss; ignites it so that grieving feels like passion; and burns down all the partitions in her head which have prevented her from seeing herself, and from recognising the implications of her own desires.

The ghostly presence of all Rhys's anaesthetised heroines — all the women at the limits of distress — is met and recognised and framed in flames (the original title for the novel was to be *Le Revenant* — 'The Ghost'):

> . . . I laughed when I saw the lovely colour spreading so fast, but I did not stay to watch it. I went into the hall again with the tall candle in my hand. It was then that I saw her — the

ghost. The woman with streaming hair. She was surrounded by a gilt frame but I knew her.

(*WSS*, p. 154)

What she sees, of course, is the reflection of herself, and this image releases a conflagration of recollections:

> Then I turned round and saw the sky. It was red and all my life was in it. . . . I saw the orchids and the stephanotis and the jasmine and the tree of life in flames. . . . I heard the parrot call . . . , *Qui est là? Qui est là?* and the man who hated me was calling too, Bertha! Bertha! The wind caught my hair and it streamed out like wings. It might bear me up, I thought, if I jumped to those hard stones. But when I looked over the edge I saw the pool at Coulibri. Tia was there. She beckoned to me and when I hesitated, she laughed. I heard her say, You frightened? And I heard the man's voice, Bertha! Bertha! All this I saw and heard in a fraction of a second. And the sky so red.
>
> (*WSS*, p. 155)

The imagery of childhood landscapes, loss, and remembered dream is all here, and the contiguity of Tia — the black friend who had betrayed her, injuring her with a stone — and the man of the earlier dream, suggests another insight. She had been promised, in childhood, that the wound from the stone would not spoil her for her wedding day (p. 39); but it had spoiled her. Loss and disappointment and betrayal had prepared her for destruction, and this is what her marriage has brought her to.

It is all a rehearsal, this dream-premonition, this symbolic narrative of triumph by igniting and destroying the power of the past. Waking from her dream, Antoinette is clear, now, about why she has been brought to England:

> Now at last I know why I was brought here and what I have to do. There must have been a draught for the flame flickered and I thought it was out. But I shielded it with my hand and it burned up again to light me along the dark passage.
>
> (*WSS*, pp. 155–6)

But as fiction, this ritual of burning is real: the climax and culmination of the novel, and of all Jean Rhys's writing.

Rhys's technical brilliance is in taking us right to the end, in taking loss to its limits and in fusing it with passion and symbolic survival, and then leaving us right at the edge. We feel, perhaps, if this writing works at all for us, that in reading *Wide Sargasso Sea* we have been put under Jean Rhys's spell; that symbolic meanings affect us as profoundly as 'real', or realistic meanings. We feel, perhaps, that this woman's writing has some magical quality, some power to penetrate to the very depths of loss, of sexuality, and of some mysterious and pervasive connection between these things. Reading *about* Jean Rhys can give us the same feeling: that somehow, her writing was *magic* for her. She told David Plante, her confidant and himself a writer, 'Only writing is important. Only writing takes you out of yourself.'[16] He asked her,

'Do you ever think of the meaning of what you write?'
'No. No. . . . You see, I'm a pen. I'm nothing but a pen.'
'And do you imagine yourself in some-one else's hand?'
Tears came to her eyes. 'Of course. Of course. It's only then that I know I'm writing well. Not really true, not as fact. But true as writing.'

(Plante, p. 31)

The 'magic' process is her justification, her centre; it constitutes her own kind of grip, her own articulation of responsibility as well as of desire. It is, for Jean Rhys, what art is made of, and the only way to be. Let alone, to be a woman.

Notes

Jean Rhys published five novels:
   Quartet (Q) (Simon & Schuster, New York, 1928). Published in England as *Postures* (Chatto & Windus, London, 1928; Penguin Books, Harmondworth, Middx., 1973). Page references are to the Penguin edition.
   After Leaving Mr Mackenzie (ALMM) (Cape, London, 1930; Penguin Books, Harmondsworth, Middx., 1971). Page references are to the Penguin edition.
   Voyage in the Dark (VID) (Constable, London, 1934; Penguin Books, Harmondsworth, Middx., 1969). Page references are to the

Penguin edition.

Good Morning Midnight (*GMM*) (Constable, London, 1939; Penguin Books, Harmondsworth, Middx., 1969). Page references are to the Penguin edition.

Wide Sargasso Sea (*WSS*) (Deutsch, London, 1966: Penguin Books, Harmondsworth, Middx., 1968). Page references are to the Penguin edition.

1. *Quartet*, p. 28.
2. David Plante, *Difficult Women: A Memoir of Three* (Futura, London, 1983), p. 22.
3. Phyllis Rose, *Writing of Women: Essays in a Renaissance* (Wesleyan University Press, Connecticut, 1985), p. 103.
4. P. A. Packer, 'The Four Early Novels of Jean Rhys', *The Durham University Journal* (June, 1979), 255. (Repr. in *A Critical Perspective on Jean Rhys*, ed. P. M. Frickey (Washington, 1985).
5. Carole Angier, *Jean Rhys*, in the 'Lives of Modern Women' series, ed. Emma Tennant (Penguin, London, 1985), p. 34.
6. Plante, *op cit.*, p. 26. *Smile Please: An Unfinished Autobiography*, Intro. Diana Athill (Penguin Books, Harmondsworth, Middx., 1981).
7. 'Let Them Call It Jazz' (1961), in *Tigers Are Better-Looking* (Penguin Books, Harmondsworth, Middx., 1982; first published, 1968), p. 60.
8. *Ibid.*, p. 63.
9. Louis James interprets this differently, in *Jean Rhys*, in the 'Critical Studies of Caribbean Writers' series, ed. Mervyn Morris (Longman, London, 1978), pp. 28–9. He identifies the entry of the lover with the return of the gigolo and sees the incident as 'a profound statement about the nature of compassion.' But I think the lover's dressing gown in fact identifies him as the neighbour (see *GMM*, p. 13; 159).
10. *Jean Rhys: Letters, 1931–1966*, edited by Francis Wyndham and Diana Melly (Deutsch, London, 1984), p. 216, Wednesday, 12 September 1962, to Francis Wyndham.
11. *Ibid.*, p. 233, Friday 16 August, 1963, to Diana Athill.
12. *Ibid.*
13. *Ibid.*
14. *Ibid.*, p. 262, 14 April 1964, to Francis Wyndham.
15. *Ibid.*
16. Plante, p. 50.

10

The Strange Necessity of Rebecca West

Bonnie Kime Scott

For Emma Stewart

I shut the bookshop door behind me and walked slowly down the street that leads from the Odéon to the Boulevard Saint-Germain in the best of all cities, reading in the little volume which had there been sold to me, not exactly pretentiously, indeed with a matter-of-fact briskness, yet with a sense of there being something on hand different from an ordinary commercial transaction: as they sell pious whatnots in a cathedral porch. Presently I stopped. I said 'Ah!' and smiled up into the clean French light. My eye lit on a dove that was bridging the tall houses by its flight, and I felt that interior agreement with its grace, that delighted participation in its experience, which is only possible when one is in a state of pleasure.[1]

This first paragraph of 'The Strange Necessity' (1928) was my introduction to Rebecca West (her original name, Cicely Fairfield). The 'I' is a fictional persona, but I thought of her as very close to the writer who created her. Simultaneously, and collision-free, she manages to be both a reader and a traverser of Paris during the critical years of modernism. She is observant of human exchanges, of a dove in flight and of her own emotional state. Her purchase gets close critical analysis, a series of descriptive approximations ending in a witty, independent, apt analogy. The intellectual work prepares an aesthetic, spiritual, renewing experience, her participation in the 'grace' of the dove.[2] Her use of 'one' implies shared experience with me, her reader. I had picked up 'The Strange Necessity' because it was supposed to be about James Joyce. The 'pious whatnot' is his *Pomes Penyeach*, which this iconoclastic young woman later faults as sentimental and lacking in taste. Already I was captivated by her active, amusing, feeling and reasoning mind; she went on, thinking her way through Joyce, Pavlov, Pruna and Ingres, simultaneously delighting in Paris, buying hats and dresses, and attending a luncheon. Here was a rediscovered model — a dynamic, outspoken female intellectual, serving as critic of literature and life. Her being female seemed an asset in my brief sample, first read in 1980. Why hadn't I heard more about her? How much more was there to find? What was her relationship to the literary age of Joyce? Had her female gender affected her writing and career? I was aware that West had special command over me as a female reader. I wondered whether she might be taken as a representative of female modernism, and specifically, how she might be related to a female sub-culture in her life, her literary criticism, and her imaginative work. My questioning placed me in a group of feminist critics Elaine Showalter has called the 'gynocritics'.[3]

There emerged several explanations for my unfamiliarity with Rebecca West, some of them related to her position as a woman writer. She was better known to my British colleages. Until her death in 1983, Rebecca West published reviews regularly in *The Sunday Telegraph*, while her activity in American periodicals like *The New Yorker* had dwindled before I read them. In the 1920s and 30s, when she was a frequent sojourner here, Americans knew her better. Some of her countrymen dismissed her to me as a 'grande dame' a role that might come with the title 'Dame Rebecca', given to her in 1959. It was not a role she played with me when we had tea in 1981. Another basis for dismissal was her politics, which since the 1930s moved from socialism and feminism to anti-communism. But far more reactionary male modernists (Pound, Eliot, Lewis and Yeats) had not been similarly dismissed.

In the 1920s and 30s she participated actively in debates about the nature of tradition and the modern in literature, challenging the authority of T. S. Eliot and the prescriptive humanism of Paul Elmer More and Irving Babbit.[4] But her essays had not made it into the text books. The critical anthology I used as a student, *The Modern Tradition* (1965), made no mention of her. But it devoted only 8¼ pages to women writers and critics. Rebecca West also missed out through her versatility. Many of her best critical judgments reside in works that can be assigned to the unfashionable genres of journalism and travel literature. Her experiments (including the female narrative persona) depart from the form of the well-made essay. Her fiction is highly varied — some neatly plotted and straightforwardly realistic; some decidedly modernist. Finally, the unavailability of many of West's papers — in restricted collections or awaiting sale — complicates the process of knowing her well, even today.

West's gender and her feminism disconcerted many of the earliest framers of her literary reputation, nearly all of them male. West herself expected 'a first crop of sniggers at the "ladies" and the exquisite humours of their attempts at criticism' when she lashed out at Babbit and More, but I think she expected that to end.[5] In 1926 Patrick Braybrooke became distressed at West's 'attacks' on men and advised paternally, ' . . . Miss West would do very well to be beware [*sic*] of the newspapers', and of becoming 'a kind of woman, to whom the Editors of the cheaper press write, when they wish to secure an article that is merely written to cause correspondence'.[6] G. E. Hutchinson recalls that 'The Strange Necessity' 'was praised as brilliant or damned as pseudoscientific, and then returned to the bookcase, for a critical work by a woman would obviously not be of lasting significance'.[7]

The discomfort with West's feminism and her identification with a female writing tradition persists. N. Gordon Ray excuses the feminism of West's early writing for *The Freewoman:* 'If she . . . expounded feminist doctrine with an assurance amounting to fanaticism, this was after all what subscribers to the *Freewoman* expected for their three pennies; no doubt she had her private reservations.' Ray also claims that West 'lost her faith in the suffrage cause', citing an article critical of Christabel Pankhurst.[8] In fact West questioned violent means and sexual Puritanism, but not suffrage. She sustained her feminism, especially economic and class aspects, as a writer for the radical socialist journal, *The Clarion.*

Samuel Hynes, as editor of *The Essential Rebecca West* (*Rebecca West: A Celebration* in the U.S.), sees West affirmatively as an androgynous writer. He cites West's statement, 'There have as yet been very few women thinkers and artists, that is to say, women who have not adopted masculine values as the basis of their work'. But his interpretation (I think incorrectly) takes as West's 'point' that it is 'not that women artists should be explicitly and exclusively feminine, but rather that, they should be free to realize their gifts without considering the roles that social definitions of gender impose'. This overlooks the implication I detect in West's statement, that alternative values — as experienced by women, not as recorded in social stereotypes — might enrich thinking and art. Hynes eagerly extricates West from the identity of 'the woman novelist', assigning Virginia Woolf to the category, as have many male critics of his generation. His reasons for respecting 'The Strange Necessity' could be identified as stereotypically 'masculine'. He applauds its movement from an opening worthy of Woolf (the opening that had attracted me) to a level of intellectual toughness and knowledge where Virginia Woolf could never have followed — 'It is as though Dame Rebecca were acting out her liberation from the stereotypes of her sex, showing us how a free mind might play upon ideas'.[9] Hynes finds West's greatest creativity, not in her feminist youth, and not in works of comparable idiom to Woolf's but in the late 1930s, beginning with the publication of *Black Lamb and Grey Falcon* (1937), and his 'essential' collection reflects this. Hynes likes works in which West radiates 'authority'. He detects wide world vision in West's faith that 'law' preserves cultural order. In *The Black Lamb and Grey Falcon*, West's persona has become a wife. This brings what may seem ironic comfort to one critic, Peter Wolfe, who like Hynes prefers West's late novels. Wolfe comments approvingly that the work 'could do duty as a marriage manual' and observes that West 'credits most of the book's best insights to' her husband.[10]

Hutchinson (whose wariness of sexist critical judgments we have noted) compares West's working with a dialectic of antinomies to the best tradition of British empiricism, 'whose tools . . . are continually modified . . . to handle new situations'.[11] What Hutchinson does not suspect is that a muted tradition of female reasoning, emphasising process and question rather than result (as in the epigraph and in Woolf's mental monologues), may be functioning as well.

The works of Rebecca West have recently been divided on gender lines, women critics embracing the early West that seemed less essential to male critics. The articles and reviews of the young West have been collected and expertly introduced by Jane Marcus, who is a feminist critic and a Woolf scholar.[12] The feminist Virago Press reprinted West's early novels — *The Return of the Soldier* (1918), *The Judge* (1922), and *Harriet Hume: A London Fantasy* (1929) — plus seven other volumes, but not *Black Lamb and Grey Falcon*. West chose as her first biographer Victoria Glendinning, who has specialised in biographies of modern women writers, including Elizabeth Bowen and Vita Sackville-West. Already a different West is emerging through contemporary women's researches.

A gynocritical approach to West can be challenged as deterministic and separatist, and certainly does not represent the only possible feminist approach to West, or to texts. My intention is not to remove West from a specious world of androgynous balance (perhaps only a fantasy world at that), but to expand our sense of her world into the underexplored regions of female sub-culture, noting her unique responses and strategies in that territory. The problematics of West's relationship to other women teach us much about her period, and are especially appropriate to a collection specialising in the reader–writer relationship of women. A compelling justification is that West used the category of gender incessantly in her writings, and was willing to identify herself in collective considerations of women — women writers, women in educational systems or in social classes.

Rebecca West's early family life offered diverse experiences of marginality (the essential position of females in relation to culture). Although she is usually designated an English writer, West liked to cite provincial origins. Her mother, Isabella Campbell MacKenzie Fairfield, 'was Scotch—Highland Scotch, which means that her family had only recently acquired the art of speaking English as their native language'. Her father, Charles Fairfield, was Anglo-Irish, and both parents had lived abroad for extended periods.[13] The family survived on narrow means in London until West was about ten, when her father withdrew to Liverpool, where he died. Isabella Fairfield, a stable, strong-minded, musically talented woman, re-established her household of three daughters in her native Edinburgh, and later back in London. *The Foun-*

tain Overflows (1956) is generally autobiographical, and
evokes a lonely childhood with few female friends besides
her older sisters, who soon went on to professions. Her
position as a strong but solitary woman seems to have
continued at George Watson's Ladies College, which she
attended only to the age of fifteen. Her criticisms of the
institution demonstrate early concern for women's collective
interests, however. She condemned the socialisation of
women into 'lady-like pessimists' content with humble work,
and identified an 'unacknowledged politics of sex-subordi-
nation'. (*YR*, pp. 154–5)

For her own lessons on life, West turned to a female
resource, the suffragist movement. Work for the W.S.P.U.
in Edinburgh and feminist journalism in London provided
West with centres for female association. The early pages of
The Judge record young Ellen Melville's attraction, tempered
with criticism, to suffragettes in Edinburgh, and her essays
recall selling suffrage literature alongside her sister. In
London, she was drawn to *The Freewoman*, brainchild of
Mary Gawthorpe, Grace Jardine, Rona Robinson and its
editor, Dora Marsden. She admired the journal's loud, clear,
repeated mentions of sex, and its shattering of romantic
conceptions of women in favour of straightforward reports
of real-life conditions. Though she resisted Marsden's pastor-
alism, she found her personally attractive, admiring her as
'brilliant in mind, saintly in character and exquisitely glamorous'. Marsden's combination of 'flower-like delicacy and
staunch resistance, even in prison' (*YR*, pp. 154–5)[14] may
have contributed to Harriet Hume, a fragile but relentless
character in West's fantasy novel of 1929. The poet H.D.
and the literary patron Harriet Shaw Weaver also staffed *The
Freewoman*. Ironically, it was West who brought Ezra Pound
to *The New Freewoman* (a later name for the journal). This
diminished the journal's feminism and its female adminis-
tration. In speaking with me, West regretted that her generation had not achieved a true feminist literary journal.
Instead, women writers and their feminist interpretations
were scattered in liberal and avant-garde publications of the
day. But West seems never to have limited herself to female
colleagues; it seems typical of her to have met and wished to
work with a man like Pound.

Rebecca West's most celebrated relationship was with another challenging man, H. G. Wells. Interestingly, it arose from sex-related criticism of his novel, *Marriage* in *The Freewoman*. West called him 'the old maid among novelists', displaying 'the reaction towards the flesh of a mind too long absorbed in airships and colloids'. (*YR*, p. 64) The iconoclastic remark seems to have posed a sexual challenge to Wells, who worked out a meeting that led in time to their ten-year intimacy; in August 1914 their illegitimate son, Anthony West, was born. These new relationships with males strained West's access to a female network. She left *The New Freewoman* partially because of pregnancy. Wells settled West and her newborn son in a variety of rustic locations convenient to himself. West's mother did not readily accept her daughter's new position, and their strong relationship diminished, though her sister Letty (a physician) attended at the birth and remained supportive. Wells represented Isabella Fairfield as a menace to their relationship, and discouraged her visits, and those of West's sisters and a friend from suffragette days, Wilma Meikle. Even West's relations with female servants were strained by Wells' desire for anonymity and the servants' sense of the irregularity of the ménage.[15] There is considerable irony in West's dependence on Wells, since she had originally identified the problem of 'parasitic' women in her review of Wells' *Marriage*, disparaging his capacity to accept it as 'the normal condition of women'. (*YR*, pp. 65–6) After 1930, when she married Henry Maxwell Andrews and settled into travels with him and residence at their country home, Rebecca West was again occupied by an alliance to a man.

It must be left to her biographers to give us a thorough knowledge of West's female contexts, especially her friendships with female intellectuals. Virginia Woolf, Katherine Mansfield, Elizabeth Bowen, Vita Sackville-West, Ottoline Morrell, Dorothy Richardson — all had husbands, but worked out strategies for exclusive meetings with good women friends; we have less evidence of this for West. She did know other women writers, especially when living independently in America. Victoria Glendinning lists Fanny Hurst, Dorothy Thompson, Doris Stevens and Emanie Arling as American writer friends, and G. B. Stern and

Pamela Frankau as English colleagues.[16] West met with women occasionally for literary dinners and talk. She gives an amusing description of modern women writers, contrasting their 'height and force and mass' to her mother's ornamental style. Speaking of herself, Stern and others, she concludes, 'Our nearest equivalent in charm was, perhaps a group of factory chimneys in a northern draw or an assembly of Fords at a parking place.'[17] The picture was unflattering, but preferable, and suggests modern women's productivity. Despite this apparent feeling of sisterhood, West intimidated women like Ethel Mannin:

> Admiring her in so many ways, her looks, her wit, her intellect, her vivacity, I wish I knew her really well — but she is not easy to know, and she appears to dislike more people than she likes. She has a mind like a sword-blade and a tongue like a whip. I feel that she would have to like and admire and respect one very much indeed before one could ever hope to get close to her.[18]

I find West's relationship personally and professionally with Virginia Woolf intriguing, not because it was close (it wasn't), but because it offers a range of female temperament, social status, and sexual experience, and brings West into conjunction with a central figure in both modernist and female literary traditions. Woolf was a less solitary woman. Her female friendships, though still problematic, seem to have been more plentiful, intimate and even passionate than West's, and her fine published letters and diaries make them accessible. Woolf explored her reactions to West, typically with female correspondents. She writes to Rosamund Lehmann that West is a 'nice woman', but 'is rather fierce, and I expect has some bone she gnaws in secret, perhaps about having a child by Wells. I couldn't ask her. Perhaps you could'.[19] The inquiry may indicate not just curiosity but empathy and a desire to provide support. Woolf followed West's more activist style of feminism with interest. Though she stayed home, she felt she should have attended a speech by West at Westminster concerning the married women's right to earn. As she put it, she was glad to have West as 'a buffeter and battler' who 'has taken waves . . . and can talk in any language'.[20] Another perceived difference was West's 'celebrity', which gave Woolf, like Mannin, a sense of limited access and a feeling of timidity. Woolf admits that she feels 'enormously wise' when convalescing in a garden, but not when talking to West. Still, they had some enjoyable all-female meetings. Woolf describes one to the sceptical Ottoline Morrell, turning West's animal-like qualities to assets:

> Rebecca was fascinating — ungainly, awkward, powerful, arborial like some sloth or mandrill; but oh what a joy to grapple with her hairy arms! I mean she was very upstanding and outspoken, and we discussed religion, sex, literature and other problems, violently, in a roar, to catch Ethel's ear, for three hours. [Ethel Smythe was deaf.] This is to corroborate my view, and in opposition to yours.[21]

West satisfies Woolf's love of talk, and moves her to uncharacteristic grappling and violence of discussion, the subjects including sex. West is more tolerable than Doris Kilman, whose feminist evangelism unsettles Woolf's Mrs Dalloway. She is not suspected of writing from only the 'virile' side of the brain, as was the 'he-goat' James Joyce.[22] As a physically and mentally 'powerful' woman, West may offer one version of the androgyny Woolf sought. Woolf's most unflattering descriptions may disclose discomfort with the sexually experienced individual, and suspicion of cultural vulgarity and modern, public, opulent flashiness, the latter attributed partly to Henry Andrews' wealth.[23] But Woolf is weighing the differences in West's identity, not just practising devastating wit. West was the only contemporary woman writer named in Woolf's study of women authors, *A Room of One's Own*. She appreciates West for assigning snobbery on the basis of male gender; the original enraged reaction of Desmond MacCarthy is recorded, as if by West's ally.[24]

Unlike many of her male contemporaries, West did not consider Woolf a Bloomsbury snob. But West felt they were not 'twin souls', and was hurt by the descriptions of her in the diaries. Even here there is likeness, however. West practised the same sharp, unflattering physical description of the young author Elizabeth Jenkins in letters to Woolf.[25] Clothing, rooms, food, and the class connotations of geographical locations were semiotics held in common, with devastating wit providing much of the life.

In her profession, West felt it desirable to promote other women writers whose work she valued, though the structure of the publishing world made this difficult. One limitation was the simple fact that West could review only the books editors sent her.[26] Her criteria for women authors are similar to hers for men, and include style, imagination, character portrayal, philosophical depth and attitudes towards women. She denounces Mary Humphry Ward early and often for anti-feminism and weakness of philosophical content. (*YR*, pp. 14–17) She repeatedly reproaches Edith Wharton and Ann Douglas Sedgwick for shallow, egotistical heroines. West defends Radclyffe Hall against censorship of her lesbian novel, *The Well of Loneliness*, but criticises her for sentimentally playing for readers' reactions rather than imaginatively recreating experience. Katherine Mansfield, Olive Schreiner (*YR*, p. 73) and George Eliot all have troublesome shortcomings for West.[27]

West gave some rave notices to women writers. Violet Hunt (a personal friend during her Wells era) and May Sinclair were hailed as geniuses for individual books. Interestingly, their strong points concern women. West praises Hunt's particularly keen representation of Victorian girlhood in *Their Lives*. (*YR*, p. 355) In May Sinclair's *A Journal of Impressions in Belgium* she finds an unusual war account, possible only from a female perspective and thus valuable to female readers. West appreciates its meticulous descriptions of 'what writers more accustomed to the battlefield' omit. Sinclair also 'writes of such a company of heroes as never lived before: of girls of nineteen who trudge over turnipfields among the bullets to look for the wounded, not in any sudden flame of courage, but as a daily occupation: of women who stayed in Antwerp at their posts until the red skies fell in on them'. (*YR*, p. 305) West's admiration of Emily Brontë's *Wuthering Heights* is based upon its transcendence of prose norms (a quality she likes in Woolf and Mansfield as well) and upon the male vs. female binary — a Byronic male vs. a redemptive, slain goddess.[28] West defends Jane Austen against critics who trivialise her. She respects Austen's sensitivity to the politics of social inequality, a pattern embracing male–female relationships as well as economics.[29]

Virginia Woolf regularly received West's praise as a nurturer of tradition, a poet in prose and a feminist. West articulated Woolf's departure from the realistic tradition of the novel in her review of *Jacob's Room* (1922), declaring her 'at once a negligible novelist and a supremely important writer'. West notes qualities that realists have held against Woolf — her failure to chart 'the long drive of the human will' (a course West followed) and a lack of 'individualised characters'. But she appreciates Woolf's creation of a 'portfolio' more typical of the 'pictorial arts'.[30]

As a fantasy of modern history, Woolf's *Orlando* (1928) takes on a theme of heroic proportions, according to West. It qualifies as poetry since it 'illuminates an important part of human experience by using words to do more than describe the logical behaviour of matter, by letting language by its music and its power to evoke images convey meanings too subtle and too profound to be formulated in intellectual statements'. West anticipates the discussions of the androgynous mind in *A Room of One's Own* and modern neuroscience by saying Woolf writes with the whole brain: 'her left lobe (which is critical) is obviously without cease letting her right lobe (which is creative) know what it doeth'. West is also interested in issues of gender presented in *Orlando*:

> People who like literalism will be most irritated, no doubt, by the passages in which Orlando changes her sex. . . . She is debating in these passages how far one's sex is like a pair of faulty glasses on one's nose; where one looks at the universe, how true it is that to be a woman is to have a blind spot in the North Northwest, to be a man is to see light as darkness East by South.[31]

West salutes *A Room of One's Own* (1929) as 'an uncompromising piece of feminist propaganda; I think the ablest yet written'. The review makes an interesting comment upon the anxieties over gender of the modernist era — a pattern rediscovered in recent work by Susan Gubar and Sandra Gilbert.[32] West finds Woolf 'brave and defiant because anti-

feminism is the correct fashion of the day among the intellectuals', the phenomenon part of 'the rising tide of effeminacy
which has been so noticed since the war'. Woolf's defiance
is celebrated as part of the cycle of traditional renewal, akin
to the seasons, a favourite image in West's imaginative
criticism.[33]

West's most interesting comments on *The Waves* concerns
its philosophical form and interest. She compares its counter-
assertions to Platonic dialogues and notes that Woolf, like
Lawrence and Joyce, examined the unexplored dimensions of
human experience. Woolf moved philosophy beyond sterile
concepts of the will, and poetry beyond the celebration of
static existence into the 'most private emotions', a realm
where traditional syntax and vocabulary fail.[34] Virginia Woolf
is always among the moderns publicised by West. At her
most experimental, where she evokes fantasy and movement
or images of the mind ('The Strange Necessity', *Harriet
Hume* and *A Letter to a Grandfather* — the last published
by the Woolfs), West resembles her stylistically.

Despite supportive reviews of women's books, Rebecca
West chose male writers and philosophers for her longer
monograph and book-length studies: *Henry James* (1916), *D.
H. Lawrence* (1930), *Arnold Bennett* (1931) and *St Augustine*
(1933). *The Court and the Castle*, reflecting the dominance
of males in literary tradition, features Shakespeare, Fielding,
Thackeray, Trollope, Dickens, Hardy, Meredith, James,
Kipling, Kafka and Proust; Austen alone among women gets
comparable notice. West's admiration for Woolf is tempered
by her judgment that Lawrence and Joyce went farther in
exploring the self.[35] In her two collections of reviews, West
selected very few on women writers, and only one of the
several good ones on Woolf. This may have reflected
publishers' assessments of the reading public, of course.

I want to turn next to West's own creation of female
character, and its impact upon a female reader. In *A Room
of One's Own*, Virginia Woolf encourages us to look for
female relationships in modern prose by women writers. She
delights at reading how 'Chloe liked Olivia', how they
worked together, their 'gestures, those unsaid or half-said
words, which form themselves, no more palpably than the
shadows of moths on the ceiling, when women are alone,

unlit by the capricious and coloured light of the other sex'.[36]
The reader rarely visits this 'vast, untouched chamber' of
experience through Rebecca West, whose heroines are usually
solitary or in male company. Where West's women do bond,
it is usually in the presence of, or for the sake of a man.
In other cases, men interrupt the relationships women have
established. Perhaps echoing West's experience, heterosexual
relationships often make female friendship inaccessible.

'At Valladolid' (1914), is an autobiographical sketch
written during an early crisis with Wells. It describes a young
woman's guilt toward female members of her family
following her unsuccessful attempt at suicide:

> . . . And those who loved me gathered round me as I lay on the
> brink of death and dragged me back, tearing my flesh with the
> sharp teeth of their love. My mother sat by my bed and cried
> from the collarbone, sobs that scald the throat. My sisters moved
> reproachfully about the room, saying to me with their deep-set
> eyes, 'So you meant to leave us, after we have gone so loyally
> with you through all these years of poverty and tragedy.' And
> sometimes the man who loved me, in whose house I had done
> this thing, came and looked at me. And from his heavy, patient
> sweetness, I saw I had committed the sin that had been
> committed against me: seduction. . . . One never escapes from
> the body of one's mother. Wouldn't my death be a brutal
> destruction of my mother's substance? My sisters and I had made
> an interesting life out of our uneasy circumstances. Had I the
> right to run away and leave them short-handed and to discolour
> our masterpiece by violent memories? And I was the heart of
> the man who loved me and if I died no more blood would flow
> in him.[37]

The responsibilities, shared experiences, shared body and
'masterpiece' of a female society are here juxtaposed with
male seductions. West's women, like West herself, are never
exclusively in female circumstances. The sketch sets up
another heterosexual drama with a hostile doctor at the Valladolid clinic where she seeks medical attention. She is admitted
by a beautiful young woman. Her attraction to this Spanish
girl suggests bisexuality, but the encounter is momentary,
the other woman is more curious than sympathetic, and their
temperaments are hopelessly different.

If I had been a man I would have turned away from all else to make love to her and capture some of her vitality. As it was I was distressed by her close, gleaming texture and the serenity with which her long waist grew like a stem from her round hips and flowered into her bosom . . . [38]

Female relationships are similarly limited in West's later work, with the previously noted exception of *The Fountain Overflows*. In the story 'Indissoluable Matrimony' (1914), written for Wyndham Lewis' journal *Blast*, a husband detests his wife Evadne's female friends and resents her recollections of her 'poor Mama'. (*YR*, pp. 269, 279) In *The Return of the Soldier* a man occasions the only female bonding. Kitty and Jenny, wife and cousin of the soldier, are together mainly to serve him, and his former love co-operates with them for his sake. In *The Judge* Richard Yaverland takes Ellen Melville away from her suffrage work and whatever female relationships that involved. Her mother, to whom Ellen is strongly attached, appears in a few scenes and then dies. Their mutual love of Richard brings together Ellen and Richard's mother Marion, but Marion's attempt to form a bond fails. Marion has no history of female friendships. As an unwed mother, she received particularly cold treatment from women. In 'There is No Conversation', from *The Harsh Voice* (1935), the narrator works her way into the confidence of a successful businesswoman, Nancy Sarle, and arouses her 'kind concern'. But it is curiosity about Nancy's affair with the narrator's former husband that motivates the interactions. Alice Pemberton of another story in *The Harsh Voice*, 'The Salt of the Earth', is a nuisance, not a friend, to her female relatives. The problems of female friendship get the most deliberate consideration from Isabelle of *The Thinking Reed* (1936). She realises that she has lacked female friends as a married woman and as a mistress. 'Perhaps men, and the social structure which men have made, saw to it that women were worked till they dropped so that there should be no force in them that was not expended in the service of their men.' Without friends, women 'were sentenced to a privacy of fate which made a living woman not so alive as a living man, a dead woman deader than a dead man. Nobody knows the whole truth about one except one's friends'.[39] As the novel progresses, Isabelle is joined by a friend whose Russian beauty attracts her. She pities Luba because she has lost her husband in the revolution, and has been rejected by her lover. Isabelle does not pursue her own physical attraction to Luba or even talk to her very much, but seeks a wealthy husband for her.

Instead of visiting the 'untouched chamber' of women's friendships, West more typically explores the 'grounds of . . . attraction' between women and men. As a young critic, she felt that non-celibate women had an advantage over the 'spinstress' writers because of their more intimate knowledge of men. 'It is not until one meets a man on the grounds of not duty, but attraction, that his faults strike one with surprise. Out of that surprise there ought to come art'. What she hoped for were male characters to match the portraits of women struggling with the universe achieved by two of her favourite 'new' novelists, Hardy and Meredith. She probably tried to fulfill this ideal woman writer's project with Richard in *The Judge* and Marc in *The Thinking Reed*.

West's female characters and the depiction of their 'surprises' over 'faults' detected in men remain more interesting to me than the men they are paired with or set against. West patterns plots around the meetings of woman with man, and records their attempts at conversation. Like Lawrence (whom she greatly admired), West depicts heterosexual attraction and the violence of 'sex war'. Violent confrontation occurs in the Lawrentian story, 'Indissoluable Matrimony', mentioned earlier. Here the pallid husband nourishes grievances against his strong, sensual, socialist wife. He refuses to let Evadne campaign for a male candidate, and fantasises that she is an adulteress. His failed attempt to drown her in a symbolic primordial pool suggests her superhuman force. 'Life Sentence' from *The Harsh Voice* presents a couple who crave the ritualised pattern of conflict and reconciliation they have developed, even years after their divorce and remarriages. The action of *Harriet Hume* (1929) is difficult to represent in realistic terms. Yet during the last of their four meetings, the male protagonist, Arnold Condorex, wishes to shoot Harriet, and may actually do so before killing himself. In *The Thinking Reed*, Isabelle thinks through her attractions to a series of men, ending with her second husband, French industrialist Marc Sallanfranque. Wealth, industrial power and gambling are some of the forces Marc's soul must struggle with, but the real battle is waged by Isabelle. Twice she has violent personal reactions to men in her life that both destroy and heal.

Many of the heterosexual relationships depicted by West offer a paradigm of female nurture vs. male destruction or chaos. In *The Return of the Soldier*, three women restore a victim of the chaos of war. The most essential and selfless restorer is his first love, a lower-class woman now grown plain and matronly. Harriet Hume. is a fragile, musical, magical fantasy figure who uses wit, fantasy narrative and a capacity to read thoughts to alert her lover to the dangers of the political, public world he has entered, and to restore him after his disastrous choices. In later works the nurturing theme is more complicated, suggesting conflicts and subtleties in the process. While considering Luba's need both to care for others and to be loved, Isabelle of *The Thinking Reed* thinks across the genders. 'Surely in each human being there is both a hungry, naked outcast and a Sister of Charity, desolate without those she can feed and clothe and shelter'. The problem is that these two halves of the self cannot minister to one another; the female requires but often cannot find a loving other.[40] Isabelle's most dramatic effort to save Marc brings on a miscarriage. But the Sallanfranque marriage is saved, with Marc learning to better return his wife's nurture. The mothering role is assumed by Luba, who expects a child, having secured the sought-for husband. *The Judge* is West's most concerted study of the ambivalences of mother nurture. Marion Yalverland (who shares a name with 'Marion' Bloom of Joyce's *Ulysses*) cultivates a strong sensual attachment to Richard, her illegitimate firstborn son, in effect transferring the passion she had felt for the local squire, Richard's father. Marion has little affection for a second son, the issue of marital rape rather than love. She tries to prevent the sons from harming one another, and to foster Richard's attachment to Ellen by taking her own life. The role of nurturant goddess survives. Ellen is prepared to take Marion's place as a single mother, and to bring forth Richard's child. There is no longer time for legitimacy, because Richard does murder his brother. As a manufacturer of cordite, a material for munitions, Richard is doubly an agent of chaos. 'The Abiding Vision' of *The Harsh Voice* describes a wife and a mistress who both begin life with 'a face unlined with care, smooth and shining flesh undepleted by self-sacrifice, restorative with youth.'[41] In turn, they nurture Sam Hartley to success in the American business world of the 1930s, exhausting themselves in the process.

The restorative woman emerges as an archetype of West's fiction; she is present in rare female relationships as well as the heterosexual ones just examined. West's early autobiographical heroine encounters her in Spain, as we have seen in 'At Valladolid'. A second travel sketch from the same trip, 'Nana', evokes the type as a performer in a Seville café:

> As the gaslight glowed off her body, whose wholesomeness immediately frustrated her attempt at indecency, and the lines of her trembled because she continued to sing deeply from the chest, I remembered how I once saw the sun beating in the great marbled loins and furrowed back of a grey Clydesdale and watched the backward thrust of its thigh twitch with power. I was then too interpenetrated with interests of the soul and the intellect to understand the message of the happy carcass. . . . Now Nana's dazzling body declared it lucidly: 'Here I am, nothing but flesh and blood. When your toys of the mind and the spirit are all broken, come back to my refreshing flesh and blood!' I clapped my hands, I wanted to touch her, I wanted to rub my tired face against the smooth down of her shoulders as though I was a child.[42]

Here the modern, intellectual woman is reoriented and energised by a female figure who is both newly encountered in travel and formerly met in a childhood nanny. The comparison of human to horse, which assists her memory of childhood sensuality, resembles the memory traces of 'The Strange Necessity', and lends physical, animal force to the archetype. As noted earlier, West herself exuded this sort of animal power to Virginia Woolf.

James Joyce's character, Molly Bloom, is received in much the same way by the intellectual persona of 'The Strange Necessity':

> Marion Bloom, the great mother who needs no trouble to trace

her descent from the primeval age whence all things come, who lies in a bed yeasty with her warmth and her sweat and sends forth in a fountain from her strong, idealess mind, thoughts of generation and recollection of sunshine. . . .

Molly's monologue is 'one of the most tremendous summations of life that have ever been caught in the net of art.' She is an engenderer like Demeter and the Chinese goddess. 'The air above her, that is to say the air above our mother earth, seems to become full of men.' She can 'draw the Son back into her body, by his consent he will become the Father, who will beget a son'. (SN, pp. 42–3) The regenerative, life-giving mother archetype has as its antinomy the father, who 'eternally' kills the son, only to have the mother resurrect him. The pattern has to be forced to make Leopold Bloom the killer of his son, but this provides another instance of West's paradigm of female-identified life and order vs. male-identified death and chaos. Molly has a regenerative effect upon the young woman of 'The Strange Necessity'. Having seized upon Molly as an aspect of art she proceeds 'along the Rue de Rivoli; still full of that sense of peace and satisfaction and reassurance which rested on me like a pencil of brightness, proceeding from the rhapsodic figure of Marion — from meeting any of whose equivalents in the real world may the merciful Powers preserve me!'. (SN, p. 375) The young woman balances art with her individual life and finds that the energy needed for her survival can proceed from 'emotional responses, comparable to sexual satisfaction, that proceeds from great art'. (SN, pp. 210–13)

While West's regenerative female is a positive figure in that she builds instead of destroys, she poses some problems for readers like me. She is mindless and selfless in many of her manifestations. She is found most often in foreign or downcast places, or in fantasy. Encountering her in *Ulysses*, a young woman expresses relief at not meeting her in life. In realistic situations, the nurturing female sacrifices herself for male rather than female survival. She is particularly vulnerable to chaotic forces in the modern world. Still, West's 'great mother' heroines speak to a neglected part of the intellectual woman's psyche. They survive in eternal recurrences in *The Judge* and 'The Abiding Vision' and reappear in travels to remote places. In their more fragile, intellectual forms, Evadne, Harriet and Isabelle, they outlast male crises and preserve an independent vision. Some of them resemble the mothers and lovers of D. H. Lawrence's fiction. But they do not glorify phallic fulfilment and female acquiescence to a male-dominated sexual destiny. They celebrate the relationship of gender opposites, and probe their problems, relating these to the survival of full individual lives and civilisation itself. Here are Isabelle's thoughts:

> It struck her that the difference between men and women is the rock on which civilisation will split before it can reach any goal that can justify its expenditure of effort. She knew also that her life would not be tolerable if he were not always there to crush gently her smooth hands with his strong short fingers.[43]

In combination with the nurturant goddess, West also provides the perceiving woman, who not only observes men with a critical intelligence, but also exerts her will against a dangerous world, its chaos created largely by men's institutions. This female persona is, for me, West's greatest achievement as a woman writer. She is more free and versatile than the sensitive female perceivers of Henry James' fiction, whom West took up in her criticism. She seems more real and accessible than the mother goddess archetype, though some of her strength comes from encountering her or playing her role of renewal. She has admirable historical and geographical mobility, traversing what could be considered the male space of the modern city in comfort and excitement. She observes Britain in the era of suffragist agitation, Paris in the 1920s, America in the pre- and post-Depression eras, Yugoslavia before and Germany after World War II. She inherits the tradition of the *flâneur* and plays the itinerant roles of T. S. Eliot's Prufrock and Joyce's Stephen Dedalus. But she is up-beat where they are moody brooders. She partakes more of the tradition of Woolf's observant women, Elizabeth and Mrs. Dalloway, Mary Beton of *A Room of One's Own*, and Elinor Pargiter of *The Years*. But, especially in her earlier manifestations, she is a more sensual, sexual, public, professional, scientifically-oriented, independent woman.

I resist some of the territories and poses of West's central persona, especially as West moves into the late 1930s. West had a long flirtation with the wealthy and glamorous, expressed in her American and continental stories and novels. Her female thinker is often adorned in designer clothes and in command of a staff of servants. She must, I suppose, be placed in a credible vantage point to observe the chaos and mechanism of the lives of conceited aristocracy, wealthy industrialists and corrupt politicians; these she alertly problematises. But this diminishes her consideration of the lives of working-class people, who received so much attention in West's early journalism. Isabelle worries about Marc's attitude towards the unions and thinks about the courtship rituals of servants, but only fleetingly.[44] West is a sensualist, and the life she would make available to all fine, perceptive beings would include fine food, beautiful clothing and art; she criticises Puritanism and would force no one into asceticism, expecially not women of the working class. (*YR*, p. 130) Still, I have to resist the feeling that her fine, thinking woman is a bit spoiled, too close to F. Scott Fitzgerald's or Ernest Hemingway's bored society women.

Despite these difficulties, an important relationship is established among the woman writer, the woman character and a community of women readers. Like Virginia Woolf, West received much of her education as a reader. She wrote book reviews for women's periodicals like *The Freewoman* and *Time and Tide*, thus setting up direct communications with woman readers, which we are now rediscovering. The immersing of female intelligence into modern chaos, espeically where the female critic renews herself, enjoys herself and survives, is a 'strange necessity' to us today. West's models of this resource have been sadly neglected, but are available to contribute to our own renewal and revision.

Notes

1. Rebecca West, 'The Strange Necessity', in *The Strange Necessity: Essays by Rebecca West* (Doubleday, New York, 1928), p. 1. Hereafter cited parenthetically as SN. I am grateful to the modernist seminar at the University of Reading which heard an early version

of this essay, and especially to Patrick Parrinder for much helpful discussion.

2. West's *A Letter to Grandfather* (1933) offers a comparable image of doves in a more obviously spiritual context.
3. Elaine Showalter, 'Feminist Criticism in the Wilderness', *Critical Inquiry*, 8 (1981), 179–205.
4. Rebecca West, 'What is T. S. Eliot's Authority as a Critic?', *Daily Telegraph*, 30 September 1932, 6; and 'A Last London Letter: A Counterblast to Humanism', *The Bookman* 71 (August 1930), 515–21.
5. 'A Last London Letter', *The Bookman* 71 (August 1930), pp. 513–22.
6. Patrick Braybrooke, *Novelists We are Seven* (C. W. Daniel, London, 1926), p. 141.
7. G. E. Hutchinson, 'The Dome', in *The Itinerant Ivory Tower: Scientific and Literary Essays* (Yale University Press, New Haven, 1953), p. 250.
8. N. Gordon Ray, *H. G. Wells & Rebecca West* (Yale University Press, New Haven, 1974), pp. 8–9.
9. Samuel Hynes, 'Introduction: In Communion with Reality', in *Rebecca West: A Celebration* (Viking Penguin, New York, 1977), pp. ix, xii.
10. Peter Wolfe, *Rebecca West: Artist and Thinker* (South Illinois University Press, Carbondale, 1971), p. 148.
11. G. E. Hutchinson, 'The Dome', in *The Itinerant Ivory Tower: Scientific and Literary Essays* (New Haven: Yale University Press, 1953), pp. 250, 243.
12. Jane Marcus (ed.), *The Young Rebecca: Writings of Rebecca West 1911–1917* (Virago, London, 1982). Hereafter cited parenthetically as *YR*.
13. Rebecca West, 'A Letter from Abroad', *The Bookman* 70 (February 1930), 665.
14. See Bonnie Kime Scott, *Joyce and Feminism* (Harvester Press, Sussex; Indiana University Press, Bloomington, 1984), p. 87.
15. Ray, *op. cit.*, pp. xxv, 50–9, 81, 191. Anthony West's version of his mother's story is less sympathetic. See 'Love and Mr Wells', *Books and Bookmen*, 21 (December 1974); *H. G. Wells in Love*; *H. G. Wells*; and the preface to the 1984 British edition of *Heritage*.
16. Letter from Victoria Glendinning, 18 July 1984.
17. Rebecca West, 'Notes on the Effect of Women Writers on Mr. Max Beerbohm', in *Ending in Earnest* (1931; repr. Books for Libraries Press, New York, 1967), pp. 68, 70.
18. Ethel Mannin, *Confessions and Impressions* (London, 1931), pp. 118–19. Quoted by Motley Deakin, *Rebecca West* (Twayne, New York, 1980), p. 38.
19. Virginia Woolf, *The Letters of Virginia Woolf*, Vol. VI, ed. Nigel Nicholson and Joanne Trautmann (Harcourt Brace Jovanovich, New York, 1980), p. 521.
20. Virginia Woolf, *The Diary of Virginia Woolf*, Vol. IV, ed. Anne Olivier Bell (Harcourt Brace, Jovanovich, San Diego, 1982), p. 261.

21. Woolf, *Letters*, Vol. V (1979), p. 261.
22. Woolf, *Diary*, Vol II, (1978), p. 202.
23. See Woolf, *Letters*, Vol. II, pp. 524, 548; *Diary*, Vol. IV, pp. 326–32.
24. Virginia Woolf, *A Room of One's Own* (Harcourt, Brace & World, New York, 1957), p. 35.
25. Rebecca West, letter to Virginia Woolf, Monk's House Papers, University of Sussex. Woolf misunderstood West's attitude towards Jenkins, and West had to explain in a second letter.
26. Interview with Dame Rebecca West, 17 October 1981.
27. Rebecca West, 'Concerning Censorship', in *Ending in Earnest*, pp. 6–12 (on Hall); 'The Strange Necessity', pp. 8–9 (on Mansfield); *The Court and the Castle* (Yale University Press, New Haven, 1957), pp. 165–6 (on Eliot).
28. *The Court and the Castle*, p. 109. West uses a similar binary in her fiction.
29. Rebecca West, 'The Long Chain of Criticism', in *The Strange Necessity*, p. 289; and *The Court and the Castle*, pp. 113–14.
30. Rebecca West, 'Notes on Novels', *The New Statesman* NS 20 (November 1922), 142.
31. Rebecca West, 'High Fountain of Genius', *New York Herald Tribune Books* (21 October 1928), 1, 6.
32. See Susan Gubar, ' "The Blank Page" and Female Creativity', *Critical Inquiry* (Winter 1981), 262; Sandra Gilbert, 'The Soldier's Heart: Literary Men, Literary Women, and the Great War', *Signs* 8 (Spring 1983), 447–50.
33. Rebecca West, 'Autumn and Virginia Woolf', in *Ending in Earnest*, pp. 209–12.
34. Rebecca West, 'With a Secret Flowering', *New York Herald Tribune Books* (1 November 1931), 1, 6.
35. *The Court and the Castle*, pp. 220–1.
36. Virginia Woolf, *A Room of One's Own*, pp. 80–1.
37. Rebecca West, 'At Valladolid', *The New Freewoman*, 1 (1 August 1913), 67; Most of this passage is in *YR*, pp. 69–70.
38. *Ibid.*, p. 66.
39. Rebecca West, *The Thinking Reed* (Virago, London, 1984) p. 133.
40. *Ibid.*, p. 165.
41. Rebecca West, 'The Abiding Vision', *The Harsh Voice*, p. 251. The same sentence, without the final phrase, is used at the start of the story (p. 189).
42. Rebecca West, 'Nana', *The New Freewoman* (1 July 1913), 27.
43. *The Thinking Reed*, p. 431.
44. *Ibid.*, pp. 42–8; 184–8.

Index

Acknowledgements

Gillian BEER: 'The Body of the People in Virginia Woolf'.

The author gratefully acknowledges permission to reprint extracts from the following:

From *The Diary of Virginia Woolf*, vol III, ed., Anne Olivier Bell. Published by The Hogarth Press, 1980. Copyright 1980 by Quentin Bell and Angelica Garnett. Reprinted by permission of the Estate of Virginia Woolf, The Hogarth Press and Harcourt Brace Jovanovich Inc.

From *Orlando* by Virginia Woolf. Published by The Hogarth Press, 1928. Copyright 1928 by Virginia Woolf, renewed 1956 by Leonard Woolf. Reprinted by permission of the Estate of Virginia Woolf, The Hogarth Press and Harcourt Brace Jovanovich Inc.

From *The Waves* by Virginia Woolf. Published by The Hogarth Press, 1931. Copyright 1931 by Harcourt Brace Jovanovich Inc., renewed 1959 by Leonard Woolf. Reprinted by permission of the Estate of Virginia Woolf, The Hogarth Press and Harcourt Brace Jovanovich Inc.

Diana COLLECOTT: 'A Double Matrix'.

The author gratefully acknowledges permission to reprint extracts from the following:

H. D., *Collected Poems, 1912–1944*, edited by Louis L. Martz, Carcanet Press Ltd., 1984. Copyright © by the estate of Hilda Doolittle. Reprinted by permission of Carcanet Press and New Directions Publishing Corporation.

H. D., *Helen In Egypt*, with an introduction by Horace Gregory, Carcanet Press Ltd., 1985. Copyright © by Norman Holmes Pearson. Reprinted by permission of Carcanet Press and New Directions Publishing Corporation.

H. D., *Tribute to Freud*, with a foreword by Norman Holmes Pearson, Carcanet Press Limited, revised edition, 1985. Copyright © 1956, 1974 by Norman Holmes Pearson. Reprinted by permission of Carcanet Press and New Directions Publishing Corporation.

H. D., *Bid Me To Live*, with a new introduction by Helen McNeill, Virago Books, 1984. Copyright © by Norman Holmes Pearson. Reprinted by permission of Virago Books and New Directions Publishing Corporation.

William Carlos Williams, *Imaginations*, ed., Webster Schott, New Directions, 1970. Copyright © by Florence H. Williams. Reprinted by permission of New Directions Publishing Corporation.

From 'East Coker' in *Four Quartets* by T. S. Eliot, Faber and Faber, 1969. Copyright 1936 by Harcourt Brace Jovanovich Inc; copyright © 1963, 1964 by T. S. Eliot. Reprinted by permission of Faber and Faber and Harcourt Brace Jovanovich Inc.

Ezra Pound, 'Personae'. Copyright 1926 by Ezra Pound in *Selected Poems, 1908–1959*, by Ezra Pound. Faber and Faber, 1975. Reprinted by permission of Faber and Faber and New Directions Publishing Corporation.

Desire in Language by Julia Kristeva, Basil Blackwell, 1982. Reprinted by permission of Basil Blackwell Ltd. and Columbia University Press.

The Complete Poems of D. H. Lawrence, ed V. de Sola Pinto and F. Warren Roberts, Penguin Books, 1977. Reprinted by permission of Laurence Pollinger Limited and the Estate of Mrs Frieda Lawrence Ravalgi.

The Diary of Virginia Woolf, vol III, ed., Anne Olivier Bell, The Hogarth Press, 1980. Reprinted by permission of the Estate of Virginia Woolf. The Hogarth Press and Harcourt Brace Jovanovich Inc.

Sue ROE: 'The Shadow of Light: The Symbolic Underworld of Jean Rhys'.

The author gratefully acknowledges permission to reprint extracts from the following:

Wide Sargasso Sea by Jean Rhys. Published by Penguin Books , 1968. © 1966 Jean Rhys. © 1929, 1931, 1935, 1957, 1966 by Jean Rhys. © 1985 this collection by the Estate of Jean Rhys. Used by permission of W. W. Norton and Company Inc. and the Estate of Jean Rhys.

Good Morning, Midnight by Jean Rhys. Published by Penguin Books, 1969. © Jean Rhys 1957. Reprinted by permission of Wallace Sheil Agency Inc. and the Estate of Jean Rhys.

After Leaving Mr Mackenzie by Jean Rhys. Published by Penguin Books, 1971. © Jean Rhys 1935. Reprinted by permission of André Deutsch Ltd., and Wallace and Sheil Agency Inc.

Quartet by Jean Rhys. Published by Penguin Books, 1973. © Jean Rhys, 1931. Reprinted by permission of André Deutsch Ltd., and Wallace and Sheil Agency Inc.

Voyage in the Dark by Jean Rhys. Published by Penguin Books, 1969. Reprinted by permission of the Estate of Jean Rhys. It is believed that U.S. copyright has reverted to the author and was not renewed following the author's death. All reasonable attempts have been made to trace the copyright holder prior to publication.